HOPELESS BUT NOT SERIOUS

Hopeless But Not Serious

The Autobiography of the Urban Voltaire

JACK McLEAN

*To Helen,
yours
Jack McLean*

"ESCAPED"

MAINSTREAM
PUBLISHING PROJECTS

EDINBURGH AND LONDON

For Brian and Richard, and brothers everywhere

First published in Great Britain in 1996 by
MAINSTREAM PUBLISHING PROJECTS LTD
7 Albany Street
Edinburgh EH1 3UG

ISBN 1 85158 664 4

A catalogue record for this book is available from the British Library
Typeset in Garamond
Printed and bound in Great Britain by Butler and Tanner Ltd, Frome

I

I am born. Well of course I am. Born at the fag-end of the War at that, and like the David Copperfield whose autobiographical reminiscence kicks off that novel I am born in especial circumstances. Copperfield was born with a caul, a strange membrane covering the infant head. I was born with a metaphorical, perhaps, metaphysical, membrane: I was born prematurely. At a time when birth was hard enough with a massive number of infant mortalities I was alive. Living at all was hard enough for the mother. We were, after all, at war. And I was just over two pounds at birth.

Today such a weight suggests that the child's chance of life is not good. At the end of the War it was impossible. I was the size of a milk bottle and possessed less colour. A few factors allowed my survival, all of them unlikely. Firstly I emerged from my mother's cavity, and after her with a long illness and all the doctors hoping to Jesus that she was still alive, bugger the baby, and her in Irvine Central Hospital, one of the few truly radical institutions in hospital care in the country. It has always been a certain source of embarrassment that I did not, after all, hail from the Magic City, but then neither did any famous and infamous and working-his-ticket Glaswegian. I was born in Irvine. Irvine is a New Town today and perfectly awful, apart from the people, who remain to this day pleasant, bucolic, and alcoholic often enough, and impervious to the disgraces of the architecture which has been inflicted upon them in the last forty years.

My mother had suffered a variety of renal failures, and I was set aside, a bundle, a baggage, a danger to a young mother. I was the second child and not only was I not expected to live, neither was my mother. My father was getting the shit kicked out of him by last-ditch Germans in France and didn't expect to survive either. The doctor was a Soviet fellow, sent across from Russia. Back in those days the level of medical development in the Soviet Union was high, or at least higher than the West possessed, but that was because British medicine was still tied to the ability to pay. Sure there were plenty of splendid doctors, but they cost money and working-class people could hardly afford the fees demanded. It wasn't that British doctors were greedy – heavens, enough of them were overworked and low-paid – it was that health insurance was inadequate. Give most doctors their due: they voted overwhelmingly for a democratic medical service, and despite some appalling fiddles by a handful of medicos who exploited this new National Health system shortly after the War, the doctors were then, and largely remain, strongly in favour of a health service which is still second to none, in the clichéd phrase. Anyway I have been, since birth, since I was born, a patient in the same practice; a worry to my doctors for fifty years. You will find out why later on.

Sometimes a cliché is a life-saver. In my case, dear Love of God, a cliché is a gift from the Gods. For the Soviet doctor had introduced a new phenomenon. He called it an incubation tent. Unknown, or scarcely thought-of in Britain. It saved my life. But your Urban Voltaire would not be here to tell the tale were it not for the most important life-saver of all. She was nineteen years of age and a very inexperienced little Ayrshire nurse from Kilmarnock . I like to think of her as having blonde hair, and virginal enough but not too much. A wee spot of petting in the picture-house with a Bevin Boy seems all right to me. Her name was Elizabeth.The Soviet doctor had brought in these rather large and odd incubation tents. But Elizabeth had brought, at the end of her childhood, not very much expertise, but what is the first sense of even very young girls, the notion to hold a baby. I was covered in hair and blood, but the lassie picked me up, despite them all saying that she was a silly girl and announced to the experienced sisters and the Soviet doctor who had last seen service in the charnel houses of Stalingrad what my mother, in her pain and grief at losing her child, overheard. The little nurse said, in a quiet and shy voice what was true. 'The baby's still alive,' she said, as she picked me from where I had been discarded. But she was right: I was still living and breathing.

I was alive, the weight of a bag of sugar, the size of a milk bottle; you could hold me in your hand. I was covered in thick black hair. My father was covered in confusion and anxiety. His only thought was for his wife, I think so anyway. It is perhaps an explanation for his later resentment of myself. I was the one who could have brought about the death of the love of his life. I might be wrong about this, but I know I am right. I was ill for a long time, longer than my mother.

Dear Sweet Mother, I was ill for near eleven years. I couldn't have inoculations, apart from the smallpox one. I never caught smallpox but I caught every other bloody thing you can think of now. I had scarlet fever and diphtheria, and polio (then epidemic), and whooping cough, and rheumatism, and the sort of influenza which kills you, and migraine, and a hernia and anything at all which could upset parents. I caught the lot. Allied to that I was neurasthenic and half the time didn't know, nor did my parents, whether I was well or not. I could have been the wee boy in *The Secret Garden*. My grandma was wont to jouk about her town stating that I was 'a miracle baby', and then recount how ill I was and how I was not expected to live. Later, when I was older, I realised how much I could have made of this. At the time I was not well and made no advantage of it. Neither did my father, who, I suspect, got pissed off having a delicate child on him.

A delicate child would seem daft now, but back then, when I was born, the Victorian experience of child mortality was yet in the mind of every parent and I was coddled a little. I really was ill in fact, slept in a different bed. Until I was nine or ten I slept separately from my young brother and my elder one. They slept together. I often slept between my mother and father because of the nightmares. When you are little and ill you get nightmares. I have them to this day but have learned to cope. Now I can control the nightmares, tell them what to do and more than that: I can start them up, unless there are bad nights. My chum, psycho-therapist Derek Rafaelli, says I can't, says I'm kidding myself, but I can – I know better about my childhood than he does, believe me.

Actually Derek knows I am telling the truth. If you spend your early childhood looking at death, nightmares are a psychic pabulum and morbidity is there when you wake, and your childhood is an early maturity. I was so ill in my baby years that I spent a lot of time with my grandma. Let me tell you about her.

She was less than five feet tall and came from Cornwall. I have seen photographs of her as a young girl with my Auntie Muriel. She had on a long skirt, to her ankles, and a shirtwaist, and a cameo brooch at her throat and she was just, and just, capable of putting her light brown hair up. For a girl of those days she was well-educated, stayed on at a girls' school until she was seventeen. She came from a well-known, and to this day, well respected, Cornish family, the Nancarrows. They were related to the Roberts, from Ireland; Lord Roberts – Bobs – was a second uncle. They owned, and the cottage lies there still, Roberts cottage, now a tourist attraction in Perranporth. And then she met a shy young man, of Hungarian origin, Kador Bennish his father was. He called himself Richard Benny. He looked, and indeed through the genes I do myself, Jewish, and despite the fact that Jews can only go through the matriarchal line, I have never quite forgotten the simple fact that I am of Slav origin: that, no matter, there is the Levant in me. My grandfather I never knew. But my grandma I did. She was very small and dainty and looked dreadful and washed-out when she was bringing up copious numbers of children and lost several through miscarriage and one through a terrible accident. His name was Eugene and I was nearly named after him. I have the photograph of him, framed. I always thought he was an angel because they said he had gone to become one, and in the photograph he has, somehow, an aureole around him. Ethereal he looks. I always felt his presence and still do. My bourgeois grandma's family would have felt that fanciful, but my grandma wouldn't have. Like myself, she had a Celtic nonsense in her head. I never said anything to anybody ever, until now, but I miss Eugene more than I can tell you. Dead twenty years before I was born and more, but I knew him well, and better than any other uncle.

Because of my grandmother. By the time she was my grandma she looked like the pretty girl she had been in her girlhood. Always beautifully dressed, gloves and hat, she was known everywhere as Mrs B. Talked to all the old men who sat around the War Memorial, waiting for the pubs to open, having outlived their wives, old widowers who had seen Paschendale. Dear Heavens, they weren't, in retrospect, that old really, some of them; but it was a different age and they just looked old; very old. Spending so much time with grandma, me a delicate child. She had a splendid bungalow, in Stevenston it was, in the well-off part, the High Road. It had a rockery at the front and crazy paving and Auchen Harvie – I think that's the spelling – was opposite. A lovely piece of woodland with an old ruined mansion house. Today it is a housing scheme, and bloody awful. Spending so much time with my grandma I spent so much time on my own, which is, I think, a good thing for a child. She taught me the alphabet for a start, and rather wicked card games like poker. The alphabet was to turn out useful. My grandma had a heart condition which obliged her to rest every afternoon, so she locked all the doors – I was a toddler after all – and left me with all these old Chatterbox Annuals. They were pre-Great War and had marvellous extracts from Dickens and other mid-Victorian novelists like Silas K. Hocking, who wrote the bestseller of the Victorian age, *Her Benny*, the *Gone With the Wind* of its time.

Almost all of the stories were about children of course, and had pictures. Almost all of the illustrations were of delicate children, just like me, who were just about to croak it or were going to recover from croaking it. Almost all of the children were girls. Edwardians were keen on illustrations of just-about-to-croak little girls. To this day I tend to favour girls who look positively tubercular. Dark eyes and ringlets, demure expressions, sad mouths, white frilled frocks, melancholy, even sulkiness: reading these stories as a child set

8

my aesthetic for life. And reading it was. Because of the illustrations. I was so intrigued by them, and so frustrated that I didn't know what the stories were, and because for two hours every afternoon I was left on my own, a very solitary child, I taught myself to read. I was four, but I had the alphabet. I suppose, like everything else in my life, I taught myself to read because I fancied the girls in the pictures. Everything I have ever done, it seems, was because of girls.

Anyway I taught myself to read. A legend in my family concerns the occasion when my father saw me gravely reading the *Daily Express*, my little four-year-old legs dangling from the chair. 'What's the news today, old chum,' he is said to have asked, amused at his tot appearing to read a blatt. 'Korea Refutes Deal' I reported. Sorted him out, that did. More than that, I had more bloody sense, when I think about it now than he did, a devoted *Tribune* reader, and Eisenhower and Aneurin Bevan put together, a most unlikely combination, except for one thing: at least two were both professional soldiers. But later my precocity in reading was to lead to an abiding passion for the process of sticking the beadies from one side of a page to another. I was six when a lodger of my grandma's, called Gwillym Owen – Uncle Bill – bought me an illustrated book of *Oliver Twist*; the drawings were by D.W. Watkins, famous for his Black Bob drawings in the *Sunday Post*. The book was fascinating.

The drawings terrified me, and these many years later still have the power to do so. Fagin with the bread knife at Oliver's throat when the boy wakes up to see the miser gloating over his jewels. The crones revealing the secret of Agnes, his mother, to Mrs Corney, later Bumble; the dark acres traversed by the boy hand in hand with Sykes; and my favourite ever character, or near it, in the Dickens canon, Toby Crackit, 'Leave the boy alone, I've seen older hands taken worse on a cold night.' The book chilled the blood, fired the imagination, drew me out of the drab world which was Glasgow, and made me read the adult book at the age of six. I understood little of the words, but I saw the way they sat against each other. And something else. Something the grown-ups couldn't manage to penetrate. I found another world. Solitary and not very well children do. What R.L. Stevenson called the Land of Counterpane. 'When I was sick and lay abed . . .'

My Uncle Bill, somehow, knew that the Other World was there for me. Uncle Bill was a small dark Welshman with a splendid moustache (he once shaved it off and I burst into tears when I saw his bare upper lip: he grew it back in a week), and he was wonderful with children because he was very, very, small himself, and shy with adults. He used to go out with my father for a beer when we visited, but it was when I stayed with my grandma when I wasn't well that he was more avuncular than any uncle, except of course the dead one in my head.

In our times it might seem odd that this young man befriended little boys. Our times are off-beam, by a long way. Uncle Bill was a lonely little Welshman who had a big family of brothers and sisters in Snowdonia whom he missed very badly, and he had been grievously half blinded by a chemical accident, during the War. He was, in fact, a chemist. My little grandmother was advised by her doctor to take in lodgers who might help to monitor her condition, should things get worse, so she took in Patrick, a rather wealthy Irishman, and Gwillym, an impoverished Welsh boy whose family had spent their all getting him to a university. He was a classic protagonist of Howard Spring or A.J. Cronin. In our times it might seem odd indeed but then it didn't seem so at all, and it wasn't. He missed his little brothers and sisters, and he was small and shy, and he was Celtic with a love of sentimentality and maybe a wee libation. He loved stories and tales and lived nearly ten years with my grandmother. My grandmother whose name was, I forgot to tell you, Beatrice, was so naive that she told the young lodgers, chemists from the nearby ICI factory where her husband had been a senior chemist himself, that she needed lodgers because the house was so big and she had heart trouble, but she couldn't afford to pay them all that much each week. The incredulous prospective lodgers told her that they were going to pay her. Her reply was wonderful. 'I'm sure,' she told them in her Cornish tones, 'that your mothers would take in my sons in their hour of need.' The two boys had to cheat by getting bacon and eggs and other things on the black market.

But The Book had an impression: I learned to read as an adult. I started to read adult books. By the time I was seven I was reading *Oliver Twist* in the undigested version. Reading teaches you more than ideas: it teaches how adults think, or want others to, and very young children who read early learn that too: we get good at adult duplicity. Dickens teaches you more sophistication than almost any other writer because he learned it in the stealthy way which people who leave formal education in younger years will never find. Dickens taught me to connive at ideas. Grown-ups think they can obfuscate in what they say and do and write and draw. But a young child can see better than that if introduced early enough to grown-up wiles. To this day I have always held to myself that special knowledge and have never admitted it before now. I could, at seven, understand your conversation, you lying, conniving bastards. There is a problem with it too. We child spectators at your adult festivals never quite grow up. That's what I knew about Uncle Bill. He was one of the Special Children: never quite grew up, and kept the secret to us. At the end of the day it has earned me a living, kidding on that I never quite know what the adults are saying: but I do. That's enough. Now I am five and ready to go to school.

No I'm not. We moved from Ayrshire to a prefab in Cathcart, a lovely little village, not a fifteen-minute journey outside of the Glasgow city centre. Next door, two minutes' walk, was Linn Park. It had a little wood and a river, and a castle, and Mary Queen of Scots watched the Battle of Langside from near there, at Court Knowe. I remember walking through this rather large park, through the woods and past the waterfall; I know to this day the rocks and trees and the idea of countryside and wildness and I still go there in times of sadness and distress. This is getting dreadfully maudlin. Memory always does that of course and what's wrong with that? But I remember walking there in autumn. The leaves lay auburn on the ground, my mother wore a tweed coat and skirt of the same colour, and she had on a tiger claw brooch, long since stolen in one of my house-break-ins, the bastards. She was young and pretty, and happy too. I wore a little suit which was blue and had a white blouse with blue buttons, and blue shoes. My elder brother was top of his class at the local school, Holmlea, which, in the strange aftermath of the War, possessed a democracy now considered wrong by both Right and Left. The big houses were up the road. My younger brother was being looked after by Helen Harvey that day. Helen worked in Kirkwood's the bakers, across the road from the prefabs, and looking after both my brother and Isobel, whose father lived in the big houses. To this day I remember those years in Cathcart: so do both my brothers, one of whom now lives a street away from where my father had brought us up after the War. I remember that particular day for no reason, it could have been any day to choose from: but I remember my mother in that brown tweed suit and the leaves and the bluebells in the wood. For it was all to change. Dickens again comes into it.

The prefab was nice and warm and the local primary was ideal for what my parents wanted for us. It was cosy and, I suppose, middle-class. My brother had finally been accepted for Hutcheson's Grammar, the apogee of academe and class. He, Richard, is four years older than me, and had been born at the start of the War. When my father came back from Germany he hadn't seen him in years. All the women in the family had treated him as a prince. There is a story by Frank O'Connor, the Irish writer, called 'My Oedipus Complex'. You'll get the idea of what Richard, and only he can tell his tale, must have encountered. From a horde of women and girls cuddling him he went immediately to Mister fucking Murdstone, telling him it was time he learned to tie his own shoelaces, rebuking my mother for kissing him every morning, a sudden hairy-arsed authoritarian in the house. I am not here to tell my brother's story, but just the way I see my own. But we didn't see my father very much when I was young anyway. He was away doing the electrification for the Western Isles, in the late Forties and Fifties. He was a cable-jointer who put in the electric for his own people really, for he was originally, or at least his parents were, from Mull. I still remember the Christmas, when snow came, and it was late, about ten o'clock at night, when he came home, bloody exhausted, and we hadn't seen him for six weeks or more. It was a good Christmas. I would be six or thereabouts, and Cathcart was lovely and I loved my mummy and daddy and my elder brother, and I had a pal, a younger brother, Brian, who had the blondest hair, and it was great seeing your daddy after all this time. My mother was used to waiting for my father after all the War years. But my father wasn't used to seeing us and so he decided to see more of us

Charles Dickens didn't know he was in the blacking factory after his father's disgrace which had sent him to Marshalsea Debtors Prison: he simply forgot about it. Can I come back to that later? No I can't. I will start again. When Dickens was forty and very successful indeed he met – with a well-clad friend, overcoat collar framed by Astrakhan fur, cane in hand, and both of them strolling through the streets of London – a poorish-looking fellow whom he did not recognise. The wretch said but few words to Dickens, but they were enough to bring back the dreadfulness to a successful and rather coarse man, who spoke, all his days, with an accent which would have passed for a Tory Prime Minister – at least one from the other side of the tracks as most have been in recent years – and caused what seems to have been a nervous breakdown. Dickens had simply blotted out – blacked out if you wish – the time he spent in the blacking factory. It was not long it turned out but Dickens could not tell, as he revealed later, whether it was six months or six years. In fact it was less than six weeks. But it was enough for the great man to turn it into a nightmare which fuelled him all his life. The blacking factory. Mine was Townhead. In the very centre of Glasgow; in the worst slums of the city which had the worst slums of Europe. At least Naples had sun.

In Cathcart, I remember we had the big houses up the road with trees and the park was a countryside in itself. My mother was used to a middle-class existence, and spent her days showing the little ones how to paint on the kitchen table with big pieces of paper my father brought back from the draughtsmen at his work, and took us for walks in the village: went down the Crescent in Cathcart, the butchers, the Electric Bakery, the Post Office for stamps and airmail letters (a lot of relations lived abroad then), Sam's the café. It was difficult in those days for any family because rationing was very restricted and food was, as it turned out when we found out about it eventually, in shorter supply than the bloody Europeans were getting. As a young child at primary school I took a penny every Monday for the Displaced Persons and the Refugee Children. If I'd known what these German rich bastards were going to end up with I'd have kept the bloody pennies to myself, not that they were much good with the rationing anyway. But we were awful good to the ex-Nazis anyway and I still feel that to this day when I see their clean and refurbished cities and their blond and blue-eyed Aryan shites who were more than willing a few years before I was born to be jouking up their arms and 'heiling Hitler'. Maybe it's my age, but it galls a bit. My daddy was earning sod all and the rapacious rich of Britain were telling him to pull in his belt while they invested,in their droves, in the new Germany. Here, that's enough of that.

But it was a very odd time for children at that time. The War was everywhere. Before the War, During the War, After the War: it got impossible in adult conversation. There were a lot of old men with curly moustaches, stained yellow with nicotine, fumbling with their gold Alberts and fobs and seals on their waistcoats, sitting outside pubs and old men's clubs. Now I know they weren't that old and had simply made themselves into patriarchs. They were the ones from the First War, the Great War. Some of them were nice and gave you silver threepenny bits. Most of them were boring old shits who blamed, well just blamed really. The schoolteachers were old as well. Miss Bringham was the headmistress at Holmlea and all I recollect about her was that she once collected all the children together and sat us down on the floor and told us that it was sinful to look at girls' pants. Immediately a small girl with flaxen hair and cornflower blue eyes looked at me wickedly and showed off her navy blue knickers. From that time I was captivated by girls, cornflower blue eyes, and knickers I suppose. Then there was Mrs Smith who told us, drearily, about Brer Rabbit and him being in a Briar Patch. It didn't take long for me to know that Brer Rabbit was a right prick and that Brer Fox wasn't as foxy and anyway, Mrs Smith was full of the sort of drivel which adults are when they think they can 'communicate with children'. Mrs Smith couldn't communicate with a fucking chip pan if it was on fire and was on top of her head. She'd still be there saying, 'Now boys and girls, I have another wonderful thing to tell you . . .' as her eyeballs melted down her bloody rosy cheeks. She told me once or all of us really, but I was only actually concerned with me, that The Ascension was the Greatest Story ever told, but I knew it wasn't because anything with Tony Curtis was and Jesus seemed a right prat to me. Why didn't he take all the treasures from the Devil and then renege on the deal and do good and give out all the treasure to poor folk? At six you are not a Socialist but you are dreadfully materialistic. I wish to Christ there were more six-year-old politicians.

But all the same it was an idyllic time really, if I hadn't been ill as often. My brothers were grand and I loved them both, and the house was cosy and warm and if we were not very well off, the rationing made sure that nobody else was. Early in my life I learned a lesson which I have never forgotten. Up the road, in the big houses with striped sunblinds, lived the Nicholson family and they were very good people. Mr Nicholson looked a bit like Mr Attlee, and so did my father, (in those days all adult males looked like Mr Attlee or Ernie Bevin except the old ones who looked like Bruce Bairnsfather's Old Bill or the way I imagined Silas K. Hocking, Ebenezer Balfour in torchlight really). Mr Nicholson was a well-to-do tailor with a family which consisted of a plump and matronly wife who was very good to you, a dark-eyed daughter called Belle, a little blonde cherub whose name escapes me,and my brother's chum Alasdair, who went on to attend my own school, Allan Glen's. He was even a prefect when I was in first year there. But there was also a modern version of my Uncle Eugene. His name was Hamish and he was smart and bright, with bright eyes, as brilliant as coffee drops. And when my father got up early one Sunday and had on his best dark blue suit and a dark big tie he told me that Hamish, who we knew, because they had told us, wasn't well, had died and he, our father, was going off to the funeral and what a funeral was, and Hamish was going to Heaven and we wouldn't see him again, I wanted to know why. It's the sort of question you ask at six years of age. So my father, who could, very occasionally be quite good at this sort of thing, told me about this brain tumour, and I imagined it as a huge purple thing and was really quite upset, that big ugly purple thing in Hamish. In those days children were rather protected against funerals and grief, and quite right too. But I have never forgotten that, and my father in his suit.

2

My father had a suit of course. On the day of Hamish's funeral it was a dark blue suit, with a distinctly demob stripe to it. He always had a dark blue suit on, for he was a school janitor. Back in the early Fifties a school janitor was invariably an ex-soldier: he was certainly an ex-tradesman. With a trade. The Jannie was not a kick in the arse off the Beadle of a previous century, and in working-class communities very important indeed. So important that the Jannie's children were regarded rather as those of a local Nazi Party official. It was rotten for Jannies' children. 'Jannie's Boy! Jannie's Boy!' they used to shout. If they'd had the sense they would have pelted Jannie's boys with mud. The Jannie was respected, perhaps feared, because the Jannie was more often than not an ex-NCO, and even the local hardmen knew the force of an NCO. And back in the days before my father became a blue-uniformed school jannie he was a blue-uniformed soldier.

He spent nearly twenty years as a regular soldier, in the Royal Corps of Signals. Mercury was the symbol of the regiment; fleet of foot. All I can tell you is that he was bloody fleet of hand as well, because it was hardly ever off my arse. He had left home at sixteen to join the army and by seventeen was a blue-patrolled dressed squaddie in the rather pleasant port of Wei-Hei-Wei in China. We used to pore over the two albums of fascinating snaps of himself as a youngster in China. I have the albums yet, crumbling a little they are. My father with a hank of hair falling over his eyes, bare chested, khaki-shorted. Christmas 1931. Photographs of Christmas Day in long tents, Chinese servants in starched blousons. Jock Penny, buttoned to the neck, a fellow squaddie who eventually rose through the ranks to become a celebrated Brigadier General in the Second World War. As a child I was brought up on those photograph albums a bit, but never did I manage to get the story out of my father, or very little until he got older and I could put a drink or two in him, about what had happened in his colonial career. A lot must have occurred. Later, as I saw him down the pub, I managed a little more, but it wasn't much. I had to do a sort of research on my own.

My father was born plain David McLean. His own father was David also. His father had come from Mull, where the McLeans come from. I have been there myself. It is a whore of a place: all you could grow there would be stones. Indeed, today it is widely known in the rest of the Western Isles as 'the Officers' Mess', because of the many English White settlers who have decided to retire there. Perfect peace and quiet. Not a breath of work or energy. No wonder the youngsters leave in their droves. When my grandfather left Mull and met the dark slums of Glasgow's Gorbals he must have thought it was bloody luxury.

He didn't have much time to enjoy the Gorbals though. He was killed at Gallipoli in the Ardenelles in 1915. My grandfather contrived to die on the same beach, on the same day, in the same war, in the same regiment (the Cameronians), for the same reason, as both his brothers. All of them left families. So much for Winston Churchill's idea of warfare. Never again did entire villages find themselves in the so-called pals' brigades. But it left me without a grandfather, my dad without a dad, and my grandmother without a husband, and four children to bring up in the middle of Gorbals, and her from Mull herself too as well. Until I was over forty I never saw a picture of my father's mother. She was a striking, handsome, and raw-boned woman in the picture, with my sloe-eyed and fair-haired father, the eldest child, with a lace collar around his neck. His mother looks stern and strong, but every inch a widow. And she was. There is my Uncle Jimmy, a sturdy, dark little boy, a year junior to my father, and Lizzie, ringlets and lawn-cotton flounces, and Sadie, the youngest, a baby. The photograph was taken in some photographic studio in Gorbals, for the husband who never saw it, the one who died on the Gallipoli beaches.

My father told me about the last time he saw his father. He was five and his father was going off that day. His father, whose image I have never myself seen, took him down the stairs of the close, round to a nearby newsagents and bought him a bar of Fry's chocolate and a tin replica of a pillar box with a slot to put money in and slid a sixpence into it. And then my grandfather went off in his kilt, looking heroic. And then my grandma, who died before I was born, got a telegram telling her about how her husband had died for honour and freedom. She also received all his medals and I have the big one framed in glory and on the wall in my living room. It's got his name on it. I'll bet not one bloody officer had the slightest clue what his first name was at all. You don't want to read about this.

But this was the romance I was brought up with, even if my father didn't know it, and it had the effect on me that it had on many of my own generation. From martyrs to mavericks was a long but inexorable process. The martyrdom of my father's father was eventually to lead to a new world. Where another sort of martyrdom was waiting. There is little point in me telling you of my father's family. My Auntie Lizzie died before I was born. She'd married a feckless Irishman and brought her daughter up in her new faith; sent her to Our Lady and St Frances' school, a highly selective school in the heartland of what was becoming a slum area of Glasgow. My father agreed to bring the little girl up as a Catholic, though we were United Free and my father was energetically agnostic, but the feckless Irish bastard saw that there was money in it, took a payment of fifty quid from my father to look after the child, and then noted that the girl could earn a living if she left her rather august school and keep him in drink, so he did all that. It was an old era and a harsh one. My father might have softened a little if a girl had been introduced into the family: who knows.

Jesus Christ, he wasn't for softening at all. I know he meant well. He did well too. His three sons have gone on to be successful in a variety of professions and were possibly no more traumatised than other children of the time in which we grew up . . . Holy fuck, did I say that? Did I actually put that down? Jesus, he scared me, he frightened me, he terrified me. Once later, when I was an art teacher in a secondary shool and had to teach religious education, and hadn't a clue what to do with the little ones in first year, I gave the weans the task of 'drawing God'. I was later reported and reprimanded, mainly because when every child came out with his and her drawing of the Almighty I looked at the effort and pronounced, loftily: 'Wrang: start again.' It wasn't just a joke though, splendid as it was. I actually knew what God looked like. He had a short, sort of Clement Attlee-style moustache and wore a blue-peaked cap. I knew what God looked like indeed. He looked like my dad. He was a just god but he was awffy keen on being the only god in the world. He was a jealous god. Vengeance was his. Well a bit of this is vengeance too. Mine. Not God's. Or Dad's either too. Here I am getting ma ain back a little.

My father had spent most of his life as a professional soldier. He'd married late in life. Was away much of the time in his children's early years. Thus he took it into his head to be what he liked to call 'a disciplinarian'. Thus it was when my elder brother didn't get a bursary to Hutcheson's Grammar School, then, as now, an elite institution of learning, my father took to ranting for days, exclaiming to us all that my brother was an idiot. 'The boy's an idiot: I knew it all along!' he declared, and plunged the household into despair. (He did the same to all of us, in an exotic variety of ways.) He was very proud of us children and we were always congratulated by other adults on how terribly well-behaved we were. And we were terribly well-behaved. Children in the late Forties and early Fifties were generally so, which is perhaps why we turned out to be such turds when we came into adult estate.

Certainly my father did not spare the rod. But then adults in those days were keen on not spoiling you. Spoiled child? It was impossible then. The food was dreadful. Apart from the deleterious effects of rationing, and no sweeties, and very little by way of healthy food, there was also the factor that few women had the slightest idea of how to cook. My mother was a sweet little lady who as a small girl had been taught Domestic Science. Domestic Science had got her confused between laundry and cookery, with disastrous results. One of the disastrous results was that I could rarely eat the food put in front of me and was ritually beaten for this failure to stagger down my throat the meagre and unpalatable repasts provided. My father was a grand man for the discipline.

I have never been quite able to understand why he chose me for the discipline. In his own way he was generally fair. He never (until I got older that is), hit me unduly, and when younger it was generally deserved. He didn't use belts or sticks. He smacked you until you cried. My elder brother rarely did anything wrong anyway, and my younger brother cried before he was smacked. I wish I'd learned my lesson. He hit me until it was too sore. A silly bastard myself. I should have gret early days.

But I don't remember a single occasion when my father lifted me up or cuddled me or kissed me, or muttered any endearment or even much encouragement; I don't remember that ever. I remember a dreadful hiding: have never forgotten it. It has taken forty and more years to dredge it up. I was six perhaps, at Holmlea School. We had a teacher called Miss Pollock and I didn't like her, not one bit. Instead of Miss McGilveray, a soft, feathery spinster with her grey hair in a bun, we had Miss Pollock. Miss Pollock had black hair and too-bright lipstick. She wore tight black skirts with a pocket from which she sported a cheap cotton lace hankie. She had high heels, and an even higher voice, and she must have been, thinking of it now, very young. But she was not nice at all. She was strident and very frightening and to my young mind – and young minds are infernally conservative – she looked a bit tartish actually. She was hardly suited to teaching. I'll bet she ended up as a headmistress. Certainly she affected my life to the extent that every time I write a short story with a villainess in it, the villainess always gets called Pollock.

Anyway this woman wasn't my teacher for long. Long enough though to traumatise me. I had asked to go to the lavatory. She had refused to permit me. In fact, I needed a crap, but didn't like doing a shite in the school lavvies because there were no doors and I was, after all, brought up in the most anal-retentive period of the most anal-retentive country in the world. But I really needed a jobby. So I asked again and was peremptorily refused permission by this fucking little madam once again. Doubtless the teacher training college which the ill-educated lassie had been accepted by had told her to refuse to allow six-year-old children to do the toilet. I watched as girls came out, pathetically begging to be allowed to piss, only to be informed that, 'You should hevv gorn et the interval.' Boys holding their willies. Eventually, desperate, I told the mad young woman that I was desperate, and she finally gave her permission, the cow. But I never made the lavatory. I shit myself. And when I got home at lunchtime I was so abject and ashamed and everything that I told my parents that I hadn't been allowed to go to the lavatory, which was true, but didn't say I had finally been let out of the class because when you are six years of age substance in communication is not subtle. The substance in my report was keech all over me.

My father of course went to the school to complain, the young teacher told a lie but one which she could edge out of (she had let me go to the lavvy eventually after all), and my father, black-ashamed, waited till after tea, when the other children were sent to bed, to administer a thrashing which, in the time-honoured phrase of 'disciplinarians', I would remember all my life. And I have. I was very small for my age, and he must have smacked my bare bottom for over ten minutes, as hard as he could. Eventually my mother had to intervene. I hope Miss Pollock is still alive and reads this. And all the rest of the curious adults who frightened me and my generation.

I don't know why I told you that: I don't know why it seems important, but it is. Or why it has come back to me. Perhaps something to do with the sheer bloody awfulness of childhood; most of it. My father threatened me and scared me and often bullied me. Oddly, what I hated more than anything else, more than the frequent spankings, were the ravings of the man, the shouting at me, the terrible silence in the house for days when his disapproval pervaded every room. The reprisals after some discovered misdemeanour (this included my mother, for she was subject too to his extraordinary fits of temper), were never quite as bad really, but the sureness of the reprisal was truly frightening. He could be very cruel too. I was painfully thin; embarrassed my father it did. Embarrassed me too, if it comes to that. He called me 'Skinny'. He liked that. Barrack-room taunting. 'Tell Skinny he's wanted in here.' He'd aye say things like that. Another time he refused to take me to the art galleries in Glasgow because, dressed in my khaki shorts and ankle socks and sandals, my legs were too thin for himself to be seen out with me. 'I'm not going out with that,' he said. I was made to put on long socks. A monster was the daddy. But not all the time, just the bad bits of it.

For there were things in the man's favour at that. Quite a lot really. He took it into his head to go in one generation from the children of squaddies and peasants to High Court judges. That's why he sent us to the selective schools. He was horribly proud of us and always supported us from outside criticism. He was loyal and brought all of us up with an exemplary morality. We were well-clothed, in a rather bourgeois way (all those years in the Army had taught him how the middle classes lived), we were well-spoken, we were fed on nourishing and sometimes rather exotic food, the result of his many years abroad. We used to go off to the expensive licensed grocers and the better stores, like Ferguson's or Massies, or Coopers, where hams hung high and the shops were permeated with the aroma of ground coffee and there were bottles of Chianti in straw coverings. This was the late Forties, early Fifties: then it was stewed sausages, and tinned cream with pineapple chunks, and we were dining off olives and salami and wedges of Stilton when my father could get it and afford it. We had books in the house, and my father was obsessed (as he remained to the end of his life) with symphonic music. We were taken to art galleries and parks every Sunday and in the holidays we were taken to every venue we could learn anything from. It must have been hard for my father, from his background to know how to treat children, how to be a father at all. Twenty years in the Army – he had a dreadful War in fact being a regular, and was elderly for a father when he had me – and had known little of a childhood himself. He was poor and putting his children through top schools and, despite his attempts at self-education through the *Tribune* newspaper and *New Statesman*, and lots and lots of improving books, he never quite understood what education was about. He thought it was like learning how to joint a cable. He thought ideas were a simple matter of learning how to do something.

I do not blame my father too much: I have forgiven him and not forgotten him. He did his best. Like every father it was simply not good enough. It would have been a bloody sight better if he had been able to earn a decent living; enough to keep children at fee-paying schools. Enough to keep us in the prefab in Cathcart, among the trees and the big houses up the road, the park across the way. Holmlea School. The pretensions of the middle class. He could have done that if he had continued to work as a highly-paid cable-jointer who had to travel all over Britain. But he had decided – years of jaunting about the world on army service had taken its toll – that he wanted to see more of his family. He decided to see more of his family with a vengeance.

Have you any idea what it is like with your father never away from you? Around every day. My mother never had to say 'wait till your father get's home' for he was there on the premises. At first he was still away, as a school janitor, and we still lived in that lovely little cocoon, the prefab in Cathcart village, but then one day we were told that he was to become senior janitor in Townhead Primary School. We were prepared, in awesome tones, by both my mother and father, about Townhead. For my father it must have been, when I think about it now, genuinely humiliating: the struggle to get away from the slums, the sheer democracy of Cathcart, his children growing up happily in leafy lanes amid the big stone houses, the local schools with Mr Brown the janitor and Miss Bringham the headmistress living up the road, the happy and carefree children with parents who held down good jobs, and now back to the dank slums of his own childhood. My mother made, I think, the best of it. I never did. I never made the best of it at all. For this was my own, my blacking factory, and I have never forgotten it.

The house was in the building itelf, part of the school. At the bottom of it. It had a part basement but the front door looked out onto the infants playground. Playground for heaven's sake. Holmlea had trees in the playground, and the teachers came out and played with you, the River Cart passed just by us and there were elderberry bushes wafting their bitter, juniper-sweet scent across. Mums and old grandpas waited at the gates for you. Townhead Primary school was black, bleak, bloody. Therein should be a gallows, as prisons had. The house itself creaked all night; the first night it had banshees in. There was a long hall and then a living room. It possessed a rudimentary bathroom and lavatory. The bath was iron and had ball-claw feet, the lavatory had a wide wooden seat which little ones like myself were worried about falling through. There were two bedrooms and a 'glory-hole' bigger than any other room, paved with stone and brick-clad on the walls. (This became a haven for me, where I read books and thought up ideas and wept when I was unhappy, and got away from everybody when I needed that odd loneliness which children sometimes need – not just being alone, but needing the catharsis of being without anybody in the whole wide, wide world, just utterly bereft of people, and sad.)

The first night I caught the first edge of what has lasted all my life since. The first night in that room I saw the ghosts. They were old ghosts, had been in that room for years, but some of them had come from other rooms too. My grandmother's, my father's mother, dressing table had been put there in the dark moonlight. There were no curtains. The moonlight shone palely against the dark mahogany. Then I knew my grandmother, as a young girl, as a bride, had brushed her hair sitting at the dressing table, her husband unwrapping his kilt only to put it on in the morning to go off to his death for 'Honour and Freedom'. There were a lot of deaths about in the room that night, my grandfather's and his brothers, my grandma, the one I'd never seen even a photograph of, my Auntie Lizzie, my Uncle Eugene, Hamish, the displaced persons, anyone who got themselves dead. That first night I lived for the first time, with a roomful of Death. I remember the voices which seemed to emanate from that piece of furniture, and the chill. It didn't frighten me really. It annoyed me. But it was the first time I saw the ghosts. If we had never gone there I would never have seen the ghosts. I would have been happy all my life. But once I saw the ghosts it was different. Sooner or later we all see the ghosts.

3

The move to the Townhead School janitor's house in Rottenrow was long and tortuous, and involved throwing out a lot of books and toys. It was a bit early for putting away childish things but I was rather forced to see through a glass darkly in my father's house anyway. I was, and I think my mother and father were too, very conscious of having gone down in the world, like characters out of a Victorian novel in which Papa loses all his money in business. 'But Mama! We shall have to move to that pokey little cottage and darn our muslins and do dreadful things like cook for ourselves. I shall simply hate it.' When we moved I simply hated it.

In place of the little prefab with its comforting paraffin stove, and the trees outside and the gardens and the River Cart burbling away, we had this dark, high-ceilinged, basement flat. Outside was the Water Board Clerk of Works building. It possessed the only tree in the district. The tree was dark green and foreboding enough for a Tennessee Williams play. It was the sort of tree you would never wish to climb. I missed the trees, and the lanes and the sheer landscape of Cathcart village more than you can imagine; than my parents could imagine. I had dreams for years, I think, about the leafy little suburb I had left, and about my grandmother's bungalow in Stevenston where the huge back garden with its beehives and compost heaps and raspberry bushes were, looking out onto swathes of wheatfields which the farming Skeoch family owned and where I used to play with their little girls in the barns and ran after the geese.

Townhead had lots of wildlife all the same. Rats, and criminals, and the ghosts at night when you were in your bed. A few years before a double murderer called Paddy Carragher, a local man, had been hung across the road in Duke Street Gaol, for the second murder he'd committed in ten years.

Townhead was full of these Bill Sykes characters. The first night in that house was as grisly as any murder. A night when the moon was blood.

The first morning my mother and father had us all dressed up. My brother Richard was going off early to Hutcheson's Grammar, clad in his cap and blazer, a toff. Hutcheson's remains perhaps the most august – academically at least – day school in Scotland – and my elder brother never knew very much at all about Townhead, about that bleak street, Rottenrow, right opposite the Glasgow Cathedral, the foundation of the Glasgow I grew up in. He had his friends in that school. My father was wont to taunt him about his 'smart pals in that hoity-toity school of yours'. Richard simply withdrew into another world entirely. This is difficult for outsiders to understand but Glasgow had then, and retains, a curious class structure which was inchoate to say the least. The top school in Glasgow was set in the middle of the Gorbals slums. My elder brother grew up middle-class, however, and called his headmaster 'The Beak' and such. He went to Sports Day in his blazer and cap and his friends had mums and dads who were lawyers and accountants and his best friend was richer than anybody because his widowed mum owned a pawnbroker business.

The first morning at Townhead Primary Brian and myself were all dressed up. We had new blazers, light blue they were, and Bannerman shirts with ties, grey shorts. New. (I quite often had shorts cut down from my father's suit trousers, and remember a kilt made out of an old tartan skirt of my mother's: a lot of the clothes I wore as a young child had been inherited from uncles from before the War, for clothes rationing was very harsh.) My mother and father told myself and my brother that we were not to be anxious about how rough the other children were going to be, after the gentler relations we had encountered with the bourgeois boys and girls of Cathcart, but we were not to speak like the urchins we were about to meet in this slum school. We were to retain our manners; our superiority I suppose. I was worried sick. I thought that playtime was going to end up with myself being set on fire. It was to be *Lord of the Flies*. Worst of all, my brother Brian was to go to another part of the school, in a different playground. At Holmlea I had looked after my wee brother, and the little feathery spinster ladies used to go round the playground and made everybody join in the games and skipping and all that. I was hardly the stuff of which timidity is made, but certainly the prospect of this version of *West Side Story* was worrying.

We were taken to meet the headmaster, whose name was Charles S. Swan. (Years later I wondered if he had a sister, Annie.) Mr Swan was well-dressed in a desiccated way. He was clean shaven and beaky-nosed, and terribly clean. He was clearly afraid of my father who was resplendent in his janitor's uniform. My father's school janitor's uniform had creases in the trousers which could have performed eye surgery, they were that sharp. The whiteness of his shirt collar would have blinded Beau Geste in the desert. Mr Swan was nervous but welcomed us two children to the school. He had a small room, which I cannot remember him ever leaving. On the walls were dark prints, one of which, I swear was 'When Did You Last See Your Father'. The other I recognised many years later. It was 'Disgraced', a photogravure of a famous painting depicting a little girl sent to stand in the corner and her sympathetic little dog who had joined her. Thus was the philosphy of the school, the black school, the one with the only tree in the entire district growing across the street from it, the blacking factory itself; thus was it expressing its purpose. Your daddy was dead in a civil war and your sister was sent to the corner. They will be putting the dog down next. Then they sent me to my class.

It was a change from the little Holmlea School where even the tarty Miss Pollock could be cancelled out by the Misses McGillveray. I was put in the hands of George Kidd, a muscular young chap of perhaps thirty who wore green tweeds for half the year and, I was to find out later, a Harris jacket and flannels for the second half. George was a splendid teacher in his own way and he terrified me no end. He had over forty-five pupils in his class and had, as most teachers, gone through a war and pretty recently at that.

Apart from Mr Kidd and the fluttery Mr Swan the headmaster, (who had been too young for the First War and too aged for the Second), there was Mr Vallance who wore a grey dustcoat and was so ferocious in his martinet-style discipline that even my father once exclaimed that Vallance was 'a severe bastard with the weans', and Mr Fraser who was in his mid thirties and had a small moustache and who was kind and gentle, and used to put his arm round the children when they were upset, and a bed in heaven to you, there were nothing but women teachers, all of them spinsters, for the rule then was that a lady teacher was forced to resign her post upon marriage, to leave it to spinsters and men who needed the jobs and the money. In Townhead Primary it was nothing like Holmlea. In Cathart the little spinsters went home with their little charges and gave them sweets and the children gave them pots of home-made rhubarb jam or flowers. In Townhead Primary the ragged children were enemies of the livid ladies who were forced into the slum schools. At least I had George Kidd.

But the first day, the first moment, had nothing to do with teachers. In place of the flowers on the teacher's table and the certain knowledge that the lilac bulbs were coming to fruition in the darkness of the light-coloured wood cupboard, and the cloakrooms where the lady teachers took off your overcoats, and helped you tie your shoelaces, in place of all that was a school and building organised partly by the Workhouse Board of the 1850s and by principles laid down by Miss Murdstone; financed by the firm of Murdstone and Dombey: Chief Executive Mr Gradgrind.

My earliest contact with an actual fellow child was cheery and frightening at the same time. He was a little boy to whose care I had been inexplicably placed. His name was Abie Matthews. He was small and dirty with torn clothes and tear-stains visible upon his grimy cheeks. He had a thicket of curly black hair and a grin worthy of a vaudevillian. 'Kin youse fight?' he asked immediately. I didn't in fact understand the question. I took it literally. I could but I didn't want to and saw no function in it. 'Ye'd better' said the urchin. 'Wait till youse see Tam Elvin. Youse urr in fae trubble.' He then treated me to a resumé of the fearsome Tam Elvin's career. Tam Elvin was the leader – not just of my class, but of the entire school and I have never understood why, because I met him at playtime. He was a small peaky-faced boy, white-faced and undernourished, with a marginally cleaner Lifeboy jersey than the others. He had flaxen hair which rose steadily from the back of his head which was large. He had steady blue eyes and spoke quietly. His officers were much bigger and meatier. Monkey-Lugs Bruce, Billy Strang the bully, Michael Collins whose dad was a well-known informal pugilist and Roman Catholic. Collins went about the neighbourhood, I was to find out later, persecuting Catholics to make up for his antecedents. Another aide was Ronald Millar who was the local bookie's son and therefore horribly wealthy. (He was too. In those days street bookies made a fortune yet were inclined to live in the same area and indeed the same houses with no baths and stairhead lavatories, but sported flashy suits and diamond pinkie rings. Danny Millar was a small and dapper chap who made as much as any Glasgow stockbroker but whose tastes led him to less respectable entertainments than the toffs of Pollokshields would have demanded.)

It was Ronald Millar, the scion of the bookie, who suggested to Tam Elvin that I might be useful. Elvin was a sagacious young fellow. The jannie's son could be an important contact. Furthermore, he had deduced early that the girls on the other side of the class – in those days boys and girls were separated on all occasions – rather liked the new boy. I had even darker curls than Abie Matthews and darker eyes and what Elvin considered a posh accent. Elvin considered a minute. I'd done extraordinarily well in the spelling test from Mr Kidd that morning too. Elvin pondered and I was admitted to the gang. The position I held from then on till I finished primary school was that of somewhat of a boffin, somewhat of a diplomat for rival gangs and, to adults, wholly as a public relations officer. It took me years to realise that Tam Elvin couldn't fight, never fought, and never had to: he was just simply a leader of men.

26

A word about people like that. Tam was absolutely fearless. He was utterly honest. He was true and faithful and brave. He saw any transgression against fairness as personally insulting. He never messed about in class and never cheeked a teacher: indeed a miscreant could expect a sherricking in the playground should an altercation take place in the classroom. 'Ye were takin' a dead liberty oot a Mr Kidd,' (Elvin was a stickler for proper nomenclature), an merr, yis goat us into trubble. Yer a deid loss, so ye urr. Youse wull huv tae pull yer soacks up, ah kin tell ye.' Furthermore Elvin himself took a pride in doing well at his lessons. ('It's easier daein' the work than no daein' it.') Tam Elvin I haven't seen in forty years but it was a young child who first taught me a proper morality which, though I may not have entirely met, I have never forgotten.

Lessons kicked off with the Lord's Prayer which Mr Kidd performed perfunctorily. (Next door Miss Kirk, an angular lady who sported steel-framed spectacles to go with her steel-framed theology, intoned the morning religious ablutions with gusto, as though it were a revivalist meeting in some dark glen. She also had clean hands inspections and rewarded those too exiguous in their toilet with a dose of the tawse on each unwashed extremity. How this cleansed the mitts I know not but I suspect Miss Kirk had the cleansing of the soul in mind.) Then, as in every school in the Scotland of those days, we plunged into the first lesson which was mental arithmetic.

It is difficult to understand now why this exercise had such a hold over the educationists of those times. Why arithmetic should have been deemed quite so important, so fundamental. They followed up the mental arithmetic with the times-table which you chanted out by rote, the whole class. Five times seven is thirty-five, six times seven is forty-two, seven times seven is forty-nine . . . Sure, there was some amount of training in it; some element of basics, but we did this every day for years and yet even now I can't count and have forgotten almost anything I was ever taught about numbers. The teacher would pace up and down among the rows and sometimes discovered that you were merely mouthing and didn't know your times-table. This was crime incarnate. Adult visitors were prone to asking you if you 'knew your times-table' as they sipped their tea and rattled down the Abernethy biscuits. Your mum anxiously looking on in case you didn't get this catechism right. Why? For Christ's sake why? I mean the entire morning was taken up with numeracy, of which far and away the worst part was the first part of it, the mental arithmetic.

Well it was for me. For a start it was public and so was your humiliation. Monkey-Lugs Bruce and Tam Elvin could answer any question involving numbers in seconds and Ronald Millar, taking after his bookie dad, could compute with even more lightning speed, but the teacher knew that and ignored their upraised hands when they tried to answer his open question which involved adding and dividing and all the other curious antics of this almost religious rite. Kidd asked the ones who couldn't do it. He didn't ask the very thick ones much, and when he did it was for diagnostic reasons – had they grasped anything at all in the last few weeks – but he was wont to capture people like myself who were bright enough and could spell and for whom there appeared no reason why they should not be able to answer questions involving six dozen bags of potatoes at two and thruppence a bag, with a discount for the spoiled ones. This was an overgrown forest of imponderables to me in which wild animals lurked ready for the kill. Partly through fear – you were belted for too gross an error – and partly through the dreadful fact that I counted too quickly for a constancy of accuracy anyway I often got the answers wrong. When I got them right I had often sort of guessed them too, something I have never understood. A whole bloody morning was, I seem to remember, taken up with this nonsensical liturgy. It ruined mornings for me for years. Thinking back, the numbers gambit didn't last all morning but it seemed like that. We did have reading too, but it followed on from the numbers and was somehow contaminated by the calculations of the a.m. ordeal, which lasted, always, from prayers till the milk break.

Milk came in small bottles, a third of a pint. It smelled, as milk still does for me, of slept-in pyjamas and was another trial to be got through. Other children seemed to like it though and vied with each other for extra bottles. They slurped it and drank it up greedily and I despised them for wetting themselves for the bloody milk and for liking it in the first place, just as I was later on when they ate all their school dinners. As I do to this day. Can't stick the sort of bloke who eats everything because it's on the bloody plate in front of them. I especially hate people who turn to you after a dish which is obviously execrable and practically inedible and tell you that their scoff was 'great. Any afters?' The sort of people who say things like 'afters'. Thus early days I learned a horror of the mob. I suspect most of us have a little quiet contempt for others in the mass as a result of some far-off disgust at seeing other children fall prey to peer conformity at feeding time.

School, before you go to the big one, the secondary one, is filled with bad times, more bad than good. For everybody. It's when you are bullied more and by more people and when you do it yourself. It's when you are often shamed by others and when you more often feel ashamed. It's when you learn how to survive the herd you're part of and the herds you will choose to run with. All the different moves you have to make. I didn't like primary and I didn't like other children and I especially didn't like adults. And what is more I was pretty sure they didn't like me. But then, I didn't like myself.

But school was a dawdle compared to outside of it. Being a jannie's boy put you into the category of a polisman's child. Or a minister's nearly. Certainly the son of the Cruelty Man. I was made to befriend the Cruelty Man's son too: he was in my class and his dad pushed him damn near as much as my father was pushing me. The Cruelty Man was the local Royal Society for the Prevention of Cruelty to Children officer and he lived in a large Georgian house set in the district which was also his place of work, his office. (There was a row of these large Georgian houses, much blackened by the soot of industry and all of them in a very dilapidated condition, used as doctors' surgeries or offices of the nearby Royal Technical College, now Strathclyde University. As the only decent bloody buildings in the entire district they were of course the very first to be demolished when they razed virtually all of Townhead to the ground a couple of decades later.) The Cruelty Man was called Somerville and his son was Gordon, a big-boned boy with a broad, but girl's, face who was even more snobbish than I was, or made to be so by his nervous father. He stood out from the other kids though, like me, being the jannie's son like, and him the Cruelty Man's boy. Not like the other kids.

A great many of the other children were very poor-looking specimens of childhood, ragged and dirty. Many of them smelled badly, hardly surprising when you consider that few houses had indoor baths, or lavatories. They were also ill-fed, filled up with jam pieces, slabs of bread with cheap red compote on them, and tinned soup and sausages. Most of my fellow pupils, however, were bright enough and street-wise enough, believe me. Oddly naive in some ways too. On our first day in Townhead Primary myself and my younger brother were taken for English, because of the way we spoke. We came from a couple of miles away, a hitch away from their social class, and the other kids thought we were English. They had rarely heard a Glaswegian accent which was different from the one in Townhead or thereabouts. Yet there was very little of a class divide. Some of the pupils came from the firemen's flats and they were, too, in a social strata which was rather labour aristocracy. The firemen's flats were part of the building which housed the fire station in nearby Ingram Street. Some of these very firemen were to be involved later in the terrible Cheapside fire disaster in which nineteen men died, one of Britain's greatest firefighter disasters ever and commemorated by all British firemen every year yet. There were other outsiders too. All teachers and officials from the factors and rent collectors to anybody from the Corporation, to clerkesses in the Post Office to clergymen and their wives and other toffs. Not politicians oddly or publicans or bookies: they came from exactly the same social background and even if their children at the fee-paying schools were going to put on airs the politicos and bookies and others didn't. Glasgow boys who get to be political and business big wigs even now don't change their accents or much of their personas but they do learn very quickly indeed the luxuries of life enjoyed by the well-off, perhaps a very street-urchin trait. Certainly the chaps with the poppy learn quickly what tailors to go to and that you get your shirts made in Jermyn Street. They fill their mansions with good quality furniture and art and their stomachs with Beluga caviare, their cellars with choice wines. But they still tend to drink regularly in the pubs and it isn't generally until the third generation at least before they lose the democratic spirit or drop their sense of the demotic. This cannot be said for most of Glasgow's villains for whom I have usually felt some contempt: all that money and they still act naff with tarted-up council houses and gaudy holidays in tacky resorts.

Most of the girls were pretty poor as well, and very badly dressed. My childhood was, in some ways, very little different from that of children born before the War though we were a lot better fed, thank God. But the cinema was still the chief source of entertainment, and football for the men. Television was still a minority medium and it wasn't until the mid-Fifties and perhaps a bit later that it was seen by most working-class people. We were still basically and culturally, as a class, in the grip of the War. The bourgeoisie might be trying to think of new ways and waiting for new plays to come out which would change their lives, or at any rate their perceptions, but as I recollect my early childhood not very much seemed very different from pre-war days. There was the *Eagle* comic, but *Radio Fun* was still being published. And women and girls didn't seem much different from those of pre-war days either. Only young unmarried working-class girls, for instance, went to a hairdressers and clothes were still expensive. It wasn't till towards the end of the 1950s that the affluence revolution came near the lower orders. And so the girls at school were ill-clad and shod, their hair was not terribly clean and hairstyles consisted of a hair ribbon, the only decoration they possessed. A far cry from the little girls I had known in Cathcart.

I remember the wee girls then, at Sunday School parties. Little angora wool bolero jackets in pale rose, flouncy, frilly, white party frocks with satin sashes, silver little strap sandals: princesses. At five years of age I had erections which would have done credit to Errol bloody Flynn and as many of them when it came to girls. I didn't, to be sure, know anything about them. There was a small girl of about my age in the next prefab called Elizabeth Green who would show you her vagina but I don't think it really registered. I think I was more fascinated by her occasional performance of crapping in front of the other kids. The child could crap at will, for heaven's sake and we used to get her to do it for sweets. This has not resulted in coprphilia for myself or doubtless for any other spectators of her show and I never thought that other girls did that anyway: I thought it was probably just boys and Elizabeth Green who did shites. Probably like most men I still in my heart of hearts sort of continue to believe that. But, Miss Green's exertions apart, no girl had displayed anything other than mystery. They had different kind of bottoms, rather fleshier than us, and perter, and I found that inexplicably, and secretly too, very secret, nobody to know, not anybody, guilt-inducing, I found that attractive. As I did their faces and their hair. Girls had soft faces and large eyes fringed with lashes which cast graceful shadows on the bloom of their cheeks. Their hair was long, I didn't know why, and it was gentle and swished. Their dresses too were softer than the sub-military hodden we boys were forced into to go with our almost shaven heads, and the hems swished too and made soft sounds like sibilants. Their sibilants were soft as well and they made whistling breathy sounds when they said 'esses' and had lispy lips and I found girls insensately lovely. That is, the lovely girls. Plain girls I didn't think of as girls, and I probably don't even yet. I think of them as another sex entirely, a sex without one. That is undeniably rotten of me but not nearly as rotten as it is being a plain girl and there's damn all I can do about that. I know you're not supposed to think like this but I do and so does everybody else especially plain girls.

But the girls at Townhead Primary didn't look like the girls at Sunday School parties, at least not like middle-class ones. They were horrid stick-like things with impetigo, (back in those days every kid got impetigo, an unpleasant facial infection which resulted in scabs which unthinking school nurses treated with Gentian Violet ointment), and whose unprepossessing underwear you could see on the clothes line each Monday. They were not alluring in any way, girls. Not far away was the selective Our Lady of St Francis School in Charlotte Street,(which my cousin, my dead Aunt Lizzie's daughter had attended), where bright girls of both working and middle class families went and they were wonderfully pretty. You'd see them wending their way haughtily through Townhead in their brown school uniforms with the navy blue edging and think salaciously of their pristine lingerie, and of their faint scent of blossoms. Of their fragrance. And then you'd be confronted with the girls in your class with their oily gaberdine too-big or too-small hand-me-down gym slips and their National Health specs with one lens covered by elastoplast to correct their squints. But there was always one diamond in the glaur. In one case it was a girl called Eleonora McGurk.

Eleonora was not only the prettiest girl in the class, she was the only pretty girl in the class. She had golden ringlets (which I later discovered are created

31

by twisting the hair in strips of rags), and nice fresh clothes worthy of Princess Grace of bloody Monaco. And she spoke nice. And her daddy – who was an officer in the Merchant Navy and something of a prince himself – was better-off than most other parents and God knows what she was doing in that school or district. And though she was nice and pleasant to the other girls nobody ever sat beside her because she was, after all, a princess. None of the children could pronounce her pretty name easily and so she became Linoleum McGurk, though I made sure I could pronounce her damned name all right.

In those days girls sat on the other side of the class from the boys. It meant, by and large, one splendidly quiescent, and quiet too, half of a room and another half a seething cauldron of intemperance, a pit worthy of Dante's most fevered imaginations. But a serious offence could result in a boy being made to sit beside the girls. This meant an offence too wicked for the belt but not quite bad enough for a letter home. God knows how Mr Kidd thought he was punishing me by making me sit beside the girls but this he did one day. It was one of those days when the mischief is upon you and the badness in your heart from the moment you stride into the classroom. Only a matter of time before the belt started itself up and it did. Normally that would have been enough for me, but this day it wasn't. Eventually I found myself with the worst, the final, admonishment. Sent to sit beside the girls. Had Mr Kidd never been a boy himself? So I sat beside Linoleum. (I never called her that myself. I called her what she wanted to be called, which was Ella.) She had these fair ringlets and wore, I remember, a print frock the cornflower blue of her eyes. Hands like little pink tea roses. But the badness was in me. Even this angel could not restrain the badness. For right in front of me, right in the seat before me, was an enemy.

'Oh, you enemy, you enemy,' I thought, 'oh, you enemy.' The enemy in question was a wee fat lassie called June: she had pigtails, infuriating priggish pigtails. She had got me belted months before for telling a lady teacher that I had muttered 'Hell's Bells' in her ear and the shocked lady teacher was so shocked that she belted lumps out of me and sent me home with a letter for my father who laughed himself sick, saying the woman was an old maid who was 'all piss and vinegar'. June had caused the outrage upon my person, and she was a fat lassie with fat pigtails, and the wickedness was in me that day. It was the work of seconds to dunk one pigtail into the inkwell.

I never knew that hair was that absorbant. Jesus, her pigtail would have absorbed the Loch Katrine reservoir. The ink went galloping up her plait like acid through metal. And then fat June swung her bloody pigtail. Instantly the other side of the class – the boys – were spattered with ink. When she turned back, her skein of hair covered all the girls and all their clothes in the blue blood of literacy. Chaos reigned for several minutes. June wept herself to death. For some reason, despite the fact that I had neither intended this result nor expected it, I found myself in a kind of existential ecstasy. Ella had of course been unaffected by the ink or the mayhem (she was the sort of girl who emerged through hellfire unscathed). So she said, and I quote verbatim after all these years: 'That was super. Fat little cow.'

Needless to say, I was taken away after things had sort of settled down and the boys and girls were washed and June was calmed down with a bar of McCowan's Highland Toffee and Mr Kidd gave me six of the strap which was very painful indeed. But I had transgressed too far. Next was Charlie Swan, a kindly man, who was kindly enough to thrash me again. By the time I got home the hands were dropping off me and I was looking for a wee quiet place where I could greet without anybody seeing me. But Mr Kidd and Mr Swan and all the lady teachers and all the weans and especially all the girls and, most especially of all, the fat lassie called June with the inked pigtails, had told my father, who, being the janitor of the school, was terribly close at hand for telling. That night I had an arse you could have fried an Irish breakfast on. All I can tell you is that I spent years trying to sit beside girls like Linoleum McGurk and the result has usually been as painful in their own ways and I am going to avoid all the Linoleums in the future or will if I have any sense.

4

There were of course escape routes out of Townhead apart from my dreams, or the appalling vision of my father's which was to get me a gaffer's job and a terrace house in Muirend. The dreams were a nightly visitation. They had me turning a corner round a crumbling wash-house and suddenly there was a grassy lane, long and winding and straight out of an illustration by the Beggarstaff Brothers. As the lane continued the trees grew thicker, the copses brighter, the sky more blue and then the golden cornfields. It always ended up at my grandma's house, its tumbling rockery, the front door with the striped sunblind on the porch, the dark cool of the hallway with its scent of the fruitbowl and Mansion polish, its air of gentility. What I always thought of as the morning room, where I was the aristocrat of the breakfast table. In fact the dreams were simply a recording of the reality, and the reality sustained me while I dwelt in that broken landscape of the slums.

Do not let anybody tell you all that crap about the warmth of the slums, about how the people were that helpful to each other, the door was always open, the soup was on the hob, we were poor but we were happy. Shite that is. It might do for reminiscences by appalling old actresses who tell lies about their childhood privations and then dress them up in couthiness and end standing on Tory platforms. It might do for aged politicians for whom the delights of slum community life were so fetching that they all fucked off to the land of the bought houses and the community of the golf club and their kids' fee-paying schools. Helpful? For helpfulness you should have seen the McNultys down the street who helped themselves to all you had if you had been daft enough to leave your door ajar, imaginary soup on the hob or not. The slums a welter of bonhomie? Glasgow's slums were foul-smelling hovels surrounded by wasteland broken up by the stark wash-houses and air-raid shelters, long since reduced to receptacles for human ordure (though occasionally a carnal tryst was made there; God knows what romance could have blossomed in these excrement-smeared chambers), by long rows of spiked railings and by the filthy middens in every back-court. The streaked sky reflected in the glassy mirrors of the cess-pools which stretched across the shriven vista. Black buildings on the outside, darker in the inside with dark lives lived there. Artists like James Morrison and Joan Eardley (a well-kent figure in Townhead in her mannish slacks and jerkin, often toting a child's pram in which she had her canvases and painting equipment), made a painterly beauty out of the nightmare of it all, and sometimes captured something of its tragedy. Sadly we were later to find playwrights and other writing hacks attempting to stir some blood, or occasionally conscience, out of the incubus. Sometimes very foolish commentators wrote of the vitality of the people who lived in these barridos. Mostly people were depressed and diminished by their struggles, pasty-faced and consumptive, their imaginations tubercular too but occasionally fired by a visit to the picture palaces. Orwell could have re-written his early books here nae bother. The working-class vitality much admired by generations of outside commentators was a mixture of fiery resentment and a goodly dose of in-bred psychopathology. The bulk of the people who lived in Townhead and the other slum areas of Britain knew all that and felt the way I do; anything to take them out of the slums was jake by them, even if it did end up with the wastelands of the housing estates on the outskirts of the cities. Nightmares too now, these once brave new worlds, and that was quite predictable.

But most people who lived in these unreconstructed bomb sites looked forward to the new estates, and a lot of the children in the school moved some four miles or more away to housing 'schemes' elsewhere, outside the town, over the margins of the city. Mostly to a scheme called Ruchazie, a big green open space. A measure of how thoughtful the City Fathers had been was that all the kids who had moved away had to be bussed back to Townhead because nobody had thought to build a school there anyway. (Or if it comes to that churches, shops, pubs, cinemas, libraries – in fact anything at all.) Along with the great diaspora of the working classes, occurring throughout Glasgow and other cities, there emerged too, in tandem somehow, a sudden sort of affluence, the rather gimmicky beginnings of it. A kind of cheap glamour started to appear and nowhere more so than in popular culture. Furniture and wallpaper and lino and cars, anything which was designed in fact, started to change after the Festival of Britain. As I remember it contemporary design – that was the big word then, contemporary – was somehow rather cheap-looking. Spindly furniture, raucous colours for interiors, motor cars which possessed neither the boxy worthiness of the pre-war age nor the flash of the chromium streamlining of the American Buicks and Chevrolets. Like many children I was reactionary in my tastes, and still find the design of that era ingenuous and jejune and too risible by half. Just witness any British black and white film of the mid-1950s and you will see what I mean, all those terrible sets of living rooms with Dansette radiograms and girls in stiletto heels and tulip-shaped dresses with hair which seemed made out of fibreglass. For children like myself there were sudden fads brought over from the United States like Hula Hoops and Davy Crocket hats. But what had grown out of the States didn't graft on easily in a Britain which seemed, at least in the days of post-war austerity, full of rain and smog and mean streets, smelling of cabbage down cheerless hallways, and carbolic and clothes worn too long. An atmosphere of 10 Rillington Place was dispelled by a flurry of Flash, as much by cleaning powder as art and artifice. Then came Teddy Boys and teenagers and Bill Haley at first and then Elvis Presley. But I will tell you later of Elvis Presley. Elvis comes much later really.

Escape routes now. My grandma's was one and as I was still occasionally ill I went there to her bungalow in Stevenston often, a respite to what was often my misery in Townhead. My grandma was a splendid source of stories and tales of her native Cornwall, about smugglers and fisherfolk, some of them doubtless culled from her reading for she was a highly literate woman for her times and widely read in poetry in particular, enjoying spirited renditions of 'The Charge of the Light Brigade' and, in its glorious entirety, 'The Ancient Mariner'. She also knew all the names of flowers and trees and was rather eccentric too in her taste for taking myself, and my other siblings as well when they were there, down to the shore at Saltcoats when there was an especially vibrant storm. Thinking about it now it must have been rather dangerous really. She was not the weight of more than perhaps seven stone and I was a very wee boy. But we would stand at the steel barriers on the shore front along the promenade and watch the sea horses roar and whirl and the spume damn-near drench us, making our way back, all the way, freezing outside but warm with the exertions of a furious pace while we walked back home. My grandma liked a wee bit danger.

We spent the holidays there too, my mother and two brothers going down on the train on the Friday, my father following on the Monday morning as he cleared everything up in the school. He always looked white-faced and exhausted and I always supposed he was. Now I suspect that he probably went out for a few drinks on the nights we were away, though he was not a regular drinker and rarely went to a pub. For a start he had no friends.

My father had no friends at all. None. I never saw as much as an acquaintance except people he met while working – tradesmen like coal merchants or glaziers or such – save the once. That was in Renfield Street in the city centre and I would be about seven or eight. I gleaned that the man, a spruce-looking fellow in a hat, a sure sign of middle-class status, had been a fellow soldier during the War. The conversation lasted perhaps a minute and a half and that is all the conversation I ever heard my father make with anybody other than relations (and that was very rare as my father had no time for his own relations, and discouraged my mother from having much for hers), or people he knew through his work. But he had, I knew, friends once. The photographs of his days abroad in China in the 1920s and elsewhere in the Army proved that. And he talked from time to time of people in his squad during the War. He never talked of these ghosts much. One of them actually was a ghost too. His name was Bill Ghost and he was involved in one of the few stories my father would tell of his Army days (and bear in mind that he spent fourteen years in the Army). It was a good story and must have said something about my father, or at least what little he wanted you to know of him.

My father was ever a little self-deprecatory about the War and his part in it, like a lot of ex-regular soldiers. He had, in fact, a strong contempt for ex-servicemen who boasted of their exploits and spoke contemptuously of those who did. 'Pay-Corps Heroes' he called them which was a bit rough on the poor buggers who got sent to fight. And he'd never wear his ribbons on his uniform though I very much wanted him to: if it had been me and I had the chance to wear a uniform I'd have been prancing about like a Japanese admiral. Anyway he told us a little about his part in Dunkirk.

He and his squad had arrived at the Dunkirk beaches late because he was in the Royal Corps of Signals. 'Men of the British Army and Gentlemen of the Royal Corps of . . . ,' he would declare stentoriously when he had a drink in him at New Year, as he swaggered with his swagger stick. It was in fact a riding crop for my father had been in the Corps when they still had horses and he was deeply proud of that and also the fact that he had been one of the world-famous motor-cycling Corps of Signals display team. But he also told us that the Signals weren't first in battle. 'That was the poor bloody infantry' he told us. It was true that the Signals were behind the infantry for it was they who set up the communications (though my father was also a dispatch rider and at the front occasionally), but obviously when the poor bloody infantry retreated it was also the Signals who were left behind to cut communications. Thus my father came to Dunkirk to discover the thousands already there. He told us, and I am now unsure that this was the truth, that he and Bill Ghost and a young fellow of about eighteen had at first tried to skip the copious queues but been thrown out many a time until eventually they were forced to face the reality that they were going to be taken prisoner by the Germans, if they survived the strafing of the beach anyway. So he and his pal and the boy started to help load the wounded onto the ships. There was nothing else to do and they were pretty much doomed to capture or death anyway. It was when loading a wounded squaddie onto one of the boats that he heard a shout from the officer commanding the boat. 'You men down there,' the captain had shouted my father told us, 'Get on the fucking boat or get off the fucking boat.' The boat was about to take off for one of the ships and my father was about to take off as well when a sailor on the boat clutched at his sleeve. 'Don't be an effing mug, chum, back home for you and yer mates.' And that's how he got home. It's a bit romantic really, but I tend to believe most of it. For he must have had friends once.

It was and is a very strange thing that, not a single friend in the world he had. My father was absurdly uxorious and horribly engrossed in his family. Undeniably he would have been a happier man, and a less demanding one, had he had adult company to talk, and share something of his troubles with, other than my mother. He was so extraordinarily dominant, and domineering, that I don't suppose my mother counted as an adult with him anyway. His relationship with my mother was, we all knew, consuming and sub-Heathcliffian, and he was bound up with her but it hardly made for an entirely healthy family life. I am never sure if his total self-reliance, indeed often self-absorption concerning his family, resulted in my own inability to make friends in my childhood and early youth, and my later tendency to cultivate quite so many friends and acquaintances but it may have been. Certainly this inwardness within the family has continued to a great extent with myself and my two brothers. All we brothers have remained very close and their friends and mine often seem to see us as a group on our own, for it was certainly a very tight-knit brotherhood. Rather an odd family altogether, and regarded as extremely eccentric by our neighbours. We followed intellectual pursuits too which marked us as different. E.M. Forster could have written about us for heaven's sake. Stuck out like a sore thumb we did. And still do, I suppose. But this oddness, this difference, made me miserable as a child, and I grew up feeling disorientated and out of synch. I was right to feel that. I was both.

But I did have some advantages. One of them was that I could draw. At the first primary school I was the best in the class at drawing. Well of course I was. I had been the best at home too. In fact at a very early age my precocity was one of my badges, you know the badges you get issued as children: 'This is the shy one, this is a holy terror. This one is slow, this is the one with the brains. This one has the musical ear, this one can draw . . .' And I could draw all right. Oh yes. I must have been about three when I drew a railway train. That isn't terribly unusual though not common; at that age most children are still haptic illustrators with drawings of themselves bigger than everybody and mummy drawn bigger than daddy and in short symbols. Every artist, art educator, and psychologist will tell you that they learn a great deal from children's drawings. What my parents learned from that drawing of a locomotive was that I was going to become an artist. I drew the engine and my dad asked me what the line sort of things were on the wheels. 'That's what makes the wheels go round, daddy,' I replied. 'They get moved by the big engine.' Nae wonder my father thought I was a bloody changeling. What I had noticed was that the pistons made the wheels go round, that's how the train worked. Such a perception is not unusual in those who are gifted with the ability to draw. It is the form in which their intelligence is expressed. If I couldn't, like many artists, understand number or abstract calculus, I was blessed with the intelligence of drawing. What that means is that I can find out how things work only by seeing how they do, by drawing the working itself. Later, I remember drawing a fireman, after an exceptionally exciting day when a red fire engine had careered past the shops in the Crescent in Cathcart on their way to Weirs works. I drew the fireman and his coal-scuttle helmet and his boots and the buttons on his tunic and the factory in the background. And as an extra individualistic touch I drew the hosepipe save that the hosepipe was emerging from the fireman's trousers and in fact he was holding a massive prick in his hands and spraying enough piss to put out the Clydebank bloody blitz. My parents found it of course and here I was to discover something very weird. I expected some kind of trouble, a scolding at least, for being 'dirty' but my father made a sort of perfunctory demur and went on to praise the drawing. He said it didn't matter if I did draw the fireman doing the toilet but it wouldn't sell any pictures in the future. (How little he knew, it'd make your fortune today. Actually almost every famous artist drew such scatalogical scenes in their early childhood, and many of them kept on doing it. Psychologists remark upon this as rather frequent among visual artists.) My parents even kept the drawing and I was to discover it among my mother's papers after she died. But I was the artist in the family and then I was the artist at the school.

It is a unique gift, a strange talent, drawing. It needs only a bit of ground and a stick and there you are marked out from the rest of the tribe: you have a kind of shaman status – it's what you are really. From the first days at primary school I was asked to draw, by the teachers, by classmates, by others in the school itself. Little girls would come up to my desk at interval and smile sweetly and ask me to draw a drawing for them, for their birthday or their little brother's for a friend in the class. 'I'll give you a kiss' they would say, or a sweet, or some such token. The boys I always made give something, a conker, a marble, something. One day a fat American boy came into the class and, being a new boy, was made much of. Stories filtered through that he could 'draw better than' me. I took the taunts for a day or two, and then could resist no longer. In front of the other children I asked him what he could draw. 'Anything,' he replied, 'but mainly Arabs.' It was then I knew my man. I'd seen his type before. 'Do one,' I demanded. He did one. I took the paper and the pencil and drew a magnificent Arab. I gave him curling moustaches to go with his curly dagger, and a hawk nose and eyes fierce as a falcon's, and striped robes. The boys and girls came back to my studio immediately and I walked the American boy home to show that there were no hard feelings. And there weren't either: I had simply seen him off.

But at Townhead school I was faced with a weightier adversary. He was a rival in other academic areas too – the boy whose father pushed him as much as mine did me, the son of the Cruelty Man, Gordon Somerville. He vied with me for the top of the class position in academic areas but that was no real problem. He wasn't much better at arithmetic than myself and his reading was less wide, and it was a friendly rivalry anyway. I liked him. I had found a friend in him in a way, for I had recognised one of the Children of the Hugely Ambitious Parent. But Gordon could draw wonderful things – things I couldn't draw, I knew he could better than me. Where I struggled to get a face right in three-quarter view, Gordon Somerville could draw whole scenes. Mr Kidd put his drawings on the wall, next to mine, for everybody to see how much better he was. Dethroned.

One of his drawings in particular was glorious, a broad battle scene at sea with furled sails and cannons firing, and foam-tossed oceans and galleons burning. Turner couldn't have done better. I held this to my breast for nights. And then one night I told my father, haltingly, not wanting him to know how much this hurt, for I made a heavy pretence that my gifts were lightly borne. Also I suppose, not wanting him to know how hard the hurt was at all. 'I can't ever draw like him,' I told my father, 'because he'll get better when he gets older and I'll not catch up when I get better. I'll never catch up.' My father tried to placate me, assuring me that, 'You can't always be the best, that's only what we aim for,' but I was not to be consoled with adult casuistry. Then I told him that an unusual feature of Gordon's work was that he always drew in black pencil, even when he did coloured drawings he did them in black pencil and then coloured in the spaces. My father considered this and then told me to get out of bed and dress. We went into the school, into the long dark corridors of the night, along the eerie walls, and came into my classroom where my father asked me to show him the drawings. He looked at them and said it was alright, everything was alright. He said I could draw better than Gordon really and he'd show me. And he did, that night, back in the house. He drew over a picture with a piece of paper underneath. And between a sheet of blackish paper. Carbon paper. That was how Gordon Somerville was doing this, the method he'd used to effect these marvellous drawings.

My father told me not to tell anyone, how Gordon wanted to show he was better than he was and that was a weakness and it would be unkind to unmask him and, best of all, I'd know that I was better, I'd have that in my heart forever. My father was very convincing on this and I never told anybody of Gordon's trick till now. I never told anyone and I never minded when other children said Gordon could draw better than I could for I knew. Eventually so did Gordon I think, for he stopped the carbon tracings shortly afterwards and never pretended to my crown again.

Another escape was there for us. We still went back across to the south-side regularly. Instead of the cinemas which abounded in Townhead we took the trolley bus to the south-side. The south-side of Glasgow is different from the north. It has larger streets and more grass and greenery and somehow bigger skies. It is also where the notorious and world-infamous Gorbals were. To this day world journalists come in their droves to explore this Naples of the North and it's crazy because Gorbals was demolished almost in its entirety over thirty years ago. In fact Gorbals was never as bad as it was said to be and was rather a thriving community with well-ordered Irish pubs and Italian and Jewish delicatessens and bakeries. The Irish and Jewish communities had lived there for generations and older people remember Gorbals with some affection. But beyond Gorbals lay tenemental areas for the better-off working man and his family, and then on to grassy suburbs, some of them for the wealthy. Some of them still are and it is a confusion to visitors to the city when they see the Randolph Hearst-style mansions which the Edwardians built for themselves and which are as well-kept as ever. Every city has its areas for the wealthy and so does Glasgow. The surprising thing is that in Glasgow such areas lie cheek by jowl with poorer estates and there is little class distinction, if a lot of envy. The south-side is infrequently, if at all, visited by the denizens of north of the river, and south-siders regard themselves as belonging to another city really, as though it were Buda and Pest. And myself and my brothers returned each Saturday to our city on the south of the Clyde. The cinemas we preferred were the Kingsway, the George, but most of all the Toledo. It is the only one which still exists, the others having been variously metamorphosed into bingo halls and churches for the Jehovah's Witnesses and once, briefly, as bowling alleys.

We liked the Toledo because it was even more of a fantasy building than the others. It was built on the outside like a Moorish town hall in Spain. Inside it had balconies and haciendas and Toledo wrought iron. The curtains were glossy and shimmering, turning from red to green and orange with the lights, an entire experience. For some reason, in an age in which children are assaulted with noise and bright lights and every device designed to get the buggers as hyper as a speed-freak on Mescalin, today's cinema interiors are rather dull. In my childhood they were aff their heid with glamour. The interiors were off the film sets, and the players were dressed as extras, from the resplendent commissionaire in his Ruritarian outfit, to the cinema manager who wore evening dress at nights. The films changed twice a week unless a film had taken in especially large receipts and you got two films, a main feature and a B film, often a British 'quota nasty' (the Government insisted that a certain number of films shown had to be British and the aboriginal film industry responded with some marvellous drivel highly watchable today on late-night TV), and a cartoon, a newsreel and adverts. My brothers and myself liked the ads and played a game in which we were held to possess the object being puffed on the screen. This was grand if they were advertising restaurants or motor cars, but not worth a turd if it was nylon stockings or kitchenware. Aye, jings it wis rerr fun tae be alive. Well it was in the cinemas of that time because you got a lot for your money. The movies then were great for kids too because there were a lot of costume pictures and even very big stars did not hesitate to act in films which had them prancing about in doublets and hose, sporting togas, or looking bizarrely out of place in union shirts and leather chaps and astride horses of which they were clearly highly fearful. It was a time before actors became artists. A great many of the films about contemporary life were in the sub-gangster genre and, though we didn't know it at the time, were examples of what is now called *ciné noir*. It was a good time for movies, the last days of the film empires, and a good time for moviegoers. Certainly my whole generation has been affected by the movies all our lives and many, like myself, have been untouched and unscathed by television. If I hungered after escape though, I am glad it wasn't the bloody TV set at that.

My father certainly had an escape in mind for his children though. He'd already sent his eldest to a selective fee-paying school where there would be opportunities for rising to the top. It wasn't a bank clerk's job he was seeking for his sons; we were to be Chancellors of the bloody Exchequer. Bit of a disappointment Richard had been. I mean he'd done well scholastically. Well, in everything except science, Maths, anything to do with what my father considered 'the real world'. In short, Richard was what adults call a dreamy boy. It was thus to be hoped that I would enter the world of technology, though how anybody could imagine me fitting into that prospect defies belief. Then, as now, I could hardly put on a light switch. Part of the plan to make me into the inventor of radium was to send me to, of course, a selective fee-paying school. Preferably on a scholarship, and preferably not Hutcheson's Grammar which had made my elder brother into that dreamy boy who was to go on to do Classics at university, and who read fiction and didn't play football. The fact that he was technically very competent (he made, and still does, model aeroplanes of quite astounding complexity), and that he was a highly regarded wing three-quarter on the rugby field, made little difference. Like so many fathers who have had ambitions for their children to move out of their class, he resented it when they did. He didn't, in fact, really know what he wanted.

It was very odd indeed in the playground at the interval. I didn't know a single child, and few of them knew each other. There was a very boisterous group of them who most certainly were well acquainted: they were the boys who had spent three years in the school already, since they were nine, and were now sitting the entrance exam to the Big School. There was another, smaller, more muted, set. They were the boys from other schools but who lived in the same well-off areas, whose mums and dads went to the same golf and tennis clubs. Most of the boys were, of course, from well-off areas, bought houses, lawns. Brothers and sisters at similar schools. Though my clothes weren't actually all that different, the same schoolboy's uniform of shorts, socks, blazer, and Clydella shirt and tie, I felt different all the same, an outsider. I felt like Pip in his heavy boots when Estella makes him play cards. I'd also been told much the same as I had when we had been enrolled at Townhead Primary; only the opposite factor underlay the injunction. Then I had been told to expect 'rough boys', an expectation fully met. Now I was told that the boys I would meet – how I was to meet any boy in ten minutes in an alien playground I cannot tell – would speak differently and be dreadfully posh and I wasn't to Let Them Down. What did they think I was going to do – spit on the ground, brandish an open razor at the teachers, swear raucously in lumpen Doric, piss in the hydrangeas? I knew what they meant. I wasn't to 'show myself up'. For I was 'as good as them'.

The playgrounds changed but not much. There were only six selective boys schools in Glasgow, if you didn't count the two Roman Catholic ones and you most certainly didn't count them. Edinburgh has a tradition of fee-paying schools and in that city's less egalitarian atmosphere they count for social cachet very much indeed. Glasgow's schools were very academic, among the best in the UK and well considered as such, but they were immensely meritocratic and competition for entry was intense. I had been put in for every school save Hutcheson's for Dreamy Boys, and for the scholarships, which were few but not so few that there wasn't a long and worthy tradition of working-class boys becoming leaders of the nation. I kind of recollect the playgrounds all the same. I mean the schools each had a different look to them. Kelvinside was Grecian with its pillars and its blazer badge. Glasgow Academy was merchant-money, even a kid could smell it. The only one I remember particularly was Hillhead because there was a boy there wearing a skirt which shocked me to the core. He was a terribly girlish-looking boy as well and seemed to me, at the time, rather as though he had been an Afghan dancing boy. Certainly I, metaphorically, had my arse against the wall all the time I spied him in the playground. Also he played with the girls. When I got home I discovered that the 'boy' was a lassie after all but had been sporting an Eton Crop, a short hairstyle sometimes affected by little girls of the middle classes.

The Glasgow High School had enormous traditions with three Prime Ministers going there and was grubbily patrician, the buildings being set just off the bustling epicentre of Glasgow, Sauchiehall Street. The only school I didn't like the look of at all was Allan Glen's, the High School of Science and Technology, the only one in Britain. It was a set of amazingly ugly black buildings, designed clearly by the sort of self-made man who stands no nonsense and wants facts more than Mr Gradgrind ever required. The halls rang with brimstone and smelled of sulphur. I was accepted, as a scholarship boy, for every one of the schools. So naturally I went to Allan Glen's.

5

Allan Glen's was at the top of a long steep hill off Cathedral Street and wasn't far from my primary school, five or six minutes away from my house and set in the middle of dreary black tenements. There were only two climates. Wet and dark, and dusty and shabby. Somehow everything was worse when the sun tried to shine; a pale sun, like a watery egg. Then it got depressing. The day I arrived at Allan Glen's it was the former, wet and dark. A bit more too; there was, I recollect, a dark red streak across the sky, a portent. 'When fishes flew, and forests walked, and fig grew upon thorn/ Some evening when the moon was blood; then surely I was born.' My secondary school career was born with just that sentiment in mind. A portent indeed.

I arrived early. Two boys stood forlornly at the massive iron gates, one dark-haired and saturnine, the other red-haired and somehow foolish looking and cheery-faced with the sort of grin that is described as lop-sided. Later I discovered that he was a bit lop-sided altogether. The dark one was called Glyn Philips and Lop-side was called Bird. I never thought of him again without imagining a bird, one of those birds with long legs forever poking its beak into sad waters. Armed with these new friends I was marched into a large hall with the rest of the new boys. There were a lot of teachers about in gowns. This was not a pretension, for teachers in the state senior secondaries were also attired thus. In fact, to its credit, Glen's had no pretensions in that way: it didn't really need them. Of all the selective schools it had the most working-class profile, with its hands covered in the lubricant of industry, for most of its pupils went into engineering and science when they left. Also it had a high number of scholarships for boys. Bursary Boys we were called. I was rather, and I suppose justifiably, proud that I was a Bursary Boy. For a start this had not only been a source of pride to my parents, it also afforded a certain financial leavening. Not only were my fees paid (they were a very nominal sum, about three guineas a year I think), but also my books and jotters and there was even some help with the uniform. My pride was about to be punctured though. A red-faced angry-looking man in a fat black gown with big sleeves addressed us. It didn't take a genius to know that he was the headmaster himself for there was a certain amount of deference shown to him by assistant masters and certainly he showed himself to be conscious of his own authority. 'Hands up the Bursary Boys in here!' he demanded. Those scholars raised their hands. 'I don't want you Bursary boys to think of yourselves as receiving charity. Being a Bursar is nothing to be ashamed of.' Very good. Instantly I thought of myself as receiving charity. Instantly I was ashamed of myself. The headmaster's name was John B. Sommerville.

In later years this man became the bane of my existence, a horror to be encountered in the school corridors. And he is the only person that I have ever hated. A blight on my schoolboy life he was, as he was to be for many, many others who came into his hands. 'Joe Boss' he was known as to his little charges and he was hated the way convicts hate the bad overseer in chain gangs. Feared too, for he could be remarkably vicious and temperamental. He had come after a rather gentle headmaster called McKimmie who had, said some governors (who were largely Corporation councillors), let the school slide. This was not in fact true, it was just that Glen's could never compete with the other schools for social status, and the school had never been intended to make gentlemen. We might be officers but we were officers in the REME, not some smart cavalry regiment. But we were the men who won wars. Well that's the way everybody except Joe Boss thought of the school and by and large the perception was true enough. In later years I discovered Somerville to be somewhat of a womaniser, well maybe not: I do know that he married twice, enough to make you Bluebeard in the Fifties. It was said he drank. In the years of his thrall I knew him to be a bully in the way that only a school teacher can be: a furtive one never found out by parents, governors, or those in authority. I got my own back though. I wrote his obituary.

The first days at secondary were no different from anybody else's then or today no doubt. You are practically witless with apprehension and don't know where anything is, or what classes you are meant to be in. It is a rude start to the beginning of the end of childhood and today's schools unwisely attempt to ease the process. Unwisely because it is still a shock to discover that you are largely on yer own-io, and there is no all-seeing figure like the primary dominie to smooth your passage: you will just have to find out for yourself.

Soft-minded primary teachers, and positively feeble-minded social workers and such, are all for cushioning the blow. But this process, doubtless as much for girls nowadays as for boys, is a great lesson to learn. That there really are bastards out there and some of them aren't even people. Some of them are the simple matter of the Way Things Are Done Around Here. ('You'll soon get to know the ropes, Carruthers.') The best idea is to get it over and done with. If that is a touch sink or swim it is the way life always is in the animal kingdom. Few people sink, most of us learn to swim.

Years later I was to discover that even a school like Allan Glen's was not quite as Malthusian as that, and there were many kindly teachers around to help a bit, without anybody noticing, in much the same way that you sometimes speak sharply to a child so that he or she doesn't collapse in tears. Cruel to be kind rather. My register teacher was called Robertson and a very nice soft-spoken gentleman he was: he once damn-near illustrated what I mean by being too kind. He told me off once for some dreadful but long-forgotten offence. It was the way he did it which was worse than whatever crime might have occasioned his rebuke. He spoke softly to me, on our own in his class after the others had left. 'Don't forget, son, you're here because your mother and father have sacrificed for you. I know your parents. Good people. Don't let them down.' Jesus, I was as near to greeting as I ever came to throughout my entire school career, both primary and secondary. Decades later on I was to discover that this was the sod's technique: he had the hardest teddy boys the school threw up, and there were a goodly few of them, going through the same scenario.

Mind you, there were certainly those masters who embraced the maxim of Cruel to be Kind with a vigorous enthusiasm. I'll never forget the shit who gave me nine of the belt for a misdemeanour, which, if it was one, was more than insignificant. The man had asked me in front of another class, and another teacher he had been visiting, why I had done so well in so many subjects and abjectly failed in his. I had enquired who had told him of my results. He said a little bird had told him. I knew it must have been Old Man Campbell, the head of mathematics. 'Was it a wee, fat bird?' I asked. Okay, a smart remark. Nine of the belt though? Six was regarded as the very maximum, and rare at that. Oddly it was another teacher, the one in whose class I had been, who intervened. It led, I discovered later, to a major row in the staffroom. The intervening master told me to go away and wash my hands or something. As I was leaving I heard Mr Prais call his colleague a bastard. Edgar Prais was to become a distinguished professor of languages, and was Jewish and knew the way that some Jews had treated others in Hitler's Germany and elsewhere. His colleague was also Jewish. Me, I was very small and the thrashing was too much for me though I hadn't flinched during it. (You couldn't let your classmates witness such a humiliation, let alone a teacher.) I went down to the lavatories and went into shock, trembling for about ten minutes.

But the first days at the school were distinctly strange to us all. Unlike most schoolchildren we knew nobody. Nobody knew anybody more or less, because unlike neighbourhood schools the only neighbourhood we shared was that of the clever working-class boys from state primary schools, a very inchoate neighbourhood with drifting frontiers. There were a good number of pupils from other social strata as well and it was probably a touch odd for them too. There was only one other boy in my year who came from a similar area to myself though, in the heartland of the old Glasgow slums, around the Townhead district. His name was Lavery and he did indeed look rather poorer than most of the other kids. I don't know how, but he did. He had thick dark hair and black eyebrows, and Romany features. He was, it quickly turned out, very bright indeed. Not that any of that mattered because, although there was the occasional idjit who brought to the school a consciousness of his background, most of us just wondered why we were there at all and tried to make the best of what was clearly a bad job.

My first friends were the ones who sat next to me in class. I can't remember their names but one was the son of a publican, and the other of a tailor. A third boy joined us whose father was dead, a Norwegian sea-captain called Peden who had been drowned at sea. There was a certain interest in this fact but when his mother married a perfectly Scottish fellow called Hunter and Peden got called by his new stepfather's name it took the shine off him a bit. They were pleasant enough companions if rather silly I thought and they knew exactly how to waste time so I joined in. At Christmas I had failed nearly every exam.

I stopped the friendships but my academic disaster that first term wasn't their fault. I don't think I'd ever have passed a maths exam or any of the sciences. I didn't know what all these valencies were for, and couldn't keep the elements in my head and never understood how to work a beam balance and all this nonsense with beakers and Bunsen burners and how to make cobalt crystals appeared so bloody pointless. I mean, if all these adult scientists knew perfectly well how to make cobalt crystals, why was I doing it too? I was bloody sure that all this tomfoolery bore no relationship to any kind of applied science and I didn't want to be a scientist anyway and sod it what was this science master doing in the room wasting his time as well if it wasn't that he himself wasn't really any kind of scientist himself and why wasn't he in a laboratory doing the things which I read about in the novels by Neville Shute.

I had then a keen understanding of what C.P. Snow was later to describe as the two cultures and I damned well knew which one I was in.

But it was different in the Art class and in English and Languages and History. Especially the Art class. There I knew – I could see with my eyes – that the art teachers were the genuine article, artists. I knew that they only appeared occasionally like, as a whim on their part, when they took time off from their own painting in their own studios and deigned to come down from their *ateliers* looking out for young, fresh talent. One of the teachers most certainly was. Looking for young, fresh talent that is. He was a magnificently epicene young chap who was wont to say things to the boys like: 'Get your bottom back in your seat, boy, before I put it to better use.' His name was Potter, and naturally he was known to the boys as 'Pansy Potter'. He wasn't there long but was well liked for his sarcasm and somewhat feminine wit.

Two other teachers were in the Art department and they were there for many years. Not only were both of them extremely skilful draughtsmen, not only did they exhibit, but they most certainly looked and sounded the part. James McGill was a military-looking man who spoke, at length, in the most wonderful Edwardian prose style. He dearly loved to argue, even with boys, and set up immensely long dialogues with his class in the dialectic style. He was also a very decent man and his occasional rages, which were a delight to behold, were much enjoyed by his charges. And they came to nothing. Far from being frightening he was very much liked, particularly for the rages, and especially those he frequently had with other, philistine, members of staff. He was joined in this disdain for many of his colleagues in other disciplines by a most remarkable art teacher, Ralph Cowan. Both men were to figure large in my school career and both of them are still around today. Ralph indeed, I know, is still painting. And in a modernist abstract style too.

Ralph Cowan was my art teacher from the start. On my first day in the art class he frightened shit out of me because he caught me talking to my neighbour and demanded to know what I was saying. I believed then that I was in trouble for speaking, as would have been the case in every other class. Later I was to discover that Ralph simply *did* want to know what I'd said. I remember it very well, that incident. It was our first lesson and he had told us to draw a market scene with people in it. This was, I was to discover later when I became an art teacher myself, an old ploy to find out in the early days who could draw, who had imagination, who had powers of observation, who of recall and I had all of them and I could draw. From the first Ralphie, as the boys called him behind his back, supported me. In the dark days I was to encounter later on, Ralphie looked after me in the face of considerable disapproval, as I found out many years later. But Ralph must have faced exactly that many times in his art teaching career, not least because of his appearance.

Cowan wore beautiful clothes, soft Lovat tweeds, soft-collared shirts, blending woven ties, crafted shoes. And he wore his hair very long indeed, amazingly so for the early 1950s. It was long and silver and extremely poetic. For some reason he and McGill didn't make any kind of contrast to me, they were both part of the same artistic zeitgeist, complements to each other. From time to time other art teachers strayed into their studios. I remember a fleeting period when the cartoonist, the late Ewan Bain, came to visit. He later became famous for his magnificent Angus Og strips in the national press. (Angus Og was in fact Ewan himself and all the characters in his strip were real people who unfortunately recognised themselves as a result of which Ewan found some difficulties in his homeland of the Western Isles.) But the daring duo of McGill and Cowan was really the art department. They were joined from time to time by a pottery expert who taught even the stupidest and cack-handed children to make pots and did so with abundant good humour. Any ceramicist who has ever taught anybody how to throw a pot will know that it takes an even temper worthy of Our Lord himself, on valium, to do it. But there we boys were in that haven of civilisation with three of the kindliest dominies you ever met.

Yet another teacher was my English master, Paddy Inglis. He had a lilting voice which we boys took for an Irish brogue. In fact, he came from the Borders but he was known as Paddy all the years he was at Allan Glen's. A big, stocky man, he never, as far as I know, used corporal punishment, save once. He called out our entire class and made us raise our hands. He then brought the strap – he must have borrowed it from a colleague – down on our hands with all the force of a humming bird's tail feather hitting its arse. 'That's you all been belted then,' he cried. 'I'll have some discipline in this class if it's the last thing I do!' He also had a sharp wit which softened at the edges, writing on pupils' essays such heavy admonitions as: 'You speakum English heap good.' Paddy was good-natured and very erudite. It was no surprise to find decades later that his chums among the staff were the triumvirate in the Art department. Certainly it was Paddy who shaped much of my later reading, as he did with many other of his pupils, a number of which have gone on to publish books dedicated to 'Paddy, my old English teacher'. Another Glen's F.P., Roddy Forsyth, wrote an inscription to me in his splendid book, *The Only Game*, an elegiac survey of Scottish football, about Paddy. Roddy was years below me, but he went on to become both an arts writer and a sports writer. There are only two journos currently plying both trades at once in this country. I'm the other one and both Roddy and myself know how much we owe to this gentle gentleman.

Paddy taught me a lot of poetry and gave me difficult novels way above my head. He issued me with Joyce, telling me: 'You won't understand this now, but it'll help when you can't understand it when you're older.' (Nae wonder he got called Paddy.) He also taught me grammar and syntax. For a boy who couldn't get his head round the arcana of mathematics or such things as logarithms, I was a blue streak at the grammar and syntax. I came to love such exercises as General Analysis and grew fond of the Adverbial Clause of Consequence and other joys. Parsing was a puzzle as pleasant as a crossword though better because I nearly always solved the damned things. I embraced such furry little animals in the undergrowth of grammar as gerunds and positively petted gerundives. About the only science I have ever grasped, or wanted to, is the beautifully precise one of words. Paddy is long dead now but I still remember him, as a lot of Allan Glen's boys do, with enormous affection and a great deal of gratitude. His widow, Jenny, is now a friend of mine, and proud I am to know her for herself let alone for her late husband. Certainly Paddy and Ralph Cowan and James McGill made life bearable for me because the bloody headmaster didn't. J.B. Somerville had taken it into his head to dislike me and there was a reason for it, even if the reason was unreasonable. Joe Boss disliked me because of the way I looked.

It can be pretty grim being a teenager at any time in any age. It is very grim indeed when you are the first generation to be teenagers. It should have been a good time too, a great time. But it wasn't, for the generation older than mine were about as sour-faced and mean-spirited as any have been since. True as it was that other younger generations had their critics among their parents and elders – enough literature chronicling the Jazz Age of the post Great War era testifies to that – there was a terrible intensity about the adults of my teenage years astounding reaction to the emergence of The Teenager. Mine was the first generation which en masse had a level of affluence which allowed for a truly discernible break with their parents' views, values, music, clothes, films, literature and much else which made up their horizons. As a small boy I saw little difference between young men and women and their parents in the way they looked or walked or behaved really. Young men wore much the same clothes, for instance, as their fathers did. The music was similar too. Frank Sinatra, even with all the bobby-soxers screaming their adulation at him, wasn't that much different from, say, Bing Crosby. Indeed this was freely acknowledged. You can even see it in the movie 'High Society' when Crosby interrupts Francis Albert in their duet with: 'You must be one of the newer fellas.' Newer, but not new. The New came very suddenly, in 1956, with Elvis Presley.

The revolution had been brewing a long time, but the way we saw it, in a very staid Britain, it burst suddenly, in brightest technicolour, like a glorious firework explosion, bright and blinding across a dull, grey sky. The first I knew of it was when the playground buzzed with argument betwixt two factions, the pro-Bill Haley and his Comets set and the fans of the phenomenon with a monicker that sounded more like a medical condition than a name, Elvis Presley. In fact, the first inkling I had that there was a change coming in popular music was a recording of 'Singin' the Blues'. Two recordings really, Tommy Steele's version and Guy Mitchell's. The latter was already a top hitmaker very much in the crooner tradition with a strong line in novelty numbers. Tommy Steele's record had what, in retrospect, was a kind of skiffle sound to it. It wasn't very good skiffle but it heralded a country-ish style which had sort of been hanging around in the background with people like Jimmie Rodgers and Hank Williams and old country artists like the Carter Family who you occasionally heard on the wireless. There was an extra beat to the new sound though and a freneticism hitherto only heard on records by people like Cab Calloway. It was a pretty innocent age as far as music went for music wasn't non-stop, covering your consciousness all day every day. There wasn't, when I think about it now, that much music about. No trannies or personal stereos, no LP records, no all-music radio stations. Therefore music wasn't as important in people's lives as it would become, and it wasn't the mega-industry which it has become over the last thirty years. And so Elvis Presley came as a genuine shock to almost everybody outside of the red-neck deep south of the United States. He came as a revelation to me. And that was before I had ever seen, as you would say now, the cat.

The Hillbilly Cat he was known as in the States. There was a lot happening there too, and emanating from it. Films stars like Marlon Brando (though I remember he and people like Montgomery Cliff being initially thought of, not as rebels, but rather mainstream new film stars). There was a change coming. Names like Elvis Presley indeed. Then we saw him. Elvis was ideal for young people – especially, probably, young adolescent males. He looked rather girlish really, and I suspect part of his appeal to young girls lay in that aspect, though he also most certainly looked sexually dangerous with his heavy-lidded eyes and sneering curling mouth. His clothes were outrageous too, pink coats and black shirts and white loafers. And his music was sensual and somehow primitive and citified at the same time. He even had a fine voice which he displayed in his ballad numbers, songs culled from the vaudeville of Al Jolson mixed in with the salaciousness of the negro entertainers. He was a bloody shock to Middle America, a dreadful upset to Middle Britain, and a fucking godsend to the teenage generation.

But with all this came a new industry, since terribly corrupted, since gone horribly wrong. It was a character in a novel by the American writer Wilfrid Sheed who claimed that rock 'n' roll had been folk music until the Beatles came along, bringing old effete European ways to bear on it. Probably true as well, and certainly a lot of today's rock 'n' roll music seems somehow overstated, over-produced, and a bit stale in place of the fresh raw sounds the early rock 'n' roll artists made. Along with the fresh raw sounds came a style in clothes, speech and thinking. There were a lot of changes about in the mid to late Fifties, from theatre and novels to what we wore and even what we ate. But what got me was what we were and I decided to be a teenager as much as I possibly could. What was more, it was a role which was made for me.

I had the right looks. Surly and discontented. Dark hair which when hair cream was applied could turn into the very apotheosis of teen rebellion, the Bop hairstyle. If my father loathed it – he once ordered me down to the barbers several times in one day – my headmaster went daft. Suddenly in his school a style, almost imperceptible at first, began to emerge: tighter trousers, slimmer school ties, a lot more hair. But that was, he must have known inside himself as must have the rest of his age group, just the superficialities. There was a change in attitudes as well, a bit like the hair. Slicker, sharper, less deferential, a lot more narcissistic than ever before, even a lot more classless. The old buffers were still coming out with drivel and continued to do so for many a long year. Nothing could exemplify it more than the films and shows which the entertainment industry came out with for damned near twenty years. There were TV programmes with back numbers, laughable nonentities like Denis Lotus and the Fabulous Yana – all that was fabulous was that she was earning a living at all. Films for years tried to update themselves with what they absurdly thought was the latest music, latest style, latest actors. A collection of merry macs they were, just like the comedians of the day. Crap. Stick Arthur Askey or Norman Wisdom onto the stage of my generation's back memory and we will laugh ourselves sick at the sight of them. Movies with 'wild parties' and Lawrence Harvey doing the twist and girls in old-fashioned but 'daring' dresses set in the same Belgravia flats we had seen in 1958 B films, lasted all the way through till the 1970s. We can see the residue of that consciousness even yet in a great deal of television, but back in my teenage years I didn't think about middle-aged culture: I ignored it. What is more, I knew then, I know now, that we looked and sounded great. I suppose that's what Joe Boss saw when he surveyed the school he thought of as his domain, a culture he thought as he stood astride, and there we were in Bop coiffures with a duck's arse at the back, and white socks, and insolent insoucience. And I came to the fore in the madman's mind because I had the best Bop in the entire school.

The style was achieved with the sort of care the Macaronis of the late eighteenth century took. To get the look right, the quiff as bold and dashing as the crest on a particularly flashy knight's helmet, took time. You needed lashings of Brylcreem, though I later patronised Tru-Gel. The advertising for this product claimed that your head didn't soil the pillows and made anti macassars redundant. Soil the pillows? Your bloody head stuck to them during the night. I used to get my mother to disengage me from the bedclothes every morning. I had enough grease on me to oil a Lamborghini. We took as much care over our clothes as Regency dandies and lavished anxiety on the cut of a bumfreezer jacket or the spearpoint of a shirt collar as Brummel ever did with his linen or his topboots. No generation had considered style as important since the days of the early nineteenth century. And there was this generation of dominies dunning Byron and Thackeray into our heads and decrying the very styles, and certainly affectations, of those literary giants as rediscovered by teenagers, while they themselves wandered about looking ineffectual and neutered, like old men put out to grass, in apparel designed to look as if their pricks had dropped off long ago. Nae wonder we looked elsewhere for models for being grown-ups. But not entirely. We were often, all of us of whatever age, in something of a time warp in those days. School was one certainly, and so was work. I came to work early. And I met other people there.

My first job was during the school holidays with a tobacconists called George Murray Frame. The company had several shops all over Glasgow and beyond, with its main shop, its flagship, set at the corner of George Square, a long large shop which sported grand window displays of boxes of cigars; Dunhill briar and Meerschaum pipes; expensive lighters; exotic packets of cigarettes from all over the world; great porcelain tobacco jars. Inside the aroma was magnificent (the neighbouring shop, two doors down in Queen Street, was even more so, for it contained a large cavern below which was a coffee shop, one of the many which graced Glasgow for many, many, years, the arenas in which real business was discreetly conducted by Glasgow's businessmen: the rich reek of ground coffee, expensive Havana cigars, and navy-cut pipe tobacco held a promise of unimaginable and prosperous adulthood.) I had simply walked in one day in my Allan Glen's blazer and asked for a summer job. I must have been well-spoken enough, and the blazer denoting one of the fee-paying schools would have helped, for Mr George – as I realise now, the middle-aged son of old Mr Murray Frame gave me a job, starting the next day at seven -thirty in the morning and it was perhaps the best job I ever had. I was thirteen.

The first duty of the day was polishing the brass surround of the windows with its embossed legend of the firm's name. Then I washed the public floor and stacked the shelves with their banks of cigarettes. Players had a naval hero on the packet; Capstan an equally nautical emblem, pale blue in medium, pale brown in Full Strength; Senior Service in white with a full-blown galleon; Admiral in blue and gold. There was a lot of sea about in the tobacco trade: Pegasus and Prize Crop; Gold Leaf in its red and gold; Du Maurier in red and silver; Passing Cloud in pink with a picture of a Franz Hals Cavalier (Passing Cloud were expensive cigarettes and, oddly, were oval in shape), the cheaper Woodbine of the children's playground rhyme. 'Fur Woodbine is a rerr wee fag: geeza light, geeza light, geeza light . . .' We didn't sell many packets of the cheaper Woodbine for our trade was very much upmarket, the Fortnum and Mason of Scottish tobacconists. And then until nine or so I helped out in the shop, serving the customers. I actually became a favourite with some of them. 'Let the boy serve me, smartest one in here,' they'd say with a wink at one of the men.

Customers were mainly businessmen collecting their daily supply of cigarettes or pipe tobacco. Many of them had their own mixtures, ready made up for them and set aside in jars with their names on them. Some had their own cigarettes with their monograms on each, though that trade was mainly for home-delivery, in bulk. Smartly dressed our clients were, the older ones in particular. One very old gentleman came in about ten o'clock on a daily visit to the coffee rooms and the nearby Stock Exchange clad in, I swear it, a frock coat and carrying a cane. Certainly there was an air of the old days of trade, the last days of it, when Glasgow was a major business centre and business was a gentlemanly pursuit, with the men doing only a few hours in the office at all. Sometimes pert young secretaries came in to collect their boss's cigarettes and joke with the staff and embarrass me with enquiries concerning my sex life. But the best part of the job was after ten-thirty, after my break in the coffee shop. It was then I was given parcels and enough money for bus fares. For I was the delivery boy.

We did a lot of deliveries to older people and big houses where they still entertained on a large scale. Then I discovered not only what a large city Glasgow was but how many different lives people lived in cities altogether. Areas I had never seen before, with huge mansions and servants answering the door. Big overblown suburbs with driveways it took five minutes to walk up. A lot of districts now with their houses split into conversion flats, or gone to seed, still possessed a prosperity then which was neo-Edwardian: Kelvinside and as far as Bearsden out to the north; Dumbreck to the south-west; Whitecraigs and south past Cathcart itself. Big houses and other worlds to me entirely. Travelling about what I now knew to be a very large conurbation indeed I lost the city boy's sense of ethno-centricity for ever. I was young to learn this, and that was good.

I worked for three summers after that too, turning up at the start of the school holidays every year and working all the way through to the last day of them. I gave all the money I earned into the house because I don't suppose anybody thought one wouldn't. And I loved it. In fact when I left school Mr George offered me a job with the firm, to learn about buying tobacco. I'd have got to travel all over the world – to Virginia, to the Balkans, to the Russian Steppes. With what was to happen to the tobacconists trade I don't suppose I'd have been in a job much longer than twenty years at most but I rather wish I'd taken up the chance. Old Mr Murray Frame himself was an octogenarian old fellow who lived in considerable splendour in Kelvin Court, an art deco block of service flats, and he had, like something out of Raymond Chandler, a uniformed nurse to look after him. I used to take the old man his weekly supply of Passing Cloud and a block of Walls ice-cream wrapped soundly in an entire copy of the *Evening News* and he always suggested I learn the business. 'Just the sort of smart lad that's wanted, m'boy,' he would say. 'There's a long way to go for a smart lad, m'boy,' he'd say. It was rather the era of the smart lad. You used to see signs in shop windows stating 'Smart boy wanted'. Today even the shops which haven't closed down don't want smart lads, or lassies either. Jobs for kids walking off the street have gone forever. Perhaps work itself has. Certainly the idea of the Scottish Calvinistic work ethic is probably so tarnished that most people would laugh at it as if it belonged, which perhaps it does, to notions of Empire.

But if I worked in the summer, and I worked all throughout the year as a paper boy and milk boy, I did not, I can admit, work much at school. As a young man I regretted that but with hindsight I don't now. I learned what I wanted to, I think, and I put a wondrous amount of industry into becoming that crassest of all creatures, a teenager. When just a wee lad I watched the older teenagers dance to the sound of Elvis on the jukebox in the glittering café in George Street, spied the up-turned collars, and the greasy hair touching the edges of them, lusted after the girls in drindl skirts, admired the teddy boys in their Saturday drapes: I knew exactly what I wanted to be. I think I probably became it to some of my coevals, but not, I am afraid, to myself. But I was to meet another set of contemporaries, away from Townhead, away at last from the Blacking Factory. We moved back to the south-side of the city, back, near enough, to Cathcart. I was fifteen. It had been eight years.

6

We moved to Merrylee, a housing estate on the edges of Cathcart on one side and Newlands on the other. A model scheme it was, set among large houses, big bought houses, with large lawns and what passed for *haute bourgoisie* in Glasgow to lounge in them. The children from the big houses went to private and fee-paying schools. Their daddies had a few bob and it showed in the cars which sat in their long driveways and the tennis clubs they went to, and in their wives who shopped and visited and might do a spot of charity work, and their children who wore school uniforms elaborate enough for the Household bloody Cavalry. Their teenage daughters looked absolutely delicious in their crisp pastel summer dresses, with their hair gleaming with shampoo, and their light make-up and flat shoes, quite unlike the brazen little tarts I was used to in Townhead. What the boys looked like I didn't give a bugger about really. I liked the look of the daughters too much to give their male siblings a thought. Merrylee was on the edge of the big houses and its inhabitants weren't but even then it was the sort of housing 'scheme' which shouldn't really have existed, too damned posh and upwardly bleeding mobile by half. There was a reason for this.

When the plan for a council estate was first put forward the posh aborigines of this leafy area had strokes, and the history of Merrylee was one of pulling them. Every fly-trick from the middle classes was perpetrated, just to avoid the lower orders. (Some of the families were very big in business with not a few millionaires residing there: the Forsyth family who owned the up-market stores in Glasgow's Renfield Street and Edinburgh's Princes Street were one, the grocery chain family, the Cochrane's, were set side by side with them.) The first thing the then Corporation put forward to assuage the fears of the big shots who lived in the big houses, was to propose to sell the houses to small shopkeeper types, inoffensive bank clerks and the like, the sort of Poujadistes the aristos were used to condescending to when needed. Keep out the lumpen, that would, the sepoys could revolt somewhere else, not in their stretches of parkland. That was in 1952 and it caused a bloody uproar, including a strike by the tradesmen who were working on the scheme; and marches in the streets; other workers in other trades downed tools in solidarity. There was, after all, still a democratic resonance from the post-war years, a feeling among many people that we were building a new world, a classless one, and even among many of the wealthy themselves there was a feeling that if workers were good enough to build the houses they were damned well good enough to live in them. The Merrylee Strike, it got called that, was an uprising by Decency really, and an impasse seemed inevitable. The new ruling Labour group came up with a solution. They didn't sell the houses, they let them, as was the policy to those who needed houses and 'had the points', to ordinary people from ordinary walks of life. But they put a rare spin on this concept for they vetted the type of ordinary people who were to obtain houses in this ordinary scheme. Some of the vetting took on a surreal dimension. If you had a job with a collar and tie in it, that was extra points, if your children were staying on at school, extra points; Jesus, a boy at university, you went to the head of the queue. It was a lot more subtle than that. What really happened was that the Merrylee Scheme (like Mosspark and Knightswood elsewhere in the city), picked the prize crop, the labour aristocracy. The result was undeniably the poshest council housing estate in Britain. Good idea for Merrylee at that and I couldn't and can't complain. By the time I got there Merrylee was just absolutely spiffing.

Nobody ever remembers their adolescence with any coherence, or at least they shouldn't. It's a period in life when things are often unbearably, unremittingly, slow; when everything takes for ever. An hour in a schoolroom lasts an eternity and there is a sort of itch in your inside you can't scratch, an itch in your very bowels. Any converse with adults, especially parents, is not only long and tedious to get through, it is always somehow disjointed and you never get to say what you meant to say. You never seem to say what you thought you would when you thought about it before or after either. Then there were interludes in which it all moved too fast, events occurring quicker than a butterfly's fart. You had too many friends taking up too much time. You hadn't a friend in the world. All too infrequent triumphs were followed by a level of unavoidable disasters which would do for the plots of Scandinavian tragedies. The paucity of comprehension on the part of others was enough to have you considering a session with the sleeping pill bottles and then there was a brief meeting with someone who thought so exactly like yourself that you wondered why there was only two of you on this planet. What I remember about my adolescent years are merely a series of vignettes chained to each other but all tangled up.

I remember the incredible desire I had for articles of clothing. A white shortie coat with a red satin lining – it was no fucking good without the scarlet lining. The desperate need for the right shirt, for heaven's sake, with cutaway collars or spearpoint collars – there was a brief and splendid fashion for stiff, starched collars I recollect. I remember paper collars which were quite smart until you perspired too greatly in the dance hall when the bloody thing disintegrated on you. You took two collars to the dancing and changed in the bogs. I never had enough money for the most fashionable and therefore expensive stuff, unlike some of the other lads who were working while I laboured away in school.

School itself I hardly remember at all save that Joe Boss the heedie initiated a campaign which meant he went crawling about the buildings looking for me, checking up on whatever misdeeds he was convinced I was getting up to and becoming apoplectic with frustration because I wasn't getting up to them or at least he couldn't discover me in the act. It was the hair he hated most, that oiled quiff, that anti-Christ of a coiffure, that rebuke to the short back and sides and some bloody discipline, some fitness of things. Jesus the man tried to nail me and never managed it. Once he had me for flooding the lavatories by blocking all the sink taps up. I had the best alibi you could imagine, the sort major criminals always have in police series on TV. At the very time the lavvies were being flooded, I was standing in front of a geography teacher called Dewar and waiting to be thrashed for being caught smoking round the back of the techie huts. This was a merry wheeze all round because I was joined in this alibi by several other solid miscreants, each of whom the headmaster had been trying to catch out for months. We could have told him that the outrage in the latrines had been perpetrated by Bill Bird, whom you last met at the school gates on my first day, and all his pals from the Debating Society. (Bird was a wily one and his gang's membership of this dialectic organisation was a scam which our mob rather wish we'd thought of first.)

The other boy at those gates had been Glyn Philips and he was one of the Bad Crowd, the ones who smoked. In The Shed. At first I didn't like cigarettes, encountering spasms of nausea five minutes after a few drags of the weed, but I persevered. Oh yes, I persevered all right, about the only time I did really throughout school. Well the Shed Boys all smoked, didn't they. Part of the drainpipe strides and sideburns. What was quite so venal about fags I don't know but it wasn't a kick in the arse off drinking beer or visiting bordellos and I was all for it. There was a definite allure about all those desperadoes who smoked in The Shed too. Davie Jack and Dunky McLean and Billy 'Buff' Barnes and Smokey and Linky and Tommy Dunbar: an entire cast of hidalgos altogether. We even had a supplier, a precursor of the playground pusher. Kenneth McKenzie, now a well-known art restorer, used to sell us single fags out of his packet of twenty. Every now and again we communards revolted and took his fags off him. He just appeared the next day and charged us a penny more for each cigarette until he'd made up his losses. We called him The Parasite, because he himself didn't smoke. But he was always better-off than us.

An expensive business the five Bristol of a morning, so we all started using our dinner money which we were meant to pay each Friday and went without lunch instead. Some of that was spent, of course, in nearby merry mansions of malfeasance, the snooker hall. There were two we patronised as a group; the Crown, which stood at the top of a series of dusty auction rooms; and the rather gaudier Imperial which lay underneath a barber's shop straight out of gangster movies. Snooker halls were then a perfectly ideal spot for teenagers to come to no harm but yet were ludicrously regarded by parents, clerics, and schoolteachers, as the sort of gaming hells Regeny bucks had orgies in. You'd have thought you could catch syphilis off a billiard cue the way the adults told you. But if you caught a whiff of the *demi-monde* in those musty, urine-reeking vaults they were indeed harmless and a lot more fun than the pusillanimous palaces for precocious young snooker players they are today. My career in snooker, though, ended with an absence of jollity altogether, especially for one fellow pupil of the school.

There was a constant dearth of money, for teenagers still at school had none. And there were the fags and the snooker to be paid for. We found a way. There was a fat myopic boy called Peters there who wore the sort of clothes that his mum bought him and who was forced into wearing his hair with what doubtless his dreadful parents called 'a proper trim'. I've changed his name actually because he might still be alive being as much a prick now as he was when he was a boy. He was the sort of wimpish chap who liked to hang about gangsters, straight out of Runyon that is, and he hung around the snooker halls with us when he could and he couldn't play the damned thing at all. So we regularly took him to the cleaners. For money, because he was also the sort of boy who bought himself some kind of faraway membership and we let him do this because of the poppy. Eventually he couldn't pay what he owed and then suddenly he could: we didn't know how, or at least I didn't. I was to find out though.

Allan Glen's possessed a school orchestra. Headed by a teacher, a lunatic called Lockie, it contained every loop in the entire school. All the sad lost boys, the incompetents and the ones with nervous tics and funny walks and ringworm and receding chins. The erks, the jube-jubes, the dispossessed. Few owned their instruments and relied on those the school provided which were kept in a large and dusty room which we smokers knew well because we had a key to it and played pontoon in there from time to time. Peters was, of course, a member of this orchestra and kept his violin in the music store when he didn't take it home to practise. Who it was who told him about pawn shops I do not know but Peters needed money to pay his billiard hall debts and he had this violin, even if it was school property. So Peters settled his first debt and absented himself from orchestra practice as best he could. But he didn't absent himself from the billiard hall. The lure of being with the hidalgos was, I suppose, too strong. And so he got into another debt. A lot more debts. And how he got out of them was pawning violins.

After a while I suppose it occurred to him that an orchestra without a strings section might not be considered viable and his, well, fiddle, would be slightly noticed. So he took to trombones. And then trumpets. And then any damned instrument at all. If the school had owned a gilded bloody harp I suppose he'd have marched that off to the pawn just the same. Christ knows what the leader of the band, the mad Lockie, must have been wondering as his maestros were trying to belt out 'The Soldiers Chorus' with what by now must have been lavvy paper and combs. And so eventually, as he must have known he would be, Peters's thefts were found out, actually because he was caught truanting, and he promptly admitted to his life of crime in areas other than merely dogging school. Thinking about it, Peters had thieved to the value of, in today's terms, several thousand pounds. And then he gave the names of those involved.

There was a fair gang of us and actually I wasn't in the business myself at all but Peters must have blurted out every name of every member of the miscreant community he could remember and I was among that number. Somerville sent for us in our droves. The reason why nothing could be proved against me was that I had sod all to do with the caper. I didn't even know about the scam and played serious snooker with a youth called Morton who worked a stall at the Barras, the local markets. The problem was that I looked the very part of the Bad Yin. A sort of pocket-sized version of Flashman. And so I was blamed at first. By now Barnes didn't know who any of his tormentors were in fact and would have fingered Billy Graham, Billy Sunday and Billy the bloody Kid, and we all got off with it while Peters disappeared for ever, doubtless sent to the Colonies or whatever version of it his mum and dad had for him. What rather rankles even yet is that there was still a whiff of guilt attached to my blameless self and those who had gleefully blagged Peters, and the school orchestra of course, were considered by this Somerville to have been led astray by me. He said so to my mother whom he had called to the school and informed her, while she wept in front of me – he liked a touch of that, mothers weeping – that I was a 'ringleader', a 'bad influence' altogether an evil genius. My mother said I wasn't of course but mothers are always doing that about sons who have been proved irrevocably to be mass murderers. 'He was always a good boy at home' they cry. 'Does a' the messages and widnae hurt a fly!' Well my mother pulled all that stuff but Somerville was having none of it. He said I was the worst boy he had ever had the misfortune to encounter. He was wrong. The worst, and certainly the smartest, was Davie Jack.

But I now had a life out of school and in Merrylee and district – a very wide district indeed covering slum areas from the Gorbals and even the city centre, the suburbs, the posh ones as well, out to open countryside. My patch in fact. It is amazing how far and wide adolescents roam, and on their own two feet at that. You never do it again, this roaming abroad. When we first moved to this pleasant area I was a bit all at sea and caused massive offence in the early days when, playing football with local lads, I fouled their best player, a chap called Sandy Fraser. Well, I did foul him. He'd beaten me after all so I pulled the pins from him. The Merrylee boys were working class lads but a lot more polite than the kids I knew either in Townhead or at school. When they remonstrated with me over my disgraceful conduct I think I was taken aback. Such rebukes in my experience took the form of threatening behaviour. So I told them to fuck off. I think I added a wee 'cunt' as well. Believe me, I got that language, at least the ease with which I used it, from Allan Glen's School and not the lush paved pastures of Townhead. There was, I remember, a riffle of disapproval. Said Sandy Fraser, now a social work boss in Strathclyde, 'You think you're hard just 'cos you can swear.' This was a puzzle indeed, one part of it rather like the question wee Abie Matthews had asked on my first day at Townhead Primary. 'Kin youse fight?' he had asked of me. Now these boys were saying that I thought I was hard because I could swear. Anybody could swear, I thought; all you did was open your mouth and, well, swear. Also, I didn't until then think I was hard, nor did I want to be thought of as such. I am afraid that others began to think it though, and after a while, so did I.

This had a spin-off in that I got to know a lot of the local youths, some of whom thought I was hard and therefore one of them, or therefore they thought they should be one of me. But I never made friends really; just a lot of acquaintances because, of course, not going to the same school as anybody else I never got much chance. So I made friends with my younger brother's ones or their older brothers. My younger brother made friends very easily indeed so I had a fair-sized pool out of which to choose acquaintances at that. Many years later I was to discover that the Merrylee locals thought I ran around with a plethora of crowds from all over, and that perception gave me somewhat of a cachet. In truth I ran around with nobody really. I hovered a bit.

My brother Brian is only a couple of years younger than me and, because I was born prematurely and was so small, I even shared a pram with him and we were brought up dressed in the same clothes, like twins. In fact until I went to school we were taken for such. Brian and I were brought up together and shared everything; for many years we shared the same bed. One of the worst things about secondary school had been the wrenching separation which I felt. I had felt that once before when Brian had to stay in the infants playground and I was in the big boys one. Despite that, Brian and I were and are not alike at all. For a start Brian was blond-haired where I was dark, rosy-cheeked where I had a complexion which would have done credit to a Victorian child on its deathbed. He also had a sunny disposition and was perpetually happy, or so it seemed. He was quiet and shy, but open and friendly and possessed the charming selfishness, which he yet does, of the non-egoist. I was the opposite in all qualities mentioned above and with an added goodly dose of pugnacity, not an attractive trait at all. I still have the pugnacity and it is still not attractive, but we cannae all be happy and sunny-natured and I'm not and have to make do with a cheeriness which, though rarely forced, holds a certain desperation in it, like singing merry songs during a bomb raid.

But the teenage years are always spent with a certain desperate edge to them because you know they can't last but by and large I had a good time during them because Merrylee was a green and grassy place with good people about and it was a very good era to be a teenager in anyway. A fellow Scottish columnist, Jack Webster, once wrote that he had not enjoyed his teenhood (also, he wrote, his young manhood), and I suspect that was because he grew up in that dark time when teenagers were cut-down wee men who tried to be just like their dads and cavorted about in gaberdine raincoats. I remember the gaberdine. A sort of Lovat grey it was, the coats shapeless, the rain came with the coats. Nothing can exemplify better that difference in teenhood than the grey gaberdine and the then sudden explosion of colour when I came to my teens. Jack was an unusual name in both Webster's time and my own and some people have sometimes talked of the two Jacks and pondered why we are so different from each other. The difference is simple. I never had to wear the gaberdine. Jack never put on a black shirt with a pink sportscoat.

It was the fag end of Elvis the rock 'n' roller and a very fecund period of pop songs. Buddy Holly, Eddie Cochrane, Ricky Nelson, Bobby Darin, Bobby Rydell, Bobby Vee, Frankie Avalon, Fabian, perfect for incipient spivs like me. The songs were rather maudlin and girls listened to them dreaming. There was a lot of dreaming going on. Well, a lot of songs were about dreaming and dreamboats. The Everlys even had a song with a wonderful chorus which went: 'Dre-e-e-em, Dreem, Dreem, Dreem, Dreem, Dreee-em.' There were Dream Lovers abounding and I intended to be one of them. So I went out and fell in love.

Truth to tell my first contacts with girls were really pretty pointless and my heart wasn't in it. I met two rather lumpen prole girls and went about with both for a while and then just the one. Her name was Marlene but I always thought of her as Marleen: she was a bit too common to share a spelling with Deitrich. She was rather common-looking too: if you can have brassy red hair she had it. Her mum and her two brothers were very nice and much approved of me – I was a steady enough boy whose dad was the local janitor. Marleen was sort of flighty though and it never bothered me because I didn't fancy her anyway which was just as well because she didn't let me do anything to her at all. But then, very few girls let you do anything to them at all, at any time it seemed. We all met in the local five-pin bowling alley on Sundays and told each other how far we had got of course – you think all those repro Fifties movies that Hollywood does so well were hooey? Think again, they are often very accurate indeed, and I remember my early teenage years as being rather American too. Maybe because Glasgow has always had a certain American feel to it. My father's generation thought they were all Jimmy Cagney. Mine just updated it. We sported ice-blue jeans and Hi-Back collared shirts we bought from Bob Fletcher's Esquire Shirt Shop in Cambridge Street across from Fusco's the hairdressers. We went to hops not a kick in the arse different from those bopping away in Philadelphia or Boston or Memphis, Tennessee. Certainly British films have either not recaptured that time or tried to, and probably couldn't.

The five-pin bowling alley was a re-furbed cinema and it was the first attempt to put Middle America into the city, in a little quiet suburb of Glasgow too. It had the alleys all right but the pins had to be put up by hand by a hapless youth who lurked underneath the hatch where the pins went down. I was taken on as an instructor which was great because a lot of families tried it out, and there was always a truculent teenage daughter with her pants wet just dreaming of bad boys like me. The alley didn't last long really because a lot of the mums and dads caught the yearning look in their daughters' eyes and garaged them up good and proper. But it remained one of the spots for the kids to come, especially for the post-mortems on Sundays in the café.

'Howdya get on with Morag?' countered by 'Got the tits'. Very robust liars said they had got the hand. Nobody ever said they got their Nat King Cole because nobody would have believed it. In fact nobody believed the bit about the tits or the hand much. And nobody ever said anything, ever, about the girls they really fancied. Or were in love with.

There wasn't all that much being in love in any case because then, as doubtless now, boys and girls in the teen years tended to hang around in groups, a lot like pals really, and most of the romances were a lot of crap: you just got fixed up as couples as a kind of executive tidying-up. Just like the movies. And in the teen films there was always some Romeo and Juliet doomed romance and it was always the two best-looking who went in for that. So I went in for that and fell in love with a dark sad-eyed girl called Elizabeth Watson who was called 'Buff' by her friends. I never tried a damned thing with her because I was so much in bloody love and I suspect that Buff got a bit pissed off with that because she chucked me and I broke my fucking heart, I really did. Just the way they tell it in the storybooks. I couldn't eat, and woke up each morning with such pain in my psyche that it was deliciously unbearable. I still had the good sense not to let any of my family know about it. I could have stood the merciless taunts of my father and brothers but the dreadful sympathy my mother would have gladly swept me up in would have had me slashing my bloody wrists.

There were of course other types of girls and I found out about them quick enough. There is always some wee lassie who will let you put your finger in her and adjust her underclothes for you, why I don't know. Some undeniably because they are a bit starved of affection at home or have bloody awful homes anyway, some because some adult, sometime, has abused her, and some because they like it. Elaine was of the last category and had me, almost, in a very quiet, secluded, little knoll near the park and not far from the bowling alley, called Courtknowe, and it was on the very spot, commemorated by an engraved cairn, where Mary Queen of Scots' troops lost the Battle of Langside. If the troops lost their lives, I lost my virginity, you could say, well in a way. I'd asked Elaine up there with many a nudge and she'd agreed and by the time we arrived at the dark little dell I was shaking with fear and anticipation and romance stirred within my loins and also in my romantic bloody head and we necked and my hands went up her skirt. For this I had waited and lusted horribly and earnestly tossed myself off in the bathroom. (The first time I had an emission I thought I'd broken the damned thing and didn't touch myself again for . . . well a long time I thought.) I had a richly romantic imagination and somehow I had considered this moment as one swathed in moonlight and gossamer but though there was certainly moonlight, there was no gossamer and in fact I hadn't a French letter with me and couldn't have got my hands on one if I'd wanted to so Elaine told me just to pull it out when I thought I was going to come. Romance dimmed a little at her matter-of-fact way. I then put my fingers in the waistband of her knickers and started to pull them down. She stopped me immediately in an unromantic whisper. 'For Christ's sake,' she said, annoyance ringing in her tone, 'jist fuckin' pu-ull them tae the side!' So I did and felt her vulva rise towards me and put my bloated penis up towards the lips of her vagina and shot the bloody lot all over her. She went bloody mental. 'You dirty little bastard!' she cried, 'my mammy'll fuckin' kill me if she sees your spunk a' ower ma skirt. Could ye no huv tellt me youse wurr cummin'!' No, Ella, I couldn't. And it wasn't me who got you up the stick either, thank God. Actually, she lived to see a perfectly respectable marriage, for in those days, very few girls ended up with illegitimate babies. Boys who got their girlfriends pregnant married them then, and I suppose it was the major reason for getting married at that. In fact about the only pregnant schoolgirls I ever remember always amazingly seemed to be terribly 'decent' girls like the daughters of the minister or some other unlikely personage like that.

Two things I took from that incident. One of them was that in the future I was going to do it with a girl I really fancied and take my time over it (it was many years before I managed the both at once), and the other was that girls were a sight more basic in their language and behaviour than I had hitherto thought.

7

I took up alcohol at an early age which was a bit surprising because my father wasn't a drinker really. He rarely went to a pub, having no friends, and it was very rare that he drank in the house and certainly not when we were younger because he didn't have the money for it. Later, he and my mother went for a drink of a Saturday lunchtime, but all in all my father didn't drink much. The only occasions I ever saw him drunk was at the odd New Year when he disappeared and went to look for my Uncle Jimmy. My mother, who came from a rather bourgeois near-teetotal family herself, imagined that Uncle Jimmy tied my dad to a chair with light flex and injected his unwilling veins with alcohol but I suspect in fact that my father was the sort of man who bought lots of rounds to show face and wasn't used to a large intake. Jimmy was, I think. He was a heavy, dark man, rather good-looking in a saturnine way and the last time I saw him was at my father's funeral. We saw very little of him and I think that's a pity. I haven't met my cousins, his children, since I was about six, coming up to half a century away.

So drink wasn't in the family at all and I can't think of any reason why or how I came to regular pub-going as a youth. Drinking was then, much, much more than it is now, a necessary part of growing into adulthood and, given common sense, not a bad route either because you learned how to get on with people of different age groups and social classes and how to conduct yourself in company. How to discuss matters of varying importance and how to win an argument. How to start an argument too, if it came to that. And when, how, and why, to always buy your round. An important element that in the democratic intellect and a cornerstone in a sense of democracy itself. It doesn't matter what form buying your round takes, though it takes the form of alcohol in this culture, but stand your round you must. That concept underlies the oft-stated criticism of the teetotaller by imbibers. Never trust a teetotaller may be a maxim which is not forever true but by and large it'll do. Certainly what Will Fyfe claimed has a ring of veracity to it if you come from the West of Scotland: 'Ach, teetotal? Teetotal? When you're teetotal ye've a nasty feeling that everybody's yer boss.' Certainly no boss or superior, or elder, or even your ain da can lord it over anybody else in the pub and it comes to his round sooner or later. Which is why, I suppose, huge numbers of the bourgeoisie take to drinking at home or maybe down the golf club. You are on equal terms in a pub, until your natural qualities come through. So I took to pubs naturally and easily and with great relish.

The first pub I went to really was in what is now called the Merchant City in Glasgow, and it is still there. It isn't all that changed now, though the Court Bar went through a period when it was, unbelievably, a gay bar. When I went there first I was fifteen. I was dark with a beard growth early on so it was myself who was sent to the bar counter by my fellow drinkers because the bum-fluff on their chins wouldn't have got them as much as a glass of shandy. It didn't take long for the bar staff to, well, tipple to the ruse, but by that time our custom was by no means unwelcome and nobody bothered a light unless we got too noisy. Anyway we didn't get drunk. At least in the bar. Some of the boys did that later on with bottles of Carlsberg Special laced with Fowler's Wee Heavy. Early days though I could drink without showing it much, a quality to be neither proud nor ashamed of, but one which can sometimes lead to heavy boozing. Although it wasn't permitted to leave the school playground at any time during the day there were ways of escaping and myself and a few of the bad boys occasionally jouked out at lunchtime and had a pint or two in The Glue Pot or The Cross Keys. So it was that on my last day of school we went to a pub after it. An hour in the Barony Church and then freedom. It was too. Young people leave school worried sick today, no jobs or college leading to no jobs but back then there was work enough. So the last day we all threw away our ties and buggered off to The Horseshoe Bar.

My coevals were lanky youths considerably older than myself but less accustomed to hard liquor and I quickly left them to their, by now slightly drunken, devices and disappeared into the maw of the south-side and adult life. I don't think I ever saw any of my fellow drinkers again. What I do know is that I lifted some chap's copy of the school magazine in the church by mistake only to discover that it was signed by the headmaster, Joe Boss himself, and all the prefects except one who must have been the owner of the document, a last souvenir of the Happiest Days of His Life. Well there you are then, life's a bitch. I can't remember the name of the prefect either.

It was now time to find a future career, or at any rate, a job. Because I had been shoved on so often at primary school (what they now call fast-tracking and a very silly idea indeed: I spent my last year at school with boys who were as much as three years older than me, and my emotional development was therefore somewhat amoebic), I had a few years to do some damned thing in the work line but I didn't know what it was. There weren't many options for an over-educated Glasgow boy who had just turned sixteen and who didn't have one single relation in the Freemasonry. I spent a time in the libraries looking through the jobs vacant sections in the evening papers. Some of them were just daft. One reply from a prospective employer came to the house addressed to a Jane McLean. Unwittingly I had applied for a job as a housekeeper. Another time I was appointed a brush salesman, going round doors. My father found out about it and the chaps who had given me the job got short shrift when they appeared at the house trying to convince my mother and father that there was a long term career in selling Acme lavvy brushes round doors. In fact my first job on leaving school was with the Dolcis shoe shop, at one of its outlets in Glasgow's busiest shopping street, Argyle Street. I lasted two weeks before I was sacked. It was months before I found out the grounds for my dismissal, which had utterly bemused me. It was the fault of a large-boned youth with no front teeth called Finbar, a fellow inmate in the Men's Department of Dolcis shoe store. Bastard. Amusing chap though, with a ready wit and an even readier will to make a bob when he saw an opportunity. Unfortunately I was the opportunity. About a year after I was sacked I met him in the street. He apologised for getting me my jotters. How could he have got me sacked? He told me. Every time a new start came he ripped the till off something rotten. Nobody ever suspected him – he'd been there six years. Nae wonder I found it hard to get work after I'd given Dolcis as a reference.

Oddly one of my next jobs was also in a shoe shop, a cheapo affair catering for the ned population of Glasgow, greasy yobs with spots looking for winklepickers with double buckles made of paper and costing £1 19s 11d which wasn't very much but was half their wages at the time. Gordon's Shoes it was and Jewish owned. The boss was one of the sons or nephews or something, a big heavy red-haired Jew, coarse and foul-mouthed. All the Jewish kids I had known at school – and my own family had a Jewish background far off enough – had been cerebral Ashkenazy academics and I wasn't prepared for this lout at all. I left after he kicked me up the arse for a laugh to show off to one of the shopgirls who he was publicly pojering at lunchtimes. He'd have done well in 1920s New York, the Garment District, but I told him to stick his job sideways and called him a fuckin' mushugenah so he said he was sorry for thinking I was a goy but I still told him to stick his job. It didn't lead to anti-semitism but I took a careful approach to big heavy red-haired bastards after that.

After that? There was a hell of a lot of after thats when it came to jobs. There were a lot of them about then. I worked for a couple of months in a cardboard box factory on the outskirts of Glasgow and met a very nice girl in the invoicing section of the office and got caught heavy petting with her in my own lunch hour in the green pastures of this garden factory and the management sacked us both for our gross moral turpitude. For another few months I collected rent for a factor in the wealthy district of Newton Mearns, well, that's where his office was, his property was in the semi-slum areas halfway in the country and halfway out of it, places like Barrhead. Mr Wilson sacked me for wearing a corduroy jacket which he thought unsuitable for his executives, i.e. sixteen-year-old youths he paid so meagrely that they, that is, me, couldn't afford lunch and walked the four miles back home every night.

I didn't even last in John Brown's shipyard where I was apprenticed as an engineer because one day Joe McCabe, the foreman took me aside and gave me a fag. 'Son, you're a nice wee boay, but' he said, 'ye'll nivver make an engineer. Ye're no cut oot fur it.' He was a kindly man and I was a bit distressed. 'Does that mean I should resign?' I asked. 'Naw, son,' replied Mr McCabe, 'it means ye're sacked. Ye're pey's made up at the office.' I was even more distressed but Joe – who must have been nearing retirement – explained that shipbuilding was finished on the Clyde, certainly the upper Clyde. What Joe, and a great many of the shipyard men, knew and the bloody Government ministers and the financial and economic experts seemed not to, was the obvious fact that soon the shipyards of South East Asia would be taking all the work. And Joe and his mates knew all this before the notorious building of the QE2 when half of Clydebank had the insides of their houses furnished courtesy of the last big passenger ship built on the Clyde. By all accounts the carpets went on one gangplank and off the next. There are those who maintain that this is a filthy lie and a slur upon the good name of Clyde-built men and probably Jimmy Reid will be boaking with litigation at the above but what would Reid know and him in the drawing office? Anyway Joe McCabe knew more about the impending economics of British shipbuilding than all the economists and politicians put together and told me I was well out of the trade to boot. And, as it turned out, so I was.

I was by now well out of a great many trades and frankly I can't remember how many jobs I had or how long I lasted or even how I got the work at all. I lasted two days at Biggar, the musical instrument and record and radiogram store, in their repairs shop because Mr Biggar spied me and sent me out to get my hair cut with the injunction to 'get these side things, these sideboard things, removed'. He gave me half a crown and I spent it in the State Bar in Holland Street and never returned. Years later I saw Mr Biggar in the city centre and he sported a pair of mutton chop whiskers which would have done credit to Uncle bloody Pumblechook. Actually I never minded much, getting fired: it was like taking a holiday every now and again and I was hardly embarking on a future career. By now my parents neither knew nor cared much either what job I had: I always seemed to have one at that. And then I started with the Glasgow Corporation, in the Office of Public Works, in the Sewage Department. Now here was fun itself.

It is hard to imagine today how it was so easy to live in a world forty years out of date back in the early 1960s. The streets were filled with soot-blackened, grimy, crumbling buildings and grimy, crumbling people to go with them. Businessmen wore bowler hats and black jackets and striped trousers for heaven's sake. In that setting they would have passed muster in a George Gissing novel. The smarter young clerks clothed themselves in cheap Burton's suits and cutaway collars, like something out of *Room at the Top*. Girls were girls but even then the fashion of the times rather led to C&A raincoats and bucket bags. I don't think there were trams then but there should have been. The rainscape – it was nearly always wet – had touches when the streetlamps reflected in the glistening streets and the sodium lamps fizzled, and the pale streaks of blue sky in the early evening shone in the puddles in the gutters; reflections of blue and gold as gaudy as an Orangeman's sash. It was as though the 1930s Depression had come to Glasgow and just stayed.

It made itself well at home in the Office of Public Works, Sewage Department. A M. McKenna was in charge. He was a cadaverous-featured Catholic man who didn't shave his cheekbones, leaving sinister triangles of sprouting hair on them. He wore, I swear it, a celluloid collar, and was tremendously religious. He and a fat red-faced clerk called Callaghan, the sort of man once described by Dickens, 'If the man did not drink, he should sue his face for libel,' used to round up Catholic boys every Holiday of Obligation and say novennas or some damned thing all morning and then take the rest of the day off as they were entitled. If Glasgow's business community, and professional classes were overwhelmingly Protestant in those days there was a haven for Catholics and that was in the Glasgow Corporation – then, as now, overwhelmingly Labour and largely Catholic and of Irish origin. It was a pretty grim Catholicism, very Calvinistic, and most Roman Catholics took a cheerfully pagan attitude towards their church, paying it little heed except at Mass on Sundays or in occasional attitudinising over issues like birth control. (I remember shocking a Catholic street acquaintance called Billy Fagan when he discovered that I had a French letter in my wallet and every intention of using it should the opportunity arise. 'Ah couldnae,' he cried, 'it's against ma religion!' Fagan carried a knife in his inside pocket and had been in Barlinnie Jail for stabbing a bloke outside the Locarno ballroom.) Anyway it was common knowledge that non-Catholics didn't last long in Mr McKenna's section so eventually I was promoted to make way for a chap called O'Hara. They promoted me into the Highways Department.

Actually I hadn't minded the Sewage Department at all. For a start two days in the week I went away, accompanied by another clerk, an asthmatic youth called Snagge, in an Austin limousine chauffeured by one of the Corporation drivers to pay out the sewage workers wages. There was Shieldhall and Dalmarnock where the sludge boats took their reeking cargo down to dump in the Clyde estuary (the reek was of lime and alumina, not excrement), and Partick Pumping Station and Kinning Park and Dalmuir. On the way we bought a bag of 'flies cemeteries', square fruit slices in puff pastry cases, and two almond slices for Jimmy Webley, who was the one-armed clerk at Dalmuir. Jimmy gave us fags for these delicacies. He got the fags in lieu of light bulbs which he exchanged with the local newsagent just as he got whisky in for bags of lime, just as . . . in fact Jimmy was a lovely, horribly corrupt, fellow who had clearly swopped his arm in the last War for the entreprenurial skills of the black marketeer. He was a great man for knowing racecourse winners and had some reputation for it but, he confided once to me, rarely put a wager on himself. 'Mug's game,' he'd say. 'Punters? Only the fuckin' horse is more fuckin' stupid.' Jimmy also tarted up the figures concerning the amount of effluent which came through all the works in Glasgow. I used to change them too in order to make counting easier. Then the engineers changed my figures, and by the time the figures got to the planners of the Sewage Department you'd have thought there was more shite egested in Glasgow than there was in the whole of bloody Africa. But the Highways Department had no such diversions available.

The overall boss, Mr Roberts, sat for half the day in a glass-fronted box, facing his workers, a bit like Adolf Eichmann on trial really, and the other half spent it in, it was rumoured – reliably it turned out later – far-distant pubs. My immediate boss was a grey-haired spinster called Miss Alexander. She wore steel-rimmed spectacles to go with her steel-rimmed brain. My job was to record every letter which came into the Office of Public Works, and to record every letter which emanated from ourselves. The only good part of this impossible and sense-defying task was summarising them because I had to record what all the letters were about anyway. I brought to this the literary arts which had been invested in me by Paddy Inglis' teaching at Allan Glen's and went on to hone my skills. It has stood me in good stead to this day, and is perhaps – I have never thought of this before – the basis of whatever style I now possess. I remember one near-illiterate letter from a citizen which complained that a local employee in the roads department should not be employed at all because he was illegitimate. Our office replied pointing out that there was no law excluding the employment of anybody born out of wedlock. I summarised this as: 'Woman claims bastard in road gang. OPW say bastards alright.' The reason why I recollect this after all these years is because it got to Miss Alexander and she onto the track of myself.

I think Miss Alexander thought rather well of me at first because she had found out that I had been to a selective school and had all these Highers (the Lowers and Highers were sat, let alone passed, by a relatively small percentage of the Scottish population in those days when most people left school at fifteen before they could pass any damned thing at all). Later, however, she found my affectations, such as corduroy jackets, knitted ties, and sideburns an irritant. Certainly my constant nose in a book upset her, as did my astoundingly solitary ways, for I ate every day on my own at lunchtimes. Also I did very little work indeed and comforted myself by drawing the people in the office, which obtained for me the title of 'Remby' – short for Rembrandt. It was true that I read all the time, (more even than she thought for I had invented a means of reading all day by placing a book in my desk drawer which I left slightly ajar and adjusted, both the drawer and myself, in order to read each page). I was also wonderfully able at making myself scarce, more often than not in the filing room where I had a kindred spirit in a very nice clerk called Kevin Coll who liked to read books too. Kevin had done his national service in Cyprus and was married with kids and was therefore a source of information about women and their periods and stuff like that. I am never very sure if Kevin got it confused or I his reports but none of it ever seemed to make any sense to me. Anyway, a combination of everything above – as well as my pert precis of the contents of our correspondence – afforded Miss Alexander the conclusion that I was by no means a star in her department.

I spent most lunch-hours reading in the plethora of bookshops around the City Chambers or, when I could afford it, perhaps a home-made sausage roll and fried potatoes in one of the many eating houses which existed then, faintly genteel and very old-fashioned indeed, almost pre-Lyon's Corner House. Wendy's or Miss Buick's, places like that. Or perhaps one of the all-male coffee rooms where one could perfectly envisage characters, dialogue and storylines straight out of H.E. Bates. I never socialised with any other clerks, and indeed, took my coffee breaks (office workers took coffee, the lower orders tea), either on my own or with Kevin in filing. On the odd occasion when I had coffee in the same room as the clerks I was filled with a sense of displacement, as if I was looking on at some scene from a play by Becket, as though I didn't grasp the characters. One of the senior clerks, a Mr. Bowd – pronounced Boad – I used to meet in the bus back home when I found him wry and amusing and well-read. Mr Bowd had been in the Fleet Air Arm during the War and I now suspect told me so little because he had done quite a bit. On the bus he was, for a man in his early forties, quite understanding and supportive about young people. At the coffee breaks he was as insufferable in his absurdly proper vocal opinions as any. Even the young clerks would pitch in with comments worthy of a Pooter crossed with Blimp. I never knew how to agree or disagree with any of them so kept silent and got the reputation of being shy. The reputation was enough to make me shy at that.

I exploded that shy reputation the day that I swore, dreadfully, at Miss Alexander. I can't even remember what led up to it. It was one of those days when things had gone wrong for Miss Alexander, I know that. Old George, one of the clerks and a very little, very nice, old fellow who had about a year to go before he retired, had enlivened the morning by setting fire again to his wastepaper bin. He did this often because he used to light his pipe with a match and then drop it slowly into the split cane wastepaper bin below his desk. Miss Alexander didn't allow the rest of us to smoke but she couldn't stop George because he was old and too deaf to hear her injunctions anyway. George had set fire to his bucket once more and panicked as he always did; one of the girls was off sick, and O'Hara, who had replaced me in the Sewage Department and quickly been promoted over my head, had been promoted again to another department and Miss Alexander had been told she wasn't going to get a replacement. So Miss Alexander was in a bad mood, the sort of bad mood spinsters with hare-lips get into. (I'm not quite sure about the hare-lip. I think I may have invented this. But let the hare-lip stay.) Anyway she spoke from the desk behind me, in the middle of a burst of badinage with a fellow clerk who had been passing. 'Stop talking, McLean,' she ordered, 'and get on with your work.' I didn't get on with my work. 'Fuck off,' I said and silenced Miss Alexander, and, of course, the rest of the entire office, which was very large indeed. Not a rustle of papers, not a single sound. You could have heard a paperclip, well, clip. Suddenly Miss Alexander threw herself away from her desk and out of the room. There was still utter silence. I got up and made my way to Mr Roberts' glass-fronted office and resigned there and then. Mr Roberts probably didn't know who Miss Alexander was and certainly didn't recognise me even though I had sat in front of his glass front for months. Probably he was too busy thinking up his defence for his War crimes or trying to imagine how he could prove he wasn't really Adolf Eichmann, but he didn't accept my resignation at all until I wrote it out which I did that afternoon. Miss Alexander didn't come back that afternoon or indeed any afternoon for the rest of the week and when she returned on the following Monday everybody knew that I was for the off and she never told me to stop talking again. In fact she never spoke to me again either. Good.

That was the end of my municipal career. It was the end of any attempt on my part to hold down a 'proper job': I have never really had one since. The other clerks put a hat round for me and gave me a few pounds but I was too shy or diffident to go round thanking anybody. (Another clerk accosted me at six o'clock when I had finished my last day in the City Chambers and told me I was a rat. Nobody had ever bothered to ask me for a drink after work before and nobody bothered on my last day and if I was a rat I was bloody glad to be deserting the ship.) My parents, at least my father, cracked up. My father was all for phoning up Mr Roberts and asking him for my job back. 'I don't know what you think you'll do for money but you won't be living off me, my lad' – all that drivel. Too true I wouldn't be. I buggered off to Coventry to make my fortune.

Actually I'd intended buggering off to London but I was hitch-hiking and after two days I had only made Coventry. I looked about for work but all I could get was work in offices or a job as a bus conductor. Coventry was then in the process of being rebuilt after the holocaust of it during the War. They had a cathedral and all around it shopping precincts and council housing and it looked then, as it does now, like something out of Eastern Europe. When I see these structures now it reminds me of a quote from Andy Warhol concerning his incredibly highly priced silkscreen prints once snapped up avidly by collectors. 'They won't last,' said Warhol of his prints, 'I was using cheap paint.' The idea of a future in this country where the very people were figured in cheap paint, plus the only job which didn't fill me with despair being a bloody bus conductor was enough for me to forget exile and I returned, unbowed, to Glasgow and became, what else, a bus conductor.

By now I was no longer in the parental household and hadn't been for some time. Matters had come to a head one night when I had strolled in (you had always 'strolled in'), with a drink in me and the usual nonsense heard and repeated a million times in a million households throughout Britain and beyond. I got the 'd'ye think this is a bloody hotel' routine and rubbish like that. I had rather unwisely brushed my father out of the way, at which point he had grabbed me by the shoulder and shown every sign of assaulting me. So I assaulted him back which was a damned sight more unwise than brushing

75

him aside in the first place because we began to fight in earnest and he knocked buggery out of me and, opening the door, threw me into the garden outside and invited me to find other lodgings. Permanently. My mother was wringing her hands in the background and bewailing: 'David! He's only a boy!' (Standard reply: 'He's all the man he'll ever be!') 'Where'll he go?' (Standard reply: 'He should have thought of that before!'). 'He's my son!' (Standard reply: 'He's no son of mine!')And all the other items in the parental prayer-wheel. He's made his bed: let him lie on it! I've had enough of this. I'll be master in my own house. The entire litany. Then my father threw a small suitcase out the door, with a few hastily gathered garments and toiletries and told me not to come back. Years later I was to discover that my father didn't mean that and in fact was 'teaching me a lesson'. I learned my lesson though. I disappeared into the night and never fully returned to my father's house. I can honestly say though that I'm glad he tossed me out on my ear: there are very few ways of leaving the nest that aren't even more painful and I left with a pleasant sense of self-righteousness and claimed I had been hard done to, though I knew full well I hadn't and had stretched everybody's patience too far by half.

8

The West End of Glasgow I've avoided ever since my brief residence there and tend when in any city to demur at any west-side at all. East side of a European city is always the poorest part, where the huddled and oppressed go, quite simply because the prevailing winds come from the west and in the days of industrial despoilation the better-off moved out to where the grime and suit would blow in the direction of the huddled and oppressed and not anywhere near them. If the West End has a different meaning in London there are those who would attempt to give a similar cachet to the district where lie the rather tawdry ambitions of the West End provincials of Glasgow. But when I moved out of my father's house where there was no prospect of any mansion for myself, it was to the West End that I didn't just drift: I propelled myself there.

Glasgow's West End had at one time been quite smart and large parts of it still were (and remain), but the real reason why it was the place to be was that it was where Bohemia chose to reside: just by the university. The entire area depresses me now. It depresses me just seeing all these students and ageing would-be poetasters being as distressingly pretentious and obvious as their counterparts were back when I went to live in the district, a sort of Greenwich Village and Notting Hill with a touch of Chelsea and a wee bit round the Sorbonne but not really making it. But I went there all the same and was just as bad, and worse, as everybody else. I sported denim jeans and shirts and black polo sweaters, suede boots, and licorice-paper roll-your-owns, so I fitted in, though of course I wasn't sure, any more than anybody else, if I did. But it was the place to be so I went.

At first I dossed down in my elder brother's gaff off the Byres Road, the main thoroughfare in the district. After a fortnight I had moved into a one-room bedsit in Hillhead Street with a bloke I had met through my brother Richard. His name was Sandy Flockhart and even after over thirty years we remain friends. Flockhart and my brother had been fellow students at some place called, I think, the British Educational Institute and Sandy was going off, as a late entrant, to Glasgow University. He was looking forward to student life after a short but aborted career in insurance. I was looking forward to student life too because, now that I was old enough, I'd finally decided to become a bloody student, at Glasgow School of Art. Flockhart was also a talented singer and had sung opera and all that. I was the painter then. Both of us had read more Romantic novels than was good for anybody so it was quickly established that we were to enact the whole of 'La Bohème'. It was the ideal stage-set for it and, in a way, we were ideal players.

Flockhart was big, at six feet he was for that era anyway, and blond- haired and attractive to women who liked broths of boys who sang tenor so well and certainly operatically. The big man had been the star of the famed opera society at Hamilton Academy and had played the Pirate King. So he played the role for all it was bloody worth and very useful it turned out to be. It was rather useful for me as well because for those girls who didn't want big broths of boys who sang at the top of their voices there was always the opportunity of getting wooed by a small dark chap who cooed gentle words. It was a good partnership. Good as well because we got on very well together but I may say that as Flockhart was a few years older than me I tended to get more out of him than I think he did out of me. Big Flo, as he was known, had lots of pals around so latching on to him made things a lot easier for me. Certain aspects of our relationship didn't though. I was pleased at his success with women and indeed he was a welcome addition to any party, for he could be very good company and well quoted among the other guys. I was also horribly resentful that I was not. I simply couldn't understand why nobody recognised, immediately, my uniqueness, my talent, my cinematic angst. They noticed my angst right enough which was hardly difficult to spot.

But it was a romantic time then, and I spent a great deal of those brief few months in Hillhead Street sharing that bedsit living in the wraith-swirling autumnal streets of what was after all a late Victorian area, full of the tall baronial shapes of the hill-clinging tenements. It was an adventure all round. We met poets and artists and musicians and fell among the folk set. The folkies played a very big part indeed in the Glasgow of that time and it was the basis, as elsewhere, of much, much more. The same thing was happening all over Britain and in the United States even. Just as the folkies and art students and kindred spirits were talking far into the night of Verlaine and Baudelaire, of Odilon Redon and Aubrey Beardsley, of Jean-Paul Sartre and the Industrial Workers of the World and of things long forgotten, so they were all over folk clubs, coffee bars, and bedsit hovels and lofts everywhere: it was a very adventurous and earnest and impossibly jejune period. So it is doubtless for all of the young, at least those worth a damn anyway.

Scotland then had an enormous influence over the folk song revival movement and hordes of the American folkies came to little folk clubs where the entrance money was a couple of bottles of beer. The Marland Bar was a focus for a lot of this *demi-monde*. I remember Alex Campbell in there, a hero he was, who played a pretty basic guitar flatpick style but who looked the part with his lengthening hair and clipped Sheriff of Nottingham beard. Jimmie McGregor, fresh from his success with Robin Hall in the *Tonight* programme on BBC. I especially recollect Pete Seeger drinking pints in there with Hamish Henderson, whom I was to meet years later on in Edinburgh when I illustrated his poem 'The John MacLean March', and Seeger's wife, June Carter, one of the legendary Carter Family whose hillbilly music I had heard on the wireless as a child. Seeger was a shocking disappointment. He had a receding chin and looked like a querulous bank clerk who had been dressed by his elderly aunt.

There were a lot of major folkies who used the Marland (in the east, in Edinburgh, the equivalent was Sandy Bell's bar in Forrest Road), and a hell of a lot of people went on to make a stir in the entertainment business later on in a variety of forms. There was a lot of talent about but it was a time when musicians and artists and writers and entrepreneurs tried each other's crafts and often crossed over. Some of the then stars in that little world never made outside stardom at all; some of the unlikeliest did. One of the stars was a guy who had roomed with my brother, Tony Thomas. He was a dashing Dubliner with a great deal of blarney and was extraordinarily handsome. He played guitar reasonably well, in a folk blues style then becoming fashionable, and pulled birds with ease. He also, unusual for folkies, had a well-paid job as a civil engineer, and came from a well-known Dublin family with plenty of connections. His charm was easily exhausted, however, and he could be unpleasant and bloody cruel with a put-down and, if the truth be known, after a while his glamour was well outweighed by my dislike of him. I haven't met him in years and can only hope he's improved. But he made friends and, like a lot of people with the swellings of talent himself, he attracted people who had the real thing around him as early acolytes before they found themselves.

One of them was Billy Connolly. Billy was then a smooth-faced, clean-shaven young bloke who was trying to learn the banjo because Bluegrass music was coming across to the folk fraternity with people like the New Lost

City Ramblers, a group of New York varsity intellectuals who had got into hillbilly music. Billy was no intellectual but he was a shipyard worker who listened to the patter of the yards and his family, especially his cousin John, a violin-maker, and also his father, were wild men with the vocal words and could enliven any party. You never got a look-in with them in a conversation unless you tried a bloody sight harder than waiting for a space. And Billy wasn't only good himself at the conversation, and very imaginative, he was a boy who learned fast. He could sop up anything anybody wanted to say, from folkies to fantasists, university lecturers to con-men, barkers to bluesmen. He didn't have the beard or the hair then, but he had the personality and the chutzpah. (Years later I met Billy in the Scotia Bar, sitting at the counter in the quiet early days of morning opening-time. I hadn't seen him for, oh, ten years or so, not since the days when Gerry Rafferty and he had dissolved The Humblebums – or a little bit after when he was beginning his meteoric career and he had since made stardom, I mean international stardom. I nodded to him and ordered a drink. 'How's it goin', Billy?' I asked. 'What'll ye have?' He turned on me with an ironic look. 'I haven't seen you in twelve bloody years and all you can ask is how's it goin'?' In fact it was the first time I'd seen Billy in over twenty years without a beard and, Godammit, he looked just as he had in the Marland Bar: you forgot with that chin, that he was The Billy Connolly at all.)

Connolly comes up to Scotland regularly to see old chums and there is, as they say, still nae side tae him but he has often had a hard time with the Press over the years and I don't blame his surliness with the hacks. I saw an instance of it some years back, during Glasgow's Year of Culture bash in 1990. The Scotia Bar, under the direction of wee Brendan McLaughlin, the licensee and publican and not a bad wee player himself, set up a short story competition which went on to all sorts of celebrations including a nice little book of the winning stories. Billy, actors Katy Murphy, Elaine C. Smith, and the late Mark McManus, and myself were the judges. The day started early in the Scotia and went on all afternoon and all of us were having a grand time and the booze was flowing. A scribe from one of the tabloids came up to me and asked if Billy would agree to a small burst of an interview for his paper. 'You can ask, but he's here with chums for a hooley really,' I told the guy. The hack got me to introduce him though I didn't know the young man's name. The opening question the creep asked Connolly was if he had any contact with his first wife. It had been a smashing day with old chums of everybody's turning up and a day when a lot of celebrities weren't hogging any limelights and then this scum tried to introduce this rubbish. We flung the bastard out on his ear and thankfully the evening went on in good humour. But it showed up the drivel in the minds of hacks like that. A million questions about people and stories and wasn't it grand to be back in his old haunts and this turd comes prepared with questions nobody except he would be interested in.

At the Art school I came across some people I'd known at school, including our old friend, The Parasite, he who had sold single cigarettes in the playground shed; Kenneth McKenzie; and another old boy Dougie Carmichael, now I believe a photo-journalist. Through them there was that strange and emerging world of art college and rock 'n' roll, and it was through art colleges mainly that the Beat boom took place because it was art students who first got into Blues and R & B and rock. It was the art colleges in Britain which led the way and I was led as well. Softly-lit winter afternoons sitting cross-legged in West-End wooden-floored flats. Sometimes the flats were mums' and dads' flats and very expensively furnished too, often rather artily. The girls all looked as much like Francoise Hardy as they could and it was girls who pioneered The Look which eventually brought about that androgenous appearance affected by groups like the Rolling Stones, the Beatles, if it comes to that, and – the archetypal art-school band – The Pretty Things. If there wasn't quite free love, and we were a couple of years or so away from what was to be called 'permissiveness', we weren't far off it, and this was happening all over Britain. It was to flood the world. The bit of it with money anyway.

Certainly it flooded me. To the extent that I did very little at the Art School, which was folly because I possessed a certain talent and we had some very distinguished tutors. There was David Donaldson who became the Queen's Limner in Scotland, and a magnificently painterly painter, and his sidekick James Robertson. David always wore dark blue shirts and little skullcaps or bunnets and cord trousers. His hair was long and he had a little goatee beard. Jimmy always wore dark blue shirts and bunnets and he had a little goatee beard . . . hell, they all did. It's taken me years to afford their paintings but both are immense stylists and prolific artists and great international names now, though back then there was only one real gallery in Glasgow at all and Scottish painters suffered from a lack of exhibition space. Another tutor was Alexander Goudie, a child prodigy and a wealthy painter today with a huge reputation, whose commissioned work goes for lots of spondulicks. Sandy Goudie was even more flamboyant than David and Jimmy, which means he was practically a young Augustus John on speed. He was and is a fabulously talented painter and draughtsman whose work, like that of many of that generation of artists, has been consistently undervalued by the very smart critics but which sells very well today and has done for a good many years. These boys aren't exactly in poverty but they all work hard to this day and are great company, cheery (even Dr Donaldson who can, it is said, eclipse the sun with his occasional moods of darkness), and like a drink or two. Ach, there were hundreds of these guys at Glasgow – big John Cunningham with his gargantuan girth and equally gargantuan paintings whose brushstrokes, like the dancing feet of big men, are delicate and silver-tongued. Or the amazingly-clothed Trevor Mackinson, whose immaculate waistcoated suits practically breathed on his slender and languid frame; the beak of a nose, the *élan* of his *boutonnière*, the glorious flowering of his tie set in his pastel-coloured shirts. There were loads more, characters all, fine painters, and models for their young charges though parents would hardly have thought so. (There was a great deal of student-teacher activity, then as now, but more so then. Certainly no art school lecturer would ever have been pulled up then for his keen interest in the very prettiest students as he doubtless would now.) I should have got a lot out of Art School but I didn't: I drank the entire grant in the State Bar in just over two months.

It gave me an in with the student world, though. And the art scene, the rock scene, the planet that youth was living on at the time. I don't know how long this time lasted; it wasn't long, but long enough. I drifted into jobs in bars and clubs, in hotels, occasionally back on the bus-conducting, sometimes with the SMT in Old Kilpatrick, other times with the Corpy – the Glasgow Corporation Transport Department whose long-time director was immortalised for all Glaswegians by having his name printed at the door of every bus. E.R.L. Fitzpayne. The other name conjured up by every Glaswegian citizen was H. Stewart MacKintosh because he was the director of education for decades and in fact used to travel on my bus every morning when I was collecting fares. In the daytime bus conducting was civilised and Glaswegian commuters then very friendly. At night it was different. Especially on the late-night buses. You'd get the drunks coming on and staggering up the stairs (drunks always went up the stairs, even when they couldn't walk on the bloody pavement without falling over). I once saw a drunk vomit over the passenger in front, all over the back of his head. The wee inebriate was nonplussed by his action and a gentleman at all times. He leaned over to his vomit-drenched victim and slurred: 'Sorry, Jim.' Then a silence. 'Nae offence meant, Jim,' he said magnanimously.

The gang boys at night were frightening a touch and would often cheerily offer you a slug from a bottle of cheap fortified wine. You had to drink it. I remember one night coasting down the upper deck and asking the chap at the front for his fare. The guy had a coupon which was criss-crossed with the old Mars Bars and very fierce he looked too. 'Fuck off!' he growled in reply to my request. I turned to the passenger behind him. 'Fares please,' I demanded.

'Same as him,' he replied laconically, pointing to my customer in front. I spent the rest of the night sitting up the back of the bus hoping the inspector would come on at a bus stop and show me how he'd handle the situation.

Occasionally the neds would be too young to frighten me in which case I'd throw them off the bus if I was pissed off, or let them stay on for half the fare and no questions. The worst time I ever got was when an aggressive Rangers fan wanted to know why I was 'fuckin' werrin' green ya fenian basturt'. Difficult it was to explain that this was, unfortunately, the colour of the uniform and tell the Corporation of your objections.

Jobs in pubs and hotels, any damned job, it didn't matter because I was running around with any number of crowds from all sorts of milieus. I was staying where I could and ended up at one stage dossing on a couch in a top storey flat in University Avenue, staying again with Big Flo who was damn-near doing what I'd done and nearly blowing his university course. It was a good time, a very sunny spring I remember, and the flat was up above a coffee bar called The Papingo which was owned by a fabulous character called Harry Turner. The Papingo never had any jazz and its coffee would have made wartime Germany's ersatz palatable, but it had lots of sloe-eyed girls trying to look like Juliette Greco, and Harry ran a sort of speakeasy as it was, and you could drink in there outside of licensing hours. Harry is now a well-known press photographer who I work with whenever I can and I suspect is still thinking up outrageous things to do. He has thought up a few in his lifetime including being one of the few British citizens who has been jailed in the Bastille, and flung out of France twice.

The flat was what had once been the nursery, and in the basement – from where she never moved – lived the landlady, a very nice old lady who wore black mourning and jet jewellery, a sort of widowed Miss Havisham. For some reason she had the walls throughout the entire house covered with fake cardboard stonemasonry and very eerie it looked too. Occasionally you would find her wandering about with a candle. It was very disconcerting until you got used to it. Early in the morning Flockhart and the two other boys who shared the flat, a wealthy Dutch medical student and an impecunious ne'er-do-well called Bob Paton who did something but we knew not what, were visited by the downstairs tenant, an elderly man of military bearing called Walter. He had a lovely modulated middle-class accent with which he used to address us: 'Good morning boys,' followed by a brisk and hopeful, 'Any gin?' I don't think any of us thought this odd. In fact, some of the girls who tried to look like Juliette Greco in the coffee bar below found the ménage intriguing; enough to visit us too. That's how, I think, I got to meet a girl whose name really was Juliette, or at least that's the name I'm calling her.

I knew her from being around and she was stunning-looking but a bit strange really and I can't remember how it came about that I moved in with her but I did. It was her who got me a job with the Corporation again, after some time working in various pubs. I quite liked working as a barman and over the years I was a barman on and off to the extent that I suppose you could call me a professional, but one pub I worked in proved to be too rough, even for Glasgow, and I resigned, which is to say that I told the man to stick it and ran for cover before the bad men could get me. Juliette worked as a town planner for Glasgow and there was a nice wee seasonal job coming up and I got it on her recommendation. It involved going round certain areas of Glasgow visiting perhaps one in ten households to discern information which it was hoped would assist the planners in their future deliberations. The information required was simple. How many in the family? What was the occupation of the head of the household? How many children of school age, how many under school age? Very worthwhile, would chart the demographic needs etc and so on. It was, I remember, rotten weather. The areas I was designated to visit were equal to the weather. Dank grey endless rows of East-European two-up dwellings set in scree. Bloody awful it was. It didn't take a genius to work out how to do this with the aid of the voters roll with which I had been issued and to do it without the backbreaking toil the task demanded. I simply sat in The State Bar or another pub and looked over every tenth house or whatever it was. If the name was Reilly or Gallagher or some such surname of clearly Irish, and therefore presumably Catholic, origin I gave the buggers five kids and accorded age levels as my imagination saw fit. Obviously Presbyterian surnames like Jamieson or Morton or whatever were less fecund in their relationships. Sometimes I imagined entire families with different jobs, different lives, tragedies, comedies, life in the raw. It was nothing but a damned soap opera I began to write after a week or two, and the week or two lasted until mid-summer. I had begun to weary of the invention required, however, and started to overdo it a little, creating occupations just a little too exotic for Riddrie or Polmadie and such, and families perhaps a touch too irregular. Perhaps this was noticed, perhaps not, but eventually what was bound to occur did. One of my surveys was cross-surveyed and it all came horribly to light. Where one of the earnest students who had been helping with the survey (most of the team had been recruited from the undergraduate population of the Town Planning Department at Glasgow University), reported that John Davidson was a plasterer and had a family of two children, I had Mr Davidson with a herd of eight brats. In my mind one of them had been shorn of a leg in a street accident and was confined to a wheelchair; the mother drank absinthe when she could get it;

and he whiled his working hours away as a stained glass painter. Time to go it was. I remember the middle-aged academic in charge of the survey went haywire. On the same day it was discovered that Oscar Mazaroli, the department photographer, was in soapy bubble for taking photographs really but not the ones he was meant to. Oscar was taking wonderfully elegiac photographs of the Glasgow which was vanishing before our very eyes and today his work is worth the fortune which this marvellous artist never received in his lifetime, and his books sell in their thousands. I can assure you of this: I never buggered-up town planning the way the Town Planning Department did and I didn't try to ruin the life of a remarkable photographer either.

But not only did I lose my job but I thankfully lost Juliette as well because she cracked up and said I had put her position at risk and all that. She threw a, mercifully cold, pan of Heinz soup over me and that was me off looking for another bed for the night and the future. I was picking alphabet spaghetti out of my hair for hours but I got a bed for the night and the next day work elsewhere. In a hotel in Dunoon. For the summer season. You learn a lot doing a summer season in a Highland hotel. Both the chefs were blatantly homosexual and alcoholic. It was the only time in my life that I have threatened anybody with a knife but, along with all the other waiters, I became quite sanguine about it because we all had to. Henry the pianist who was the nightly cabaret until he got too pissed – he was a knife-threatener as well – ran away with the head waitress who took the month's 'trunk' – the staff tips – with her. The two middle-aged ladies who owned McColl's Hotel seemed not to notice these staff changes and the customers, who were almost entirely American Navy officers from the nearby base (with the occasional bewildered elderly English couple thrown in), enjoyed the farce immensely. I ended up as the cocktail barman and learned how to mix a dry martini rather well. Also how to avoid drunk homosexual chefs and keep my own tips. I'll bet you think this was something of a shallow life. It was.

Dr David Donaldson, sadly died shortly before publication of this book.

9

Life wasn't all that shallow, though, come to think of it. Politics played a larger part in our lives then perhaps than it does now, certainly among the young. I'd been active in my teens in the Labour movement, in the Labour Party even. I remember doing posters for a by-election campaign for Dr Maurice Miller in North Kelvinside. The late George Brown turned up to support the candidate. This was before the Wilson General Election victory and Labour were cock-a-hoop with the scent of it, for what was called the 'thirteen years of Tory misrule' was clearly coming to an end. George arrived after what was reported in the next day's papers as 'a rousing speech' and was already pretty rousing with the drink when he entered the Labour rooms in Dumbarton Road. He and Dr Miller were handed a cup of tea and cakes and a large whisky for the deputy leader of the Party and then George was introduced to 'our young artist who has done so much in our campaign'. I was a young fellow, probably the youngest helper for Miller. George shook my hand vigorously upsetting his cup and saucer in the process and the cakes on it and the large whisky. I saw the scalding tea course down the candidate's trouser seams. Saw the pink Co-op meringue on George's saucer make a wide parabola and land on Miller's suede shoe. The fern cake, a sweetmeat with a very sticky icing top inherent in Labour Party tea parties, fell sticky-side down onto Miller's other trouser leg, clinging there like some strange crustacean. George continued, oblivious to the disaster, pumping my hand up and down. How he achieved the legerdemain I know not but he managed to hold on to the large whisky, and went on to consume several more during the evening. Years later I met George, by then Lord George, in London and reminded him of the incident. He remembered Maurice Miller's by-election, it being so close to the general one, and spoke highly of Dr Miller. 'Jewish doctor, wasn't he?'

he asked. 'Could do with more doctors in the House. Bastards are all bloody bankers now.' I couldn't tell whether he meant Jews or doctors.

Certainly it was true that a large number of the radicals in Scottish politics, certainly in Glasgow's, were from the Jewish community and I am still, after all these years of so many Jewish ministers in Tory cabinets, surprised when I hear of a Jewish Tory. I mean, the Woolfson family in Glasgow, a well-known Gorbals family, may well have produced Sir Isaac Woolfson but it also spawned more Marxist academics than you would have found in the communist bloc for heaven's sake. And Marxism was still alive in the Glasgow of the early 1960s; had never really gone away.

Tied up with the folk-song people and the rock 'n' roll revolution and all the posturings of what would later be called Youth Culture was a great deal of concern about the world, and though a lot of crap was talked, the concerns seemed to be less crankish than a lot of world concerns appear to be now. Today we are possibly, hopefully, going through a bad patch when idjits seem to think anti-smoking or vegetarianism or some other bloody fad is of global importance. There might have been a wheen of idiosyncrasy abounding in the Aldermaston Marchers but it was, after all, a little important at that. A new Labour government had touched a lot of blue papers, even if it was beginning to bugger things up a bit, but front page news was about what politicians were doing or trying out. The Profumo scandal of the last year or so of the Conservative government was mainly confined to the inside pages of the blatts: the Profumo Affair was initially, and mostly, about State security, and Profumo resigned because he had lied to the House. Papers didn't report what sexual peccadilloes MPs got up to, and I don't think anybody would have given much of a toss about such concerns if they had. World politics played a major part in British lives too. The Cuban missile crisis had been close. And then the assassination of President Kennedy. Somehow that was a watershed. I had been brought up, after all, in a post-war world in which there had been, after that world conflict, dedication to a tremendous stability. There had been hiccups – the partition of India, Hungary, Suez, Krushchev's outburst on Stalin, but they were perceived as the normal vicissitudes we could only expect, more important than but as much part of the normal world changes as the sudden explosion of continental soccer talent, or the advent of new American popular music. With the death of Kennedy a very unreal reality entered our lives. You just didn't ever think of a President of the United States being assassinated. The subsequent events with Jack Ruby and then of course the assassination of Martin Luther King; of Robert Kennedy; the shooting of George Rockford; the burning cities of the USA; the turmoil in Czechoslovakia, Paris and Cohn-Bendit; the Red Army faction – all this was heralded in my mind by the assassination of Kennedy. If that could happen, what the fuck couldn't? It was an end to my own sense of infinite security: Attlee and Churchill and then Eden and Gaitskill and onwards, and all in a seamless series of And-thens. Kennedy was a Suddenly. There were a lot of Suddenlys to come.

IO

The very sky looked new-washed that London morning. The smell of a new morning had other, concrete aromas intermingling. The smell of clean disinfectant from the newly mopped floors of the shops I passed; the scent of stale beer from the still-closed but about to open pubs; the leaves of the trees; the smoke from the steam trains going by; the very eau-de-Cologne of the girls in the street – the smell of London – which I can remember in my nostrils yet and which I always recognise every time I find myself in the metropolis. Sir Fitzroy MacLean once told me that Russia always smelled of Russia to him; its special effluvia had been fixed on his first day in the land of the Great Bear. London has the same for me: just as it was when I first arrived there. Walking down West End Lane with the Labour Exchange to visit to fix up work and a new start in my life to look forward to, and the knowledge that I was where it was happening. In retrospect it was the first mewlings of the infant Swinging London which was to grow into the monster it did: it was 1965.

Sandwell Mansions in West End Lane in West Hampstead. Very central really for north London. Hampstead near, and also Kilburn, a bus journey away from Marble Arch. The City and Westminster not far off. Piccadilly, Bond Street, The Strand, Knightsbridge, Chelsea. In fact to a provincial exile London is a small city and the parts of it you want to go to are easy to, well, get to. It is, as in every city, only the aboriginal inhabitants who don't explore their native heath. West End Lane was where I kicked off in London, where I dossed for a week before moving into my own bedsit. In Belsize Park it was, near Swiss Cottage tube station. Belsize Park was shabby to shabby genteel but it was *en route* to smart Hampstead and a lot of Hampstead people came down to drink in a couple of pubs there. I once saw Kenneth Tynan, the critic, in one of them and the girl I was with asked him if he was he. He said he wasn't but on leaving told us he was. I never said a word to him. About six months later in the blues club across the way (which advertised Curry and Jazz; maybe Harry Turner of the Papingo in Glasgow owned this as well because there wasn't even a packet of bloody crisps on the premises and I never heard anything other than very immature R & B played there), Tynan was one of the audience when I was playing blues harp with the band. He was with the same American girl, presumably his wife, he'd been drinking with in the boozer those months ago. 'You're that Scottish chap, aren't you? How did you make out with that popsie you were with?' he asked, which meant not only that he'd remembered me but had obviously been listening in to our conversation. Impressed me no end that did.

It was a nice little area with a kind of village feel to it and besides the pubs possessed a splendid small Israeli restaurant which was very cheap where I discovered that kosher food is absolutely vile. Cheap though it was, and I ate a lot of kreplach but not a lot of lox. One problem emerged in the form of a fellow tenant in the house, a one-eyed American on a GI grant who said he was trying to be a writer. He was, I thought, middle-aged, with lank hair and his good eye usually as glassy with alcohol as the glass one was. The only way you could tell his eyes apart was that the glass one sort of suppurated with an oily sweat. There was a great deal of sweat about him and he always wore a thick khaki sweater which reminded you of why a sweater is called exactly that. He stank of sweater. It wouldn't have mattered except that he once lent me five quid when I couldn't pay the rent and subsequently appeared at my door and asked for 'you know, that thing'. I hadn't an inkling of what he was talking about, I really hadn't. He made a hand motion which was unmistakable. Genuinely shocked, I told him that I would poke his other fucking eye out and, dammit, he started to greet, tears flooding even from his glass eye. He said he was sorry, truly really sorry, and that it was hard being homosexual. He got urges he told me, he didn't realise about me, he said and he didn't mean any harm please say I forgave him and to put the incident out of my mind. It wouldn't ever happen again. I felt very sorry for him. But if he'd tried anything at all I'd have poked his other eye out at that. (I'd encountered homosexuals before but none of them had ever made a pass at me and I suppose I didn't know how to react, so naturally my response was a little bit like that of a sixteen year-old debutante squirming away from some aged roué who'd tried to steal a kiss in a dark corner of the ballroom.)

After a few jobs in pubs I started work for a firm of civil engineers and architects as a pay clerk. Llewellyn-Davies Weeks and Bor they were called. The firm was headed by Lord Llewellyn-Davies, a socialist peer. His wife was

90

a very active socialist as well but it didn't stop the pair of them from paying their pay clerks starvation bloody wages. I suppose they had a lot on their minds, thinking up socialism as it were. The department manager was a Scot called Alasdair Anderson, a grossly honest thin-lipped chap who was the first to teach me what a set of shits many exiled Scots can be. I don't blame a lot of English people from rather disliking Scots because a great many of the ones who come down to London end up as bosses. In politics and the trade unions and, indeed, in journalism, the aggression of the Scotsman on the make is a winner but it often makes for very unpleasant high achievers. Back in the mid-Sixties I found the southern English rather racist, even towards Scotsmen and northerners. Very racist towards the Irish, and more often than not quite uncomprehending of West Indians or Asians.

The receptionist at the company building, a vast concrete monstrosity opposite Euston Station, was a glamour pin-up called Robin Gaye Burge. I asked her out once and she looked me up and down and said, in very withering tones and the trace of a Dagenham accent: 'With you?' and I withered instantly. Two meagre little pleasures were afforded me with Robin Gaye Burge, however. One was when she arrived flustered and late one morning and hadn't had time to put on her elaborate make-up revealing the fact that she had no face, no discernible features, at all. I enjoyed that. The other was upon the occasion when I inadvertently chanced upon the little trollop bouncing her skinny arse off the reception desk with the thin-lipped Alasdair Anderson giving her a right good seeing-to. They were undeniably made for each other. Thus shall the enemies of McLean perish. A small comfort though. Llewellyn-Davies Weeks and Bor had a fire about a week after I had witnessed the liaison of the receptionist and the Scottish lickspittle and this proved a grand opportunity to resign because I owed about six weeks' stamp money which I'd been borrowing out of the petty cash. It is ironic then that the only time I have ever, I suppose, stolen, was from a socialist.

I got a new job though through a young bloke who was studying to be a ballet dancer. It was a job with a lot called Domestics Unlimited, a firm owned and operated by a Jewish actor whose name I forget but he was a really nice guy and he helped hundreds of artists and would-be writers, musicians, dancers and performers. For the agency hired us out to clean people's flats when we were 'resting' while we signed on the dole and grabbed the loot. Oddly I condone this because I couldn't find any other way of earning enough to feed myself and pay the rent and there must be thousands upon thousands of young people in an even worse position nowadays.

My first job of work I remember was in a lovely little cottage sort of house in Hampstead, the sort they have in Hampstead, for a Miss Karen Fernauld.

She was a well-known, though not particularly successful, actress whose dad was the Canadian actor-producer John Fernauld. Rather snooty she was but what the hell I got paid and the work was anything but arduous. She was about ages with me and I felt like Pip in *Great Expectations*. A great many of the clients were actors, and a number were Jewish, and some of them were both. I met a lot of quite famous entertainers and actors and so on. Very strange some of them were. A radio producer called Michael Raper had an array of leather gear: I foolishly took him for a motor-bike enthusiast. He paid a tip though. I cleaned Julie Christie's flat in Paddington once or twice. While the lads out there were salivating at her image on the silver screen, because she was really hot in the movies at the time, I was clearing up after her, including on one occasion, having to deposit her panties in the laundry basket. Never gave me a buzz: it was work. Spike Milligan proved to be as amusing, and as weird in real life as his reputation had him, and a very good bloke who often made me give up cleaning and drink Irish whisky while he ate ginger snaps for an hour. There were some very strange interludes. I remember clearing the guttering for a middle-aged couple just come across from South Africa. Myself and a musician were working away when the lady of the house told us to come down off the roof for something to eat. To our amazement she wanted us to sit down at the dining-room table for a full meal and her husband insisted. So we did. A couple of workies and they started to ply us with this four-course meal and wine, and gave us a smoke after dinner. The husband had just been released from a South African jail and expelled from the country. Their children weren't allowed to leave. The pair of them were kindness itself.

Most of the customers weren't. Some of them could no longer afford the servants they once had and treated you as a skivvy. Sometimes there were heartbreaking scenes though, a guy whose wife was dying and who was trying to look after her and the children, and work at the same time. We did a lot of cleaning up after somebody had died and the widow, usually a widow, had to move. There were a few elderly people too who just needed a help around the house. The old Jewish people in Finchley and Golders Green were great. Two of my customers were old Russian Jews who not only knew each other but both had known Lenin and had signed photographs of him and themselves. There was an old Jewish jeweller who hired me two days a week to be his bodyguard while he wandered about with this small attaché case full of magnificent diamonds which he had for customers in the trade in Covent Garden. At lunchtimes he used to take me to the Savoy and feed me smoked salmon sandwiches. When he got home his wife used to sit him down and make us tea. 'It's good he has a Scottish boy, so intelligent, so honest, not like these goyim.' I think she considered Scots, as my father certainly did and as Highland anecdote has it, to be one of the Lost Tribes of Israel.

It was a customer called Martin O'Neil who got me real work, for perhaps the first time in my life. He and his young wife and toddler son lived in a terrace house in the then slum area of Islington and Martin had a technical advertising business which was beginning to make very real money indeed. He was among the first to recognise the possibilities of gentrification and bought the entire house top and bottom. The house was a strange combination of Edwardian, 1920s, and Sixties cool: it was a style which has come rather to prevail and so it should, eclectic but classy. It was his wife, Gwen, who designed it all, from the large tiled kitchen with its Aga and rows of herb bottles, to the dinky chintzy bedrooms, to the gracious drawing-room. She had a lot of class, and Martin, an Ulsterman, a lot of energy.

I got on especially well with Gwen; once, when I'd been ill the week before and turned up the next week looking thin and peaky she sent me home with a food parcel and a thermos of stew. I used to draw to amuse the wee boy, who was called Michael, so ended up occasionally babysitting for the O'Neils. It was no trouble at all. I kept the wee bugger up with drawings till he fell asleep on the carpet and that was it. They'd come home and Martin would pour me an Irish and talk. Gwen found our accents so strange and liked it and I think it was her who suggested that Martin give me a job, drawing for his firm and that was how eventually I started off to become an artist – through, at the end of the day, a mother and her wee boy.

My younger brother Brian had come down to join myself and my other brother so that was the three of us in the Smoke: it was the time when you had to be in London. You would open up the Sunday papers – the colour supplements chronicled London and virtually nothing else for a spell – and there you were in its pages, or thought you were. Visiting Yanks, and they came in their hordes, would practically bend at the knee when they encountered a native. The Swinging London movies were in full spate and very ludicrous they were but it was still an exciting feeling knowing that you were at the hub of the then universe. (On my twenty-first birthday in a little harbour town called St Valery en Caux, the spot where the 51st Highland Division had fought a last stand in two world wars, the French pop group in the local casino adopted us and borrowed our clothes. They had strange ideas of *Le Style Anglais*. '*Le* Oxford Bags, yes?' Or, '*J'aime le*'acking *jacquette, hein?*' We hadn't a scooby what all the fuss was about but an enormous élan had been thrust upon us so instead of pointing out that *Le* Oxford Bags were an anathema to the Swinging Brit we just simply took the plaudits and shagged all their birds. For once the French put up with it.)

The changes that were occurring were going so fast it was difficult to know how to get off the roundabout, and that was just us. Christ knows what it was like for the pop stars and their hangers-on whom we saw parading down the King's Road in Chelsea on Saturdays. You had to know a little about where the *cognoscenti* were going to be. There was a really tacky period in London when all these ludicrous fat Spanish bints wandered up and down Carnaby Street buying crap like purple flounced shirts and plastic replica street nameplates. Portobello Road was big for a while for those in the know but eventually the nerds discovered that was where you bought the fashionable military tunics from boutiques with titles like 'I was Lord Kitchener's Batman'. Mind you, Notting Hill Gate was very much the place to be, and pubs like the Sun and Splendour or Donaghue's were the pubs to drink in and buy hashish.

I was signing on at Marylebone Labour Exchange, the Executive Register part of it where the actors and artists and musicians got their money, and working at the flat-cleaning, taking Fridays off to wander about New Bond Street and the Cork Street galleries.My brother had got a job as a clerk in the Labour and used to sign me on from time to time. The little bastard delighted in asking me if I could show evidence that I wasn't working and was available for interviews. He was living with me in the same flat. In Kilburn.

Kilburn was, and is still, the Irish part of London. Right up and down Kilburn High Road there are to this day Irish pubs with the same, I swear it, Irish cast of extras there were thirty years ago. The last time I was there, in the mid 1990s I revisited the North British Hotel, a spacious Irish pub and the juke box had the same, but scratchier, records of Brendan Shine and Johnny Logan and the showbands it had in 1966. Behind the counter the same Irish boy with the big sideburns and the face like Rory Gallagher, the same pink-cheeked colleens, the same well-heeled Irish subbies in cheap, workie trousers but with Rolex oyster wristwatches on tattooed arms. Central casting, the lot, but there, and unchanged.

We lived in Cavendish Road, just before Kilburn station, on the ground floor of a big semi-detached house. A fellow tenant lived upstairs, a large fat man who dressed in an improbable yellow check suit, like a bookie, or maybe Evelyn Waugh. He also wrapped himself in an Inverness cape when he was cold and was wonderfully stagey which was hardly surprising because he was a bit of a legend among his fellow thespians. He rarely had currency of any kind upon him and could be found regularly adding to his slate in the nearby pubs, which knew him well. His magnificently fruity tones could be heard from one end of the pub to the other as he demanded, 'Another pink gin, Eammon, dear boy, a gentlemen's measure. Just –' and the Churchillian tones would float easily to the other side of the boozer, 'put it on my account.' No wonder his voice was Churchillian for he was none other than the actor Felix Felton, a lovely man, who had been the voice of Churchill on the BBC throughout the War. Some of the most famous broadcast speeches which generations of Britons, and others further afield, have always taken for the mellifluous Churchill himself, were in fact Felix. He would often amble down to our flat to drink thick tea, into which he usually poured a spot of spirits from a battered hip flask he carried and which he claimed had been given him by the Great Man. When slightly more sober it was Brendan Bracken. If he didn't have the hip flask he'd borrow what he could from us and wander off to the North British at the corner for fresh supplies. A gentleman, but most certainly of the boards, one could have imagined him enticing the young Pinocchio down the Milky Way to the land of greasepaint and lime lights, straight out of the movie itself. To this day myself and my brothers occasionally toast his memory in a pub, joined by a few pals to whom we have told of the glory of our forgotten mountebank. A raising of the glass and the one word. 'Felix!', and another round to buy. Cavendish Road was the unlikely setting for this portly mountebank who figured, so curiously and in a strange offshoot, in the history of this island race. Cavendish Road was a façade for less merry endeavors by less charming residents. Years later we were to discover that a few doors down was mass murderer Denis Neilson's residence. But then, though hardly a cheery district, it was respectable enough. Except for us.

Myself and my brother Richard had let it from a Mr and Mrs Hertzman along with another Glaswegian, none other than Bob Paton whom you last heard of in the flat I had dossed in above the Papingo. At first we had started well but, as young men will, eventually the house became a haven for fun, frolics, and a lot of friends and folk and fucking. Richard was by now a young civil servant on the way up, having come out second in Britain in the Civil Service Executive Officer exams and on to Admin grade in the Ministry of Defence. What the secret service security in the Civil Service was like one shudders at, because my brother used to emerge each morning to go off to Whitehall, clad in his smart coat and Hornes suit with the black and gold university necktie, when a few hours back he'd been blowing his bloody head off with hash and listening to John Peel's programme 'The Perfumed Garden'. I was cleaning actors' flats and cavorting about Cork Street galleries. Brian was signing me on and buying the shit from a West Indian pal called Sam – a small island man who earned a respectable living selling grass and dope, but no pills. 'No junk, man, I got my rep, man.' Bob Paton was a representative for the British Tie Manufacturers' Federation. In his spare time he was also 'Robert Patou; Antique Spoon Dealer'.

Paton had a penchant for role-playing, and though he really could be a pretentious pain in the arse he was also a very credible con-artist of a sort: the sort that cons itself. His latest wheeze – he'd got in with a minor public school Chelsea set – was that he would make his fortune selling antiques to his new-found chums. Bob was good on words and make-believe but not so hot on the reality. His wares, what he was to kick off his antique business in, never amounted to anything more than a silver Georgian spoon. But he had cards made. We called him of course 'Robert Patou, Antique Spoon Dealer' and acres of amusement was to be had out of the jape. In this we were now joined by none other than Tony Thomas, the Dublin bloke down from Glasgow, and his brother Gerry. Gerry Thomas spent much of his time in japes. An engineer, he whiled away the hours in the spartan flat designing a bridge on drawing paper. He never knew where he was going to put the bridge and when asked what he was going to call it always replied, 'Sure, Gerry's First Bridge.'

It was one morning when Bob Paton stirred himself from his filthy bed that he discovered Gerry, myself and Brian, by now men of leisure – that is to say only occasionally in employment – sitting round the table stirring our tea with, what else, his Georgian spoon. He went haywire, I don't know why to this day, and mayhem resulted. Nobody since can explain it but somehow it was the beginning of the end of the Cavendish Road flat. Somehow the hazy spell was broken and we all began to split up. Within weeks Mrs Hertzman was having breakdowns at the sight of the flat, which she had let to three sober young Scots, turning into the Paris bloody Commune with often as many as a dozen people living there and beds shared with all sorts of mini-skirted girls. I think the final straw was the discovery of the buried bottles. We'd been living in this, by now, hovel for about a year and a half and in all that time nobody had ever returned a milk bottle, ever. We kept them in serried ranks all over the kitchen and into the hallway. Unwashed of course. There were hundreds. Mrs Hertzman kept on at us to get rid of them but eventually there were so many that we really didn't know how to dispose of the bottles. But Mrs Hertzman was going demented about the bottles and eventually we buried them at dead of night, in the spacious back green. A single torch, four of us sweating away digging this bloody great pit, six doors up as it turned out from where Mr Neilson was indulging in rather more macabre excavations. Sir John Moore had no more regimental an internment. But even at three in the morning there was bound to be a nosy cow across the way, observing all. The next day the police turned up ready for the worst bearing warrants for an exhumation. Mrs Hertzman had finally had enough and issued an eviction notice.

On the last day, a bright Saturday, Mrs Hertzman arrived with two bemused helmeted policemen. There was no resistence. Oddly, even then Mrs Hertzman was saying: 'I know Mr McLeen' 'Yoeu hev tried to keep your friends on the right path. It's not yoor fault,' she kept saying to me. But, I'm afraid, it rather was. It took a couple of hours to oust us from 45 Cavendish Road and all the locals came out to watch, leaning or sitting on their garden walls, cheering occasionally when we saluted them by raising our beer bottles aloft, for there had been a massive party the night before and all in all there must have been about sixteen people coming out of the flat. We even had a bluegrass band playing because Billy Connolly and his pal John Gibson, an art student and folk guitar maestro, had arrived down from Glasgow the night before, and Tony Thomas and the rest of us joined in on guitars. Dickens again: it was a kind of innocent rousting of the Fagin gang without Fagin. But it ended any lightheartedness which London had for me.

After that I dossed anywhere I could, staying with friends and brothers a few days at a time. But the days, the years, of drifting had taken their toll. I became what I can only call unwell. I was still a very young man but painfully thin is the best description of my physique and the same holds true of my mental state, when I come to think of it. I'd even, after a party when I'd been high and drunk and my latest girl had abandoned me and I felt particularly friendless and at my wits' end about finding somewhere to sleep on a more permanent basis and how to get money for a cash advance for a room somewhere, gone home on my own to the flat where I'd been sleeping on the floor and attempted to gas myself with my head in the oven. I don't know if it had been a half-hearted go at it, or if I'd been serious. I can't really remember, and I was overdosed on self-pity right enough. But I certainly wasn't well.

We hardly ate, for God's sake, and though penury had ensured that we didn't smoke as much hash as would do us harm, if it does, and though I was largely still what you would hardly call promiscuous, not in today's terms anyway, I'd had a couple of bouts of venereal disease which didn't do my health or my psyche all that much good. I was unlucky that way. One of the doses of VD had been caught from a young and very lively nurse of impeccable background who was and is the sister of a prominent member of the present Tory cabinet. When I gave her name as a contact there was a groan from the youngish hospital doctor. She was a nurse in that very hospital.

On my second occurrence of gonorrhoea my groin ballooned and I started having what I took to be palpitations of the heart. It is not uncommon in young men, especially those under stress for some time, and in fact this particular type of neurasthenia was known as 'soldier's heart' in the First

World War when the young men of the trenches were placed under impossible pressures. A good many young men experience it – the young Disraeli, for instance, changed his entire life after a similar sickness, and it changed my life too. It had been self-indulgence and not the old men of the High Command which had pushed me into the trenches but in a way I had been under fire for too long and it was time for sick leave, time for recuperation, time for rebirth. I went home.

II

Ask anyone who has ever been a mature student, who has gone to university or college after being in the adult world for some years, what it is like at first and they will tell you: it is frightening and bewildering and the kid straight out of school wouldn't have the smeddum for it, would have to wait for that kind of balls. You are, in fact, going back the way; you are regressing. And you are out of your depth. For some it can be very bad. Those who are unsure of their academic ability in the first place, of whether or not they have a sufficient standard of education to begin with those who felt failures when they were at school – possibly a majority of mature students in the last category. Those who have had to stand the taunts of family and colleagues over their decision to go back; those who see it only as a last chance; those who think they have failed in their post-school careers; those who expect to fall down in this new venture. For all those mature students it is a nightmare. I had none of those disadvantages when I embarked on my studies at Edinburgh College of Art, and yet the first month was very difficult.

I'd chosen Edinburgh for a variety of reasons, one of them very silly. I'd seen the Maggie Smith-Robert Stephens 'The Prime of Miss Jean Brodie', the film of a book I'd read years before and much enjoyed, experiencing a certain yearning to find out about this seminal city for Scots which Glaswegians hardly know. (Until recent years the same could be said for virtually every Edinburgh citizen about Glasgow, the sister city which Edinburgh men only visited for a football match, and Edinburgh women not at all.) It was a good movie, one of the last for a decade and more which had a coherent plot and sound recording you could recognise. It was in fact the sort of smash hit which it deserved to be which Hollywood once turned out and thank God has discovered how to turn out again. But the movie gave a visual sense of Edinburgh which intrigued me, which I wanted to find out about. So I chose to go there though I'd had confirmation at the other three Scottish art colleges, Glasgow, Aberdeen and Dundee as well, rather as it was when the choice came up for my secondary school, except that this time I chose right. You couldn't make a bad choice with any Scottish art college though, then or now, for the Scottish art colleges are just the ticket. Everybody should get an art college education: it'd be cheaper than borstal too and a lot more hard work. I signed on for that, and the first few weeks weren't easy.

The bewilderment came with the sudden change in my age. Lecturers and tutors found it difficult to vary their range of communication, much as dons had when the servicemen came back from the War. The young fellow students were dreadfully callow and came from a quite different cultural ethos. They knew so much less it was rather intimidating, but not nearly so much so when you realised that they had aspirations and heroes you had never thought about or heard of. There's only one real way of coping with that, the way the older conscripts did in the Army during the War. For a large part of yourself you simply become their age, and very enjoyable it was too. So enjoyable in fact that I continue to do just that to this day, and still find it easy to shift age identity, easier down than up in fact. Art colleges are ideal for that, believe me. And I'd had one particular advantage to what could have proved to be, and does in some mature students' cases, a genuine problem: your relationship to authority. I had spent a long time clearly rejecting and resenting any kind of authority and then I'd experienced a little authority myself. What is more, the major advantage I had over the eighteen- and nineteen- year-olds was that I'd already had my trauma, and had healed myself. Scars of course, but the wounds had closed, more or less.

12

It was on a visit to Glasgow, hitch-hiking up to see my parents, something I had not done in eight or nine months, that I first hatched the plot to get out of London. I met a few old acquaintances that long weekend in a West End pub, old art school people and folk club friends, and been told about a good old wheeze whereby you could get a teaching job without possessing the necessary qualifications. It was called 'uncertificated teaching'. At that time Scotland, like England and Wales, employed teachers who had not been to a teacher training college and had not obtained their teachers certificate, their 'parchment' as it was known. Scotland also had, I discovered, posts in which you didn't even need a degree or diploma but only, I think, in Art and Music you know, the unimportant subjects. These latter positions were for 'Tutors', and all you needed was some evidence of having been at some bloody art school or other: you didn't need to have completed your course at it. A great many folkies and all-round bohemians had done exactly that. There was Dougie Carmichael and once again appearing in the movie, 'The parasite of the School Shed', Kenny MacKenzie, both ex-art school as well, and both, what else, sometime unqualified teachers of art in Scottish secondary schools, tutors in fact. It was a bit like P.G.Wodehouse heroes or Evelyn Waugh characters slipping into a schoolmaster's job in a very minor public school when needs became too great. And it was just the very chap for myself wasn't it? Sure, Kenneth and Dougie said the wee bastards made your life misery until you had thrashed a class or two but after that life was a veritable skoosh-case. My life in London was a bloody incubus and I couldn't think of any way of getting back to Glasgow. (I can remember on a previous occasion up north I'd almost, but unspokenly, pleaded with my father to take me in. My father, and I knew it at the time, had quite rightly put me on the bus going back to

London, ill and pale, miserable and unwell as I was, for nobody can live with such an abject failure, back as a beaten dog.) Here was a way so I took it.

I telephoned Lanarkshire County Council from London on the Monday morning and got an interview for the Thursday. I went back up to Scotland and made the interview, having made up a nice list of lies for it, for which it transpired there was no need. (I told the Lanarkshire people that I had been at Hornsey College of Art, which school had but recently been the subject of a long Paris-style student revolt and occupation as a result of which there could not possibly be any files on former students available. Actually the unrest spread and Hornsey was the fire which lit an entire conflagration in further and higher education.)

Back in 1968 teachers in Scotland were in incredibly short supply and they would put a bloody dog in front of a class if it could bark. This was bad news for teachers really who were then very badly paid, even worse than they are now, and the dominies had long been campaigning for an entirely graduate and teacher-trained profession, partly because they could up the wage demands that way and partly, it must be said, because they could up the quality of the profession as well. But classes were huge and teachers were needed and nowhere more so than in darkest Lanarkshire. It was a two-minute interview. Short of wearing your tadger outside of your trouser-fly or actually assaulting the interviewers you couldn't fail to be appointed as a tutor at some bloody establishment. I was to report, that next Monday, to a school in Hamilton, near the County Buildings complex itself, to St John's Grammar in Almada Street.

Monday morning in a great blackened red sandstone building and along the corridors into the school office. I introduced myself to a wizened little man in an academic gown which was going green with age, who seemed, however unlikely, to be the headmaster, Dr Gilmour. He appeared to be having a dispute with whom I took to be the school under-janitor, an incredibly slovenly looking fellow who I could hear growling with a strong Lanarkshire accent. 'Be reasonable, Mr Simpson, be reasonable . . . ' the small headmaster was saying to the truculent under-janitor, who was retorting: 'Therr's nae reason aboot it. Don't ye'se come yer Monkey Brand soap wi' me. Ah knew ye, Gilmour, when yer erse wis hingin' oot yer troosers . . . ' The under-janitor left Doctor Gilmour with a smart back-heel and the headmaster at last took notice of me. 'Ah, heard all about you, Mr McIntyre,' he said. 'We have, eh, a class waiting. Perhaps you might wish to start right away? No time like the present, eh? In at the deep end, eh?' he said jocularly, and before I could reply anything at all he had marched down another corridor and into a large room containing thirty plus adolescent boys and a stand-up piano.

There was total mayhem going on with boys hitting each other, standing on the seats, running around all over. 'Silence!' demanded Dr Gilmour with a savage cry and indeed silence, uncanny silence, was immediately substituted for the cacophony of but seconds before. Gilmour pointed his bony finger at a few of the youths, clearly chosen at random. 'You, you, and you!' he thundered and the youths slunk out of the classroom (to be thrashed by Dr Gilmour later no doubt). 'In your seats!' he bellowed and, by Christ, the boys were in their seats I can tell you. He then turned to me and in a voice so calm, so utterly reasonable, told me that this was 3AB, not bad lads as a whole he said. 'Mr McEwan is here,' he announced to the open-mouthed schoolboys, 'to teach you the rudiments of music. I understand,' he continued blithely, 'that Mr McLellan is a noted violin player and I hope you boys will find his instruction efficacious. So. Mr, er, er . . . ', he tailed off and left me with a group of boys as dumbstruck as myself. (Later I was to discover that Gilmour always knew full well what he was doing and that his occasional bouts of absent-mindedness, like his bursts of Pecksniffian rhetoric, were all to some purpose unknown to all but himself but undeniably by no means injurious to himself at that.) The silence prevailed for perhaps a minute or more. A boy with red hair, a little godsend to me as it turned out, began stabbing a fellow pupil with the point of a compass. I summoned up what I could remember of teacher-speak. 'Hey you, Ginger!' I reprimanded. 'Chuck it. What do you want to do, boys?' I was at a bit of a loss myself, and the piano was out of the question. The touch about 'Ginger' had the ring of the genuine teacher about it. One of the boys, a large one with a greasy Beatle hairstyle, put his hand up. 'Hey sur,' he said. 'Kin we huv a quiz?' We had a quiz, and I enjoyed it. It was the first time I had been called 'sir' in my life.

All was sorted out at interval and I met the Art department. It consisted of the principal, a remarkably handsome and well-spoken fellow with a military bearing and a rather military moustache to go with it, who gave his name as John – John Rae, and a tall odd-looking cove with red hair, a long upper lip, and a sports jacket of a highly original pattern and design called Ian – Ian Nicol. I gave them my name. 'A bit confusing that really,' said John Rae; 'There's a hell of a lot of Ians about here, and more than enough Johns' he said, and so something happened, on my first day at St John's which I suppose rather changed my life. This cannot happen often. But that conversation in the supply cupboard of St John's Grammar, that one sentence really, changed my life, it really did.' That was a memorable day for me, for it made great changes in me. But it is the same with any life. Imagine one selected day struck out of it, and think how different its course would have been. Pause you who read this, and think for a moment of the long chain of iron or gold or thorns or flowers, that would never have bound you, but for the formation of the first link on one memorable day.' On that day I started something which was finally to lead to Expectations, if not great, at least to what I had not thought of for many years, since young childhood, a future. In the cupboard, as we lit fags, myself and the two new, just-met colleagues I was to work alongside for two years, I turned round to the both of them and said: 'Just call me Jack.'

I don't know why I thought up the name, not really. I had an uncle Jack whom I think I'd seen twice. His name wasn't Jack either but then, in those days, whose was? It is a diminutive for John, sometimes Jacob, in old Scots occasionally for James, but not, save but tenuously, for the name I had been christened with, which was Iain. I have not been called it for thirty years and don't – can't – answer to it, anymore than anybody answers to a name not their own. I do in fact react to 'John' for many people think that is my original name, the one I was born with. I don't like being called it on the very odd occasion that someone attempts to do so because I can smell something from anybody who uses the name to me, people who somehow don't like the idea of anybody not only changing their name, first or second, but having any kind of control over what they are. When it was once pointed out to the painter James McNeil Whistler that he was in fact born in Lowell, Massachusetts, and not St Petersburg as he had claimed, the artist replied loftily that he 'did not choose to be born in Lowell'. John Lennon, in that cruel phase he had when he went off to work on his own, once castigated Bob Dylan for not reverting to Zimmerman. Dylan has been Dylan so long that the Zimmerman was probably practically somebody else. And I cannot think myself an Iain at all. I did not choose the name my parents gave me. I chose, almost without thinking, the name I have carried ever since it arrived. And with it came a change in many things, not least within myself.

I didn't notice this change at first at all. It was Christmas, the end of my first term in St John's Grammar, when Ian Nicol, out for a pint, told me that everybody liked me in the school. A revelation this was for not only had nobody ever told me this, I'd never have believed them if they had. I didn't like myself, but in that first few months in Hamilton, back in Scotland, I had simply worked away and worked hard. I had also, for the first time in many years tried for once to please somebody else other than myself, and without any sense of reward. What had crept slowly over me in those months was happiness in fact and a sense of purpose and fulfilment. I liked having responsibility for the children I taught. I liked the children. I liked the staff. I liked the school and the city I had returned to, and I liked myself. Without thinking, I had begun at last to like myself, for the first time ever in my life, and it gave me a glow of pleasure to me to discover that I could make other people happy or at least quite content to be in my company. I discovered another thing as well. I had always been able to make people laugh, but it was my misanthropic barbs they relished: now I found I could use the undeniable energy I had for fucking people and things up for making things cheerier. In my darkest moments since, that has been a comfort to me, the fact that people expect me to be cheery and it seems a shame to disappoint them.

For another element developed, slowly at first, in my character. I enjoyed cheering others, and I most certainly enjoyed performing, and still do. Some changes were easily noted, even by myself. One night, late into it, in Ian Nicol's house, a splendidly artistic decor and some damned good paintings for Ian was a very talented artist, not often encountered among art teachers, over a whisky, I suddenly observed that my fingernails were too long. Since that night I have always looked after my nails because I had hitherto bitten my fingernails till they bled – common among nervous under-achievers and something I often notice. (I once interviewed Sir Leon Britten and was appalled to see that he not only bit his nails but what nails he had left were filthy.) The grown nails were the first physical sign that I was now growing straight and free but not absurd. Well not all that absurd anyway, not enough to damage myself. It was a good time.

I made a lot of friends, initially rather against the odds now when I think about it for I was easily the youngest person on the staff and what was more had come up from London with what for them must have seemed long and wild hair, and outlandish clothes. In the late Sixties Glasgow, anywhere outside of London indeed, was years out of synch with the capital. Today you can find yourself in the wilds of Orkney and the kids are dressed as though it was Los bloody Angeles. But I proved to be an excellent and hard-working teacher and mucked in with everybody else when it came to socialising. Back then a great many of the teachers had been through a war – the young ones had done their National Service at the least – so you didn't get so much of the Man amongst Boys, Boy among Men syndrome which blights many a school staffroom today. The under-janitor I first spied giving the headmaster, Dr Gilmour, such stick on my first day was indeed an abrasive rough-hewn character. His name was Tam Simpson and he was the extremely well-read Head of English, and his gruff Lanarkshire exterior was a bit of a put-on. The under-janitor in fact wore a smart blue suit and had rather a cultured accent, at least for Lanarkshire. I made friends which I have to this day, good bright fellows, and a lot of fun was had – and what was to prove a lot of contacts in darkest Lanarkshire. One of the friends was an English teacher of enough nervous energy for the National Grid, Gordon Murray, who was to be influential in many things for me over a good few years. It was he who kept me in touch with outside life when I was shooting lightning through the sky at art college later on.

Towards the end of my time there was a great deal of pressure on me to become qualified – the day of the uncertificated teacher in Scotland was drawing to a close and quite right. Not a few of the unqualified teachers were very good and a few managed to find some course or other which allowed the grateful education authorities to keep them in the classroom. A great many such teachers were fly-by-nights, incompetents, chancers and schools are all the better for not having them anywhere near them. The root of many of the educational problems experienced in England and Wales can be laid at the door of the system which permits any old idjit to stand in front of a classroom full of weans. I can still remember the casual teacher taken on to teach science who somehow allowed one of his pupils to fall down a trap-door in the floor of his classroom lab. When asked how the boy had managed to meet with such an accident the lunatic revealed that the scholar had been 'only looking for a place to hide'. They'd been playing, I swear it, hide and seek. But it was time to go, and time to do the damned thing properly. So I went back to art school, and glad I was to do so.

The first couple of weeks at Edinburgh College of Art were very strange to me. The other students were very much younger and from the beginning I was looked on rather as an elderly soldier in the trenches would be, not quite Old Bill but possibly H.H.Munro (the writer 'Saki' had inexplicably joined up as a private in the Great War and served in the trenches), and it was a role I came to enjoy. As such I was treated, by the younger lecturers at any rate, rather as a senior NCO and liked that too. I was experienced in such matters, utterly fresh to my fellow students who were virgins in almost every respect, as housing and how to get accommodation cheaply, how to drink and where, how to find quick ways of doing slow things, how to pull girls. The last expertise I didn't vouchsafe to my new friends but it didn't take long, not in an art college, for them to find that out for themselves. And it was a burst of a marvellous freedom for them of course, though perhaps a little less for me, because I knew the price you pay for whatever freedoms you obtain. But as the last days of summer spread into the autumnal months and then to the dark of winter Edinburgh, especially beyond the college, I came to feel the power I had, the vitality most of us have but often fail to use or do so wastefully or with malfeasance in us. In short I was an energetic wee bastard.

The first year was a general year as was, in those days, the second year of an art school course. We did drawing and painting and design and sculpture and clay work and a hell of a lot of things. Also anatomy and art history, the last which was demanded by the academic qualification bodies. It was held by the lecturers themselves to be somewhat spurious but made so in reality by the college practice of reading out the art history questions in the exam and reading out the answers as they went along. I found out some years later that a lovely and aristocratic but very thick girl called Carol – whom we all liked actually – contrived to fail this exam but the lecturer in charge, Fred MacDonald, 'lost' her paper. The entire year of students wasn't much more than perhaps forty so we all got to know each other in a way impossible at a university. The astounding hours you have to work at art school, the amount of time you spend in each other's company, and the intensity of your relationships during those first few months, lasting into the years at the college, makes for a peculiar bonding which lasts you for life. Yes, again, like National Service. That first year we had, what had not occurred for many years, a Christmas Revel.

A few lecturers at Edinburgh had discussed this in a pub one night. For years there had been Revels but they had fallen into desuetude some time back due possibly to a certain lack of vitality in the student body itself. The lecturers, among whom had been the august and legendary head of Drawing and Painting, Sir Robin Philipson, remembered with doubtless dreadful nostalgia the Revels of old. The Revel was a beano, a feast and cornucopia of excess in every field, and one in particular: you dressed up and so did the college. It was the fancy-dress ball of the year and Edinburgh society had danced itself to a standstill at the yearly Revels throughout the decades. Until the wishy-washy Sixties came. Elsewhere in the UK students were literally setting fire to their colleges. It was just in Scotland they weren't. While there had been the Paris revolution and the riot-torn cities of the United States; while the students at the London School of Economics and Hornsey and Guildford had been joining Kent State and UCLA and the Sorbonne and Bologna; while all that was happening, the Scottish students were going home at night to their own beds and getting their bus money from mum. It was said that Edinburgh, for instance, never had one single student who had been a Cubist. Cubism had simply gone unnoticed. And the other Scottish colleges were damn near as moribund. But there was a new student consciousness about to emerge in Scotland and it was to come from our lot of them. I was damned sure it was and I was going to be there if I had to start it myself.

In fact it was the lecturers themselves who called a meeting and demanded we do something. They would give us paint, material, support, physical help and most of all, time, to do it, and create a Revel, the biggest ever, a night of fun and frolics to the backdrop of one of the biggest stage-sets ever created in the college, in the centre of the somewhat ugly and very non-aesthetic art college itself, in the Sculpture Court. And it was at that very meeting that I ventured to suggest that it would be a help if they had a committee to organise, and another one for an even bigger organisation, a Students Representative Council. Thus I started the ball rolling for what was to become a Soviet in the Edinburgh College of Art, and thunder on to every other small college in Scotland, from the art, music and drama colleges to the institutions for nursing education, food technology, nautical engineering, polytechnics – any damned place where there were students. It was to affect all the institutions of higher learning. Where once there had been very cosy little student clubs calling themselves Men's Unions and the like, full of smug little bourgeois using their membership of such bodies as springboards to good jobs and politics, the new student politics was to be led by young men and women of revolutionary fervour and often ideology and was, as it turned out, a springboard to good jobs and politics. But now beyond what had ever occurred before.

The Revel was an outstanding success but it was what grew out of it which was important. There had been student unrest in England and Wales, but it was largely unstructured. When the demand for change started in Scottish higher education it was quickly taken over by that fairly recent phenomenon, the mature student, usually from an industrial background, with a knowledge of trades unions and political structures, and aided by working class boys and girls who had learned politics at the knee. Easy the peasy. What had been a pleasant bunch of youngsters meeting in the principal's room for tea and jaffa cakes became in some cases seething battlegrounds in which in so many instances the gentle but unblinkingly conservative authorities lost, and lost too easily. In other situations the challenge to the old orthodoxies was not only overdue: it was, in hindsight, and by not a few sensible academics of the time, a shot in the arm. With a bit of bloodletting to begin with. True, some university dons gave in to some of the more lunatic posturings of youthful Trotskyists and the like, and probably most fought a losing struggle without enough backbone on their part, but a few academics there were who could see that the future lay with the young students at that. It did too, for better or worse. A lot of it worse.

The first step in setting up a new student body was to find out how to do it. I went off to number twelve Dublin Street, at the fag end of the New Town and saw the National Union of Students Scotland, represented by its first ever Scottish Chairman, Dougie Henderson, a slightly built sandy-haired chap with the fashionable long sidewhiskers of the time and a bright ambitious look in his eyes. He had just come through the merger of the old Scottish Union of Students, long a Tory front, with the until then English NUS, and was for a young fellow already skilled in political intrigue. (He is now of course the MP for Newcastle Upon Tyne.) Dougie and another chap, Stuart Paul, an ex-Allan Glen's boy as were so many in the student politics of those days for my old school was ever a hotbed of political radicalism, gave me the gen on such arcana as Constitutions and standing orders and the basic structure of the democratic process. I read and re-read the material they had given me and discovered the first law of politics: it is Law. The importance of the Law is hardly stressed, in fact is rarely touched upon, in the education of our young, and few citizens realise its importance. For all those who rabbit on about Scotland's history and the romantic events of it, there is one in a thousand who understands that my country's history, perhaps more than anywhere else in Europe, is bound up with the Law which is why Scotland still thinks of herself as a nation, and why, indeed, the powers that be in the European Community do as well. Forget that the Master of Stair was the name on the order for the Glencoe atrocity, it was Mr Dalrymple's father, and later he himself in the push towards the Treaty of Union, who framed much of what gave rise to modern Scotland. And I discovered that things like constitutions which might seem inconsequential were not ephemeral at all but power itself. I studied hard at this, probably the first time in my life that I had really attempted to grasp the consequence of Logic. So I came up with a constitution which was simple to explain, which fed the college authorities with self-regard whilst in fact establishing extensive powers to the students – well, not the students, the student representative council. Which I was going to make sure I represented. I did too, for all the years I remained at the college. We set up the student council with the blessing of the college authorities, and in fact the Secretary of State for Scotland for Edinburgh was not only one of the central institutions which fell directly into his remit, but it had a royal charter to boot.

The college principal, a dear man but no politician, and no artist either if it came to that, Professor Stanley Wright, was as woolly as the circlet of white fluff which fringed his woolly head, often topped with a Glengarry bonnet. Stanley also affected plus-fours, probably the last man in Britain to adorn himself so in daily life, and was courtesy itself. But he was aware that something had to be done in the college and, though he didn't know what, saw me as at least less troublesome than the power-brokers in his various departments. The college Secretary, John Hunter, an extremely affable but exceptionally wily administrator, knew this too and supported me in ways often unseen by the staff and certainly by Professor Wright. If the perspicacious John had been listened to and the colleges had thought, as belatedly they do now, about the astounding financial potential they had and have, the colleges would be a bloody sight more sound, fiscally and aesthetically, than I am afraid they are.

Though the Drawing and Painting school took no part in overt politicking, it was indeed powerful and could be extraordinarily vocal headed by Robin Philipson as it was, and he an almost unassailable figure. Sir Robin could be seen around the corridors in the mornings in his paint-covered smock, but in the afternoons for his positively gubernatorial visitations to the studios he would appear in his full regalia: beautifully cut and marvellously dated/undated suits with waistcoats filled with fobs, tight trousers, flowing handkerchiefs, another peeping from his sleeve, pointed suede boots, and the leonine mane of polished silver hair, worn slightly too long. He was a magisterial sight – more, a vice-regal one. He would have passed for an even more cultured Lord Curzon. His position in reality was almost thus. In the corridors of Edinburgh College of Art, as in the Royal Scottish Academy of which he was of course President, he was, I imagined, rather like Sir Lancelot Spratt in St Swithins, and he had to be won over, which was going to be difficult because he was an astute man, as most artists, don't let the vagueness and vapourings of the buggers fool you, are.

I got him on my side though, partly through appealing to his vanity which was not inconsiderable and partly because he wanted above all to get on with what art schools are for, producing art and artists. Sir Robin was, apart from being one of the finest painters in Europe, and one of the few international names from Britain, at the time perhaps the only one from Scotland, a very kindly man. For years I gate-crashed into his end-of-term cocktail party along with a couple of other students, leading my little group to the champagne cocktails and canapés and getting fed and pissed at them while the school janitors trailed after me trying to throw me out. Sir Robin's end-of-term parties were packed full of dreadfully distinguished men and women and anytime I saw the jannies descending I simply joined a group of the most important and shoved another glass down me while the college flunkeys fumed in frustration. In my last year, just before I was leaving, Sir Robin sent me a gold-edged invitation, with the request for the pleasure of the company of 'Mr Jack McLean and partner'.

The D & P staff were on the whole supportive of the students and I got on well with them. There were students, especially those who did not receive the praise they thought due to them which means most art students, who would criticise their tutors for the apprentice ever thinks himself superior to his master, but they had no cause for that. I got to know and enjoy the company of most of the staff in the college and, despite many a dispute with them, came to have a genuine respect and admiration for most. It was difficult not to respect their ability as artists for a start. David Michie, who went on to become the head of D & P, and for a spell the Principal of the College itself, was a wonderfully fluid painter in the Scottish, Francophile tradition, and a lovely if loud man, as well as an inspiring tutor. You'd see his large frame bouncing into a studio, even those for the lowly first years, and standing in front of each student's painting. 'I like it, boy, I like it,' he might finally opine, 'It sings to me!' And he'd finish with a burst of the song with which he thought it sang to him with, concluding all with an open packet of cigarettes. 'Have an Embassy!' He was a bit bloody when he didn't like the work, and could, unthinkingly reduce some hapless wee girl student to tears but he still gave you an Embassy. I wrote about this open-handed benevolence of his in a newspaper piece twenty years later and pointed out that David had long since given up the fags. Two days after the article appeared I received a small package through the post. Exquisitely parcelled, it consisted of a little box once holding tubes of gouache, but now containing what else but twenty Embassy.

Besides these two colossi were grand lads like my own first-year tutor George MacPherson who took me off for pints often and talked long into the night of painting while contriving to dally with the female students. He managed the two conversations with ease and satisfied both groups. Bob Callender, John Johnston, a fantastic man called Alan Alexander who was a ballet dancer as well as a fine draughtsman and who was epicenely gay, and Eugene Carolan, a very frail old gentleman who taught us life drawing and who had studied with Matisse. A lot of others. I was a bit distressed to discover that John Busby, who was perhaps the youngest lecturer in my time, has recently retired from the college as Head of Drawing and Painting and made me realise that a lot of time has passed.

But despite the fact that I had done well in D & P I opted to do Graphic Design, then the up-and-coming area in almost every British art school, and very difficult to get accepted for. To be honest I have always regretted it a little. For a start the painters had a better and easier time cavorting about being artists and just thinking all day. Graphics was often boring – all that design for print technology was well over my head and today must be even worse with the levels of new technology bursting into the subject every day. When I was a graphics student photosetting was of recent date and Letraset a new invention. I decided on Graphics because it was a form of applied art and furthermore it could be used with a political edge. The Graphic Design department didn't like a political edge, however, and I am not sure it liked me. There was Bob Balderston who was the head of the department and whom we never saw more than, say, five or six times in our two years in our specialism. But Stuart Barrie, a world-renowned calligrapher and rather semi-detached bourgeois though extremely affable at all times, was always about and very helpful he was too. Andrew B. Chisolm was the main lecturer and a very nice fellow but a bit square and very much commercially-minded, and Harry More-Gordon, a languid upper-class type Scot related to Sir Nicholas Fairbairn. I knew More-Gordon to be a fine illustrator but a crashing snob. He made rather a pet of an angular young boy called MacKenzie-Robinson or some such double-barrelled name because of it and ignored the one real talent there. (He rather reviled me for my origins. I liked that because I used to taunt him by being more crass and guttersnipe than I could have got away with in any Glasgow pub.) The one real talent was my pal, rather he became so, Grant Hicks. Grant had come over at the start of his Third Year from Glasgow because he was living with an Edinburgh student called Catherine King-Clerk. Catherine King-Clerk was not only double-barrelled with an accent straight out of a girls' expensive boarding school (art colleges still had the debutantes sent by daddy to round them off), but was beautiful, stupidly beautiful, with big round blue eyes and hair the colour of a shining wheatfield; the sort of stupidly beautiful which makes you feel your hands and feet are too clumsy and your linen too coarse. She was one of the boarding school set which included Jane Imrie – about whom I had instant orgasms with her dark haughtiness, straight out of the Victorian novellas I had brought myself up on – and fluttery, but still pretty, just nicer, girls like Katie Mathieson. These girls were oblivious, as girls from such backgrounds invariably are, to the effect they were having all around them, the boys who were having wet bloody dreams at night over them, but they were by no means ignorant of their charms when it came to the boarding school boys with a bob or two. The public school students were few in number but always sat with each other in the college refectory. There was a sort of sad insecurity underlying such behaviour but it didn't stop a lot of them from being snotty. Certainly Catherine and Jane were impenetrable except, I suppose, by Grant Hicks. It was later that Katie Mathieson and one of her chums from one of the posh girls' schools, Helen Lees, both smashing girls, introduced me to the debutantes and I found that Catherine and Jane were all right too, but very shy of me, for God's sake.

Anyway, Grant Hicks was the goods when it came to talent. He wasn't as good a draughtsman as me, not by a long chalk, but he was very, very imaginative, and especially inventive, and could call on a variety of styles, as indeed he did in his erratic love affairs. But when I first laid eyes on Grant I couldn't stick him, a bloody gigolo, a bit of a hippie popinjay, a smart arse, and one of the public school set. I was up-front with him and snubbed him at every turn. To this day neither Grant nor I can remember what the turning point was, how it occurred, what we said to each other, but it was not long before we were bosom chums, partners like Starsky and bloody Hutch or Butch Cassidy and the Sundance Kid. It might have been after Catherine gave him the bump; I think it was. Anyway that was always happening to Grant because he was a demanding little fucker and fell in love very easily indeed. In fact Grant couldn't tell the difference between love and his hole and often made himself thoroughly miserable as a result.

Despite his obvious talent Harry More-Gordon didn't like either him or his work and Grant ended by failing to get his post-diploma for Alan MacKenzie-Robinson, jings what a surprise, was awarded that. Grant was, of course, suicidal for he did absolutely nothing by halves and his passions were what one would expect from a very wee chap from Wishaw, which is where he was from, who had decided to become an artist. Apart from hailing from Wishie, as they cry it in that dreadful little industrial glitch, Grant's first name was Harold, I found out, and he was 'Arry 'Icks from then on. Grant instead started designing for the Young Traverse Theatre and did some great work which inevitably led to him going down to the major theatres in London's West End, where he still works from time to time when he's not making commercials and the occasional award-winning film. Grant and myself did a lot of damage in Edinburgh to the girls because he introduced me to his upper class stable, and I introduced him to the political girls and the student politics groupies who abounded in the early 1970s. For not only did I get myself involved with a lot of girls in the political scene, I soon became embroiled in the student politics of the day, at a time when student conferences used to make front-page news. It was my first experience of being close to front page news and was ultimately to lead me to what became my trade, pompously and I am not sure accurately, my profession.

13

We'd started only with a student council to get a dance organised. But somehow there were more things which needed to be done and it was myself mainly, I suppose, who did them. It was at the beginning of my second year I remember and I simply created first a newsletter, then a meeting, and then a *fait accompli*. I made a girl called Myrtle Eadie the President. Myrtle was well off, well spoken, and well endowed with brains and bottle. Thus she and myself were the student representatives on the Board of Governors, a very august body of men and one woman. We had the same number of representatives as the staff did and accomplished a great deal more. The governors were charm itself and very welcoming. We never had a problem with them, and in fact they began to throw money at us, including a genuine set- up for the students club, a kind of Students Union though not quite. (Art schools are strangely authoritarian. Students were expected to answer a roll-call in the morning or sign a register and were not permitted to cut classes. The regime would have caused mayhem in the Yooni's.) And the students club was unlicensed, save for particular occasions when a special licence had to be obtained as, claimed the governors, there were young people under eighteen etc and no amount of pointing out that university unions possessed a similar difficulty but overcame it with ease could budge them. I knew it didn't matter anyway because we had total control over the club and even staff couldn't be admitted unless invited. The club could have been awash with alcohol, and anyway most of the students smoked dope rather than drink regularly, but generally art students act relatively responsibly save in sexual matters. Work is the main thing among art students and socialising came second. But we obtained office and admin services and premises and telephones and then the agreement for a full-time sabbatical president. I persuaded all my chums, most of them exaggeratedly ignorant of politics, to be Council members and Gus MacLean, the son of Callum the minister of Cramond Kirk who appeared regularly on television, to become the first ever sabbatical officer in the art college. With hindsight, I should probably have done this myself but I felt myself too old to throw away a year. However, as I was becoming increasingly active in the national student movement, at that time very much on a roll, I could have used the year to considerable advantage, certainly in terms of a future career. It was not easy to work myself through a course which was already at least five days a week and more, from 9 a.m. to 9 p.m.; be Vice-Chairman of the National Union of Students and get to all the meetings; visit other colleges; produce papers for conference; act as Scottish Vice-Chairman; advise students, chair the National committee for Art and Design; and run the film society and start up the first ever film production unit. Oh and be on the executive of the Youth Committee of the Communist Party and help establish a Glasgow Trade Union Film Group and Publicity Committee including a poster group. Time for sleeping with girls and getting well bevved up was no problem: I simply did that while I was being the Huey Long of Edinburgh College of Art. I didn't tell you about the Communist Party, did I?

It would be splendidly romantic should I claim that the Party set me to an organised infiltration of the various organisations in which I rose to prominence but it would not be remotely true. The British Communist Party was then incredibly ineffectual in itself, and often damaging to its cause due to what was to prove, in Britain as elsewhere, terminal conservatism. The British party was perhaps the most concerned of any about ideology, though the French party too was riven by groups and sub-groups within its structure. I recollect the Althusser faction well. (Louis Althusser finally showed his firm grasp of Scientific Socialism and the Marxist Methodology when he axed his mistress to death and then committed suicide. Took a little of the shine off his theories that did.) Then there was the Gramsci group who were deeply theoretical though surprisingly ill-read when one actually came to discuss his *Lettere del Carcere*. I liked this group very much because I'd always read just that touch more than any of them to confuse the fellows. The biggest mob though were those who stood steadfastly by the British Road to Socialism and they were absolutely rip-roaring, led as they were by the Scottish housepainter Johnnie Golan who had taken over from the legendary Harry Pollitt. To sum up Golan's vision of socialism one would have to look at his concrete vision of it – a mural he had painted on a wall in the Edinburgh party rooms. It showed a fat capitalist in top hat and gold watchchain, an absurdly gold-braided admiral, and a slimy fat prelate of some kind, all of them writhing and wringing their hands, cringing from the radiating bars of a massive red sun in the background. So that one could hardly make a mistake in interpretation a banner slogan across the top of the mural read 'The Golden Sun of Socialism'. Comrade Golan's style was adolescent-primitive and would be much admired by parodying illustrators today who could never hope to catch the innocence of either content or intent. The CP held a large number of misfits and odd-balls, of malcontents and Happy Utopians, brain-dead dogmatists, and folk with a simple belief in the natural goodness of mankind once freed from the shackles of, well, whatever was shackling them. Also trades union bullies, social fascists, opportunists, careerists and all round boys on the make. Those were the ones who finally saw me kicked out the Party. That had been on the cards anyway because I had no commitment to this aged brigade at all. I remember once getting flung out of a Party party because after they had asked me to sing a nice wee song I had obliged with possibly the least Party party song I knew which was 'I Like New York in June, How About You?' Yet at the same time there were a very great many thoroughly decent men and women in The Party and many honoured ones who had sacrificed much in their lives. And you got to meet a lot of intellectuals, genuine ones, some of them highly respected academics, ever revered among Communists until, that is, they came up with something not approved of by, frankly, Moscow – not that the British Party was considered as anything other than a stamp-collecting club by the Kremlin. But in student politics the Communist Party was wonderfully effective as well as fashionable and was an ideal stepping stone for opportunists altogether.

It was at the first National Union of Students, Scotland, conference I ever attended that I was elected onto the Scottish committee as the member for art, music, drama and paramedic colleges. Simply done too. My Party comrades spoke to the comrade, a large rumbustious Dundonian mature student from Travelling stock called Adam Williamson, who was to say a few words in support of another candidate, whose name I entirely forget. Adam stood up and said his few words of support for his official candidate. 'I realise,' he said, 'that Jack McLean is the right candidate for the job . . . ,' (thence followed a panegyric which would have got Rasputin a seat), 'but I agreed to speak on my pal's behalf because he is my pal. I know he is weak and vacillating and hasn't any experience, and doesn't like art much, unlike Jack McLean but . . . ' (a speech such as would ensure the heave-ho for Mother bloody Theresa), and I was elected. It was not entirely unreasonable, for the fortnight before at a students grants meeting in Edinburgh I had spoken in the Usher Hall and a crowd outside which added up to an audience of perhaps four or five thousand, and what is more, had been rewarded with the biggest hand of the day, representing as I did, and was puffed so, the 'ordinary student, trying to make ends meet, after years of hard work in the mines and factories' – oh, all sorts of shite. I had, then, few illusions on entering politics. I did it for the fun and excitement and, following my experience after the Usher Hall speech, a sort of fame and my nookie.

The Communist Party, and every politician of today who had anything to do with the Comms will tell you this, was good training for a future career in, well, anything. In the Scottish NUS I remember we had a good candidate for our full-time Chairman on the Left in a certain Richard Cotter. Dick was bright, academic and handsome as buggery. (In certain quarters he was nicknamed Ricardo di Poncellini because he was very much the ladies man type.) But he was not going to be easy to manipulate because as well as being bright and academic he was very much his own man and had social democratic tendencies. So we persuaded him not to stand in favour of a genuine apparatchik, Doug Harrison, a Party stalwart and of the Tankie Tendency (thus named after the Stalinists who rolled the tanks into Czechoslovakia). Doug's background was impeccable Party if of the aristo Palme Dutt/Lytton Strachey type – his father had been killed by the terrorists, or Freedom Fighters rather, during the Communist Insurgency in Malaya and Doug was ex-public school but he was solid Party. He isn't now of course and is an assistant general secretary for the STUC, a position owed to his intellectual quality, and by no means to his political background which, in mainstream Scottish politics, would be considered highly suspect. By the 'We' I was speaking of I mean some people in the Party and some not in the Left caucus, and especially myself and Jim Mowat.

I first met Jim at a meeting in I think Telford College and he was wild. With his long raving hair, his longer woollen scarf and his somewhat hippie cloth hold-all bag with the North Vietnam flag on it, he stood on the platform and waved his hands. And he spoke with such abandon and such ultra-Leftism and with a great deal of market-trader style fluency that he commanded more than enough attention. We met on a couple of other tub-thumping occasions and after a while both of us became the rabble-rousers of the student scene and what is more both of us came from Glasgow and talked a lot, said 'merr than wur prayers' as the saying has it. It was a meeting of rather over-elaborate minds. Thinking back now, it was in fact a merger because otherwise there would have been a bit of a metaphorical bloodbath: both Jim and I were limelight cases of the most rabid kind and would have brooked no competition from anybody. We made a good partnership. And we were most definitely the Young Turks of the student movement but it wasn't long before we were quite Old Turks indeed, and in fact became the best-dressed and besuited Turks in the business.

We both became, and remain, well-dressed fellows and there is a reason for this, many really. One is that I always was – I regularly painted in the art college in a three-piece suit – and found myself more at ease in an attire which could not be faulted, or not much by those in authority, and I suspect James was the same. We both came from very similar backgrounds. A photograph I once saw of the young Mowat revealed he and his brother aged about eight and twelve or so, and both with glossy side partings in their hair and glossier footwear, smart little short trouser suits and long parental aspirations. (Come to think of it Mowat's parents were a little better-off than mine or maybe he was just that few years older and came to working class semi-affluence at an earlier age. Suits for Chrissake.) It says something about us both that while thwarting authority, and indeed confronting it, we hardly wished to be thought socially beyond the pale. There remains something of the snob in me, and a considerable amount of it in Jim. Undeniably, though, this deference to the social niceties helped Mowat and myself to foster an idea among authorities from university principals to the government officials and ministers with whom we negotiated from time to time that we were responsible fellows who might very well go far. I know now that both of us were pin-pointed by Civil Service mandarins as possibles for the future. I was quickly discarded and have remained an outsider ever since but Jim has gone on to become the National Secretary for the Transport and General Workers Union and, I understand, though he will hate me for writing this, rather an *eminence grise* within the Labour Movement.

Mowat took to the Arts immediately, moving easily, as he still does, in artistic circles though in our student days those circles had to involve lots of women because Jim, despite being married to his first wife at the time, was horribly promiscuous. But then the student politicos often were involved in, and many of them continue to engage themselves so, contrapuntal serial relationships. Most of the student politicians were endowed with a great deal of energy anyway and those who went on to major positions in public life, or to success in business or the arts and entertainment industries, have, I suggest, achieved their prominence through just that dynamism, alongside which often, though not always, goes a sexual exuberance.

The next two years were spent in a welter of politicking. Jack Straw was NUS President for a time, and largely well considered, especially by his future employers in the Labour Party (though he was not, in my view, as talented as his brother Ed with whom I worked on the Arts committee), but Straw was indeed the man who politicised the National Union of Students, and therefore students really, for his predecessor had been a chap now President of the European Union in Britain, Jeff Martin, whose avowed intention was to keep the NUS as a sort of focus for student athletics clubs. (Previous incumbents included the disgraced cabinet minister John Stonehouse who was eventually to be revealed as an American Cold War agent when NUS President.) Jack Straw was followed by the first Communist candidate, Digby Jacks, a large blustering red-bearded intellectual who is now Regional Organiser for MFS, the merged union of ASTMS and TASS. To replace Digby with another Communist was the task of the then Broad Left, whose members now fill a huge number of senior positions everywhere, especially in highly capitalist organisations. Jim and myself were among the most powerful brokers along with a number of other Scots lads, (like every union then as now, Scots, though numerically small, had an undue influence), and we rallied solidly behind a candidate, John Randall. We lost out to Charles Clark. Randall is now the Director of the Law Society – it is probably only a matter of time before his baronetcy comes up – and Charles went on to be the *chef de cabinet* for Neil Kinnock. (Charles' father was Sir Richard – 'Otto' – Clark, oft regarded as perhaps the most far-sighted senior civil servant of the post-war years.) If the truth be known, even at the time, we all knew that a great many of us were earmarked for glory. Or at least a right few bob.

There was a lot of talent in the student political ranks then. I remember young Deyan Sudjic, recently appointed as Director of the European Year of Architecture for 1998 and the actual schoolboy involved in the *OZ* magazine trial and, when I knew him, the aide-de-camp to Jonathan Wills, the multi-talented journalist who was in fact the first student Rector of Edinburgh University and not, as is so often stated in the press, Gordon Brown. Brown I knew slightly for he took virtually no part in student politics and confined himself to being secretary of the Labour Club. I didn't like Brown then and see no reason for changing my belief that he liked the idea of power more than anything else (fuelled by that canny wee Presbyterianism which makes its adherents want to be the meenister, especially a cabinet one), and I think Brown confined himself to Labour Party activities because he saw his career in that organisation more than he did in doing much for anybody else. I may be wrong and undeniably he is a clever and persuasive fellow, but he doesn't persuade me, and give me Jon Wills for the better man at that. Will Stevenson, now Director of the British Film Institute, was another boy set for stardom as was that handsome youth, Al Stewart, who stood for election on the vague promise that he would look out for the interests of gay students (just emerging as a lobby in any sphere), and who, when dreadfully in need of electoral support, would hint slightly that he was gay himself, a truly mendacious reversal of the truth. Al is of course now Alastair Stewart of the BBC and authoritative enough on the box to satisfy Lord bloody Reith. A good lad though, Alastair: I remember him asking me if he should join the CP. This was shortly after a triumph for the Party when we got John Reid, now the MP for Motherwell, to join just before the NUS Scotland executive elections. Dr Reid was a clever comrade though: he joined the Party two days before the voting, and resigned two days later. As it happens we knew this in advance anyway so, while we publicly confessed distress, in actuality we were cock-a-hoop. I told Alastair not to be so fucking stupid – you only needed to join the Party in Scotland. But he and Mowat and myself were there, in a college meeting in Northumberland, I recollect, on 11 September 1973, when news of the murder of President Allende by the Chilean junta came through and tried to drown ourselves in drink but remained sober and very depressed. I haven't seen Alastair in a good many years but somebody told me recently that he had got right-wing. I wouldn't think so, just adult really.

But also emerging in those days was a female political force too. Sue Slipman, who went on to be the Director of the Single Parent Association and is now something shockingly important somewhere was already a silver-tongued and very, very charming girl politico and a member of the Communist Party too. It came as something of a shock to many former comrades when she joined the newly-formed SDP. It shouldn't have for Sue was ever a slippery sort of Slipman anyway but still very, very, charming and nice. Pretty too.

That last statement was the sort of phrase which got me into trouble then. I remember when I chaired the first student Women's Conference (for which I had designed a poster using a still from that scene in which James Cagney sticks a grapefruit half on the cherry lips of Mae Marsh, and been terribly criticised for it, the then women's movement not possessing much sense of irony). The meeting got off to a bad start when one of the delegates at the entirely female conference questioned my presence, let alone my chairmanship. She announced to the sisters that I was a bloody sexist who 'treated women as sex objects'. I refuted this. 'Miss Bloomfield,' I said, 'I wouldn't treat you as a sex object. You're too ugly to be a sex object.' The moment I'd uttered this I knew. Jesus, McLean, you'd hang yourself for a good phrase, I thought. I spent the next hour and a half on Carlisle station platform waiting for the train home.

It was perhaps for reasons such as the above that I never quite made it in politics, though I think I can claim to be a little bit influential, even, I suppose, as regards some of the current crop of leading politicians. I certainly don't regret it. Though I was never quite away from active politics for many years it was always because something needed to be done or said, and there was nobody else around who would take it on, the universal but truthful cry of every shop steward who has ever taken on the thankless task. But apart from such idealism, and some of my involvement arose from just that, there was a great deal of merriment to be made out of student politics. And some invaluable experience of hitherto unseen life as well. I mean, the first time I ever stayed the night in a hotel it was through the NUS. It was in Dundee and I was on the Executive. Towards the end of the night I'd captured a girl and gone upstairs to the room. What does one do in hotels? Well I'd seen the movies with Humphrey Bogart and I knew what one did in hotel rooms so I did it. I picked up the telephone and rang the night desk. 'Night clerk,' I spoke into the phone, 'Send up a bottle of bourbon!' My brother Brian, a delegate at the conference, had for a jape and unknown to me manned, quite illegally, the switchboard. 'Fuck off,' he said, succinctly. I'll bet that never happened to Humphrey Bogart.

How I managed to combine politics with my work in the college I don't know except that I enjoyed them both. The college itself, including the governors and the Principal, faintly basked in each fresh success of mine outside the college, and we continued to set up new initiatives among the students. There was a college Art Week which was a great success for the students who had organised everything, with a wide number of prominent guests like Richard Demarco and the composer Ronald Stephenson. Much of it was sabbatical President Gus MacLean's doing, but it showed the college up well. The visitor I liked best was the actor Roddy McMillan who had a marvellous outburst against the critic Cordelia Oliver in the Sculpture Court which involved him berating her and then getting pissed with us in Clark's Bar on Student Council money. But I was embarking on a national career or hoped it would be at least and spent a lot of time and energy on such an ambition. That ambition deepened, perhaps coarsened too, after my father died in my second year at the college. Somehow I wanted then to make it to whatever top was available; one up for my da, one up for us.

The old line about 'when I was twenty my father knew nothing: when I was thirty I was surprised at how much he'd learned in ten years' was true enough. There was a reconciliation, easily made, between myself and my father in my early twenties and though it was for a few brief years I'm thankful for it too. For some years, when I could, I met him every Saturday in the Horseshoe Bar in Glasgow's Drury Street, a famous bar, one with a long history and with a wide-ranging clientele from workies to advocates, from teenagers to Great War veterans, though no women save barmaids. In fact, my mother used to meet up with him about two in the afternoon but would not enter the bar at all but wait outside till a respectable-looking gent was about to enter when she would ask the chap to tell 'the gentleman with the hat and the moustache, about your height, wearing a grey Crombie . . .' that she was there. In fairness I have to tell you that my father joined her instantly. It was just that decent women didn't go into a mans bar then at all.

Sometimes I'd bring pals with me; he liked that and was oddly very good in the company of young men and women, though I can assure you that the chums were ever a little afraid of the wee man in the immaculate suits and hats, and the trimmed moustache. (To this day people from Merrylee, where he was the school janitor, remind him to me. 'You're Mr McLean's boy, aren't you?' they say, never his first name, and ever with a tone of respect as though for some past national leader.) But, despite occasional jousts, we eventually got on well. He was still as demanding of perfection, and could be just as awesome as well as awful, but he tempered his demeanour with some measure of tolerance. Certainly a great deal of his advice was sound enough but nobody under thirty listens much to advice and by and large nor should they. He was fit and healthy-looking. Could and did still kick a ball about in the school playground at sixty. And then he had his first heart attack. I suppose it was on the cards: it was a heavy job with long hours, made a lot longer by his refusal to sleep but continue to stay awake to listen to the records of classical music, especially Wagner – he regularly enlivened the neighbourhood by giving it the nearly uninterrupted *Der Ring Das Nibelungen* – from early in the morning till 2 a.m. the following day. Merrylee Primary also had manual coal 'hoppers' for the boilers and he wasn't as fit as all that. I remember his first heart attack. I think I've always blamed myself for what was to lead to his death. I think my mother did too but she never said anything to me on that: I suspect she did blame me too.

I'd been staying in the large ranch-style school house for about a week, during the college holidays, and we'd been wrangling over nothing for days. Arguing I suppose the Oedipal way that fathers and sons do. He erupted into scorching fury every three hours or so, and I did too, and clearly this wasn't going to last. I was going to push off: I'd never found him easy to live with actually day by day in his house. It was about two in the morning that my mother woke me to tell me to ring the hospital. 'Your dad's not well,' she said. 'I don't know what . . . ' The doctor came and gave him an injection which made him vomit. For some time I'd known somehow that mortality was close at hand: I used to go to bed touching the wood of the bedside table as a kind of useless pagan eschatological prayer. But though he made a good recovery he was never the same. The second attack a year later was worse and he didn't go back to work for six months. Today nobody would have let him, but then you literally worked till you dropped. He was unwell after the second attack. The change in his diet which had been recommended made him scraggy and old. He looked ill, and the drugs he was given effected a change none of us really admitted to ourselves. When drugged up he could be almost senile, with that sly, cunning look old people can take on, and even when he was perfectly lucid which was most of the time for it was only on occasional days that he took the medicine, he looked old, with that scrubbed, clean look which men take on when they are old and finished. He went back to work though and the school and everybody in Merrylee knew he wasn't well. I came back to Glasgow on the Friday and stayed the night. I'd been out late and come back soaking wet. My father had waited up for me, the first time he'd ever done that, and made me a cup of coffee. We sat and talked, as increasingly we had done, long into the night. Three, four, I don't remember, my mother woke me up again and I went into my parents' bedroom. My father lay sweating and breathing heavily, just as he had sometimes when I was a small child and he was going through bouts of the malaria he had contracted many years ago in China. 'I'm going to get the doctor,' my mother told him. 'Don't,' my father gasped, 'don't get the doctor!' He said it vehemently. I had my arms round him and he let out a grating sound and then expelled all his breath and died in my arms.

My mother didn't seem to realise that her husband was gone. It was the first death I'd been present at, and that word is what it seemed like to me. He had gone. But my mother went on fluffing up pillows, and then checking cushions around the house, waiting for the doctor. 'It'll be all right when the doctor comes, David. It'll be all right.' But my father was gone.

I finished Art College on a bit of a downer actually, with much of the last year writing a lot and trying very hard to get into the academic world. I wanted to embark on a PhD on Visual Education (that's what I pompously though accurately named it), and had applied to Leicestershire Poly's Centre for Cultural Studies to do so. I had support from thirteen leading academics including E.P. Thompson whom I'd met in Sandy Bell's Bar, and Hamish Henderson who was a chum who'd introduced me to Eddie Thompson and there was only one problem. I didn't have a degree; I had or would have, a diploma. Ironically it was slightly due to some of the papers I wrote and some of the negotiating I did, along with fairly senior lecturers in the four Scottish art colleges, that art schools in Scotland eventually – but after my time – began to award degrees and I suspect rather specious ones at that. I later spent over two years attempting to study what everybody agreed was a very neccessary study and agreed too that I was the very chap to do it, but the madness of scholastic nomenclature denied this to me. In fact I received my diploma from Jimmy Seatter, the college jannie, because Edinburgh didn't have diploma ceremonies, following years of outrages during them. (One year the students had dropped mice on parachutes made out of hankies onto the dignitaries sitting below during the pageant. The mice had all died of heart attacks on the way down, and a few of the nobles and their wives below had nearly followed suit.) So I signed for the rolled-up bit of paper to Alice, a young college secretary with whom I had occasional liaisons when she wasn't doing the business with Grant Hicks, and Jimmy, a lovely man who was, as it happens, a member of the CP too.

My Diploma Show, the high point of your art school career was good though, rather a triumph. For a start I had put on a good display and the Graphics department took a number of my works for their own collection (though I later stole some back for a portfolio to go round the commercial studios looking for work). A number of them were illustrations of Billie Holliday and rather decent work if I do say so. My work was perhaps a little more cerebral than that of the other students but then I was older, and undeniably more, dammit, cerebral. The night of the Diploma Show I had invited my mother and my landlady and it was a great success. Well for my mother and my landlady. In other ways it was pretty bloody and certainly it left a bad taste for many of the students. The governors and most of the lecturers had a smart beano upstairs to which the bulk of the students and their parents or sweethearts or whatever had not been invited. That was pretty bad but worse was that some of the students with especially influential or 'society' mums and dads were asked to take a glass or two with them, bringing the influential mums and dads of course, and it pissed off a lot of the students. Let us give George MacPherson and Johnnie Johnston and a few others their due: they went across to the pub with us all and chatted up the mums and dads a bit and all turned out well.

I had become very close to my mother since my father's death and tried to get through to Glasgow regularly though in my final year I was obviously more often in Edinburgh at weekends. But I knew she'd love the Dip Show and she'd never seen the Art college before. As for my landlady, Mrs McCarthy, I'd been with her for four years, a wonderfully eccentric lady. I'd gradually moved all my pals into her other rooms: big Ken MacLennan from Drawing and Painting and from Dingwall; Alex Girdwood from Grangemouth and also D & P whom I later replaced with Tam Crockett from Glasgow doing his teacher training year at Moray House. A happy ship it was, not least because of Jean McCarthy who was an elderly woman who had been the head of ladies outfitting at C & A in Princes Street, and would have fitted into any sitcom. She liked a drink did Jean which is to say that she shoved a bottle of licensed grocer's sherry and more down her throat each day and often woke me up at two or three in the morning enquiring if I wanted 'a wee glass or two to keep company'. Mrs McCarthy was extremely genteel and a little sad. She once bought a refrigerator to keep up with Miss Graham next door but never turned it on because it was 'a waste of electricity'. Her husband, a fine looking major in the Irish Guards (I know because I'd seen his photograph which she insisted she kept 'for reference'), she had divorced because he had come back from the War 'without a penny, without a penny!' which wouldn't have surprised anybody save Mrs McCarthy because he had spent four years of it in a German POW camp. Myself and big Ken had once been sitting in my room (as the oldest I had the biggest room), drinking cans of beer for perhaps three-quarters of an hour when we heard a scratching sound from inside the large mahogany wardrobe. Investigation found Mrs McCarthy inside there for God knows how long it had been. We asked her what on earth she was doing in there. 'Oh,' she told us nonchalantly, 'just tidying up.' Her exploits were the source of many true but unlikely stories. Such as the time her aged boyfriend had arrived at the door wondering where Jean was. 'Wan meenit she wis in the taxi' he'd vouchsafed to us, 'the next she wisnae. Like a puff i' smoke!' Two minutes later Mrs McCarthy came in the front door, bleeding, her stockings torn and her dress dishevelled, in a foul mood. She hadn't closed the cab door properly and at Haymarket had shot out of it into the night. A lovely lady. And she enjoyed the Diploma Show no end with my mother. A right good night on the gin it was, and my mother stayed the night. The next morning Mrs McCarthy gave me two tins of Campbell's meatballs and my mother a mink stole. My mother had considerable difficulty in returning it at the time. 'Naw, naw!' cried Mrs McCarthy, 'I wouldn't wear it from that no-good husband of mine. When you marry a Catholic, you marry a bad Catholic!' This was a constant refrain from her and I never found out the logic of it. But she was a lovely woman all the same and good company even at three in the morning with a bottle of cooking sherry in her hands.

14

The move back to Glasgow was grand and it was good to find myself in my old patch. I started up another affair with my city, then as now often tempered with despair at the abysmal priggishness with which the City Fathers spin a priggish and joyless Calvinistic cocoon around what could be one of the most exciting cities in Europe if she was allowed to dress up all the time and not merely upon special occasions or when the authorities take a plunge into showing her off to the visitors. Just that could be seen when Glasgow had its Garden Festival, and then its glory year of the European City of Culture. But this was well in the future, and what I refreshed myself with was the vibrant behaviour of the streets, and the splendour of the city, its architecture, its huge areas of greenness, its buzz. It does not do to honour your own place too much and Glaswegian pride seems too often to countenance a dreadful hubris. In much of its character Glasgow is a rather American city, and sometimes very cosmopolitan. It is a city of immigrants after all, with 17,000 people of Italian extraction; 12,000 of Polish or Lithuanian; 10,000 in the Jewish community, most of them from the Ukraine; and a large Asian, mainly Pakistani, population. Over 40% of Glaswegians are of Irish origin in some way, and the rest are largely Highland. It can be an explosive mix. It was damned good to be back though and no amount of Glasgow provincialism and self-satisfaction took away from that.

It was in that frame of mind that I did my year's teacher-training at Jordanhill College in Glasgow with a great deal of commitment to education. I am hardly ashamed of my enthusiasm of the time but I am of my innocence. I went into the world of education as keen as a boy soldier at the Somme. (I left it years later as an undisguised old lag trying to get a blighty one just like everybody else who hadn't managed an officer's pips on his shoulder.)

126

The Beau Brummel pub was where we usually met. It was new and one of the first neo-Victorian pubs in Scotland and therefore quite hideous but it was near the *Times Educational Supplement* Scotland offices and Thorburn didn't like the nearby poetasters' pub, Milne's, where people talked of its most famous customer the late Christopher Grieve, that is MacDiarmid, as though he was fucking Gandhi. Thorburn didn't like MacDiarmid, or poetasters, though he most certainly liked pubs. The first time we had met there was the first time I had written for the press. And Thorburn had commissioned me to write for it.

Iain Thorburn was of average height and of deceptively light build: it must have been the way he held himself, a slouching, donnish posture, because in seconds you could see that he was of powerful and athletic build and in fact had been a useful shinty player for the Kyles club in his native Tighnabruaich. (His brother Russell was a former Shinty star, a kind of Billy McNeill of the Highland game.) Thorburn had a desiccated beard, a bit as though he had eaten his All-Bran without a spoon, and was ever a little dishevelled. On the only occasion on which I saw him smartly dressed in a rather expensive Chester Barrie suit and spotless white shirt, a new black and gold necktie of Glasgow University Graduates Association (his wife Christine must have bought him that), he had just come from an interview for the post of editor with the *Times Ed.* Surprisingly he hadn't got the job and he was understandably a bit pissed off. 'What the hell,' he said, 'let's have a pint.' At that he came from behind the table, got to his feet and strode off to the bar for an order. Then I saw why, perhaps, he had been knocked back for the post which everybody thought must surely be his – he had been deputy editor for some time. As he walked up to get the drink I noticed that he was wearing, as a little comment from Thorburn this time and not his wife or his aspirations, a pair of beer-stained scuffed corduroy shoes, the kind normal people wore in the back garden. It was exactly what anybody would have expected from Thorburn if they knew him but the smart London bastard who'd interviewed him wasn't to know that. He also didn't know that Thorburn not only knew more about education than anybody else in the newspaper business, he probably knew more than anybody in the education business. Certainly his opinions, which were scathingly cynical at all times, were much sought after by those active in educational politics. He was a very downy cove indeed. Downy enough, I should say, to have discovered me. (Once or twice he tried to discover other likely chaps but, as he said, 'They were always rather a disappointment. A lot of them went into parliament.')

The meeting in the Beau Brummell I am thinking of was early in our relationship and was the result of a telephone call I had made from the Art

College. I had phoned him to find out how he liked the piece I had written for him, the piece which he had asked me for, about: 'Art: The Basis of Perception', the subject of a stirring speech and document to go with it which I had provided for the NUS National Conference. I had asked Thorburn what he had made of it. 'It's crap,' he said, and my heart fell. 'Come down here and talk to me about it.' Over a couple of drinks and in half an hour Thorburn showed me not only what was wrong with it but had shown me how to write for publication. It is all the instruction I have ever had. Arnold Kemp, my editor in both the newspapers with which I have been associated, once wrote of me: 'As a writer Jack is an original. He went to no school of journalism.' I must admit I didn't understand what Arnold meant then, and barely do now. I didn't think at Arnold's time of writing that anybody had to go to a school of journalism. I still don't. Certainly I can't do much of what most journalists, and all reporters, can. I have no shorthand for instance, and don't know how to take down notes very well, and would find lengthy verbatim reportage impossible. I don't ask the right questions for much of the work of newspapers and cannot sustain sufficient interest in anything I find dull or unimportant to me, no matter how important it may be to the public interest. (Though I have, I confess, occasionally confounded my colleagues with an accurate report on a story which does interest me.) But then no sensible newspaper would employ me in such a capacity as a reporter. And whatever newspaper sense I have is largely that of a newspaper reader, with maybe twenty years' experience of peddling my wares in the broadsheets to go with it. But the only education I had in writing for the blatts was that half-hour with Thorburn in an empty bar in Castle Street in Edinburgh.

The article which appeared was rather well thought of in some circles, and I began to do other pieces, ranging from book reviews to conference reports, with quite a bit of opinion stuff thrown in. I even became known to journalists on other papers and considered as an occasional contributor, in a specialised field of course, but one of that band of reasonably newspaper-worldly chaps who could string a word or two together and which journals such as the *TESS* uses, and could not really do without. There's a lot of them and every national newspaper needs them from time to time. Specialists in some sport or academic area or profession who can do soundbite stuff which has either an informative point or a slightly controversial one. In many cases the writer can become something of a pundit in his own field and it can be a good springboard for further career opportunities. (In my case my endeavours were so at loggerheads with the education establishment that any career I may have had was doomed from the start.) There are perhaps thousands of these writers *manqué* in this country. I have never heard of anybody other than myself who has gone on to become a leading national journalist from such a base, certainly in the last, say, thirty years at least and I would advise any such hopeful to give up the idea and try another way.

I was meeting a number of journalists in the educational area and there were a number of them because education was at that time a very hot issue indeed. Apart from the student conferences and the grants demos and occasional college revolts and sit-ins, and in one exceptional case, the Cambridge University house party affair in which several well-connected Bright Young Things were jailed, students were news at the time anyway throughout the world in the aftermath of Paris, in the States and elsewhere. And a similar turmoil was happening with the lecturers and then the teachers. In Scotland there was the first real teacher strikes and the eventual Houghton Agreement. Every paper by now had their education correspondents and I found myself going along to some of the same meetings which they reported, and socialising with them. Many had known me as a star performer in student politics who could always be relied upon for a rousing speech demanding the overthrow of whoever was in power. One of them was John Pirie of *The Record* who as far as I know is the only journalist ever to be honoured by a teachers union when he became a Fellow of the Educational Institute of Scotland. I am always glad to see him, long retired now, in Babbity Bowster's hotel bar every time he comes to Glasgow which he does when Dundee United are playing in that city. One of the others was to prove the major player in my journalism career, Harry Reid.

Harry has been the Deputy Editor of the *Glasgow Herald* for some years now, but when I first met him he was education correspondent for the *Scotsman*, and probably the most prominent of all the educational journos at the time of the Houghton dispute. He was a tall, urbane, good-looking chap with a background of Fettes and Oxford and one of the first ever batch of the *Scotsman's* graduate entry scheme, (another member of the same elite was historian, right-wing iconoclast, economist and journalist, the appallingly dissolute and gluttonish Michael Fry whom I count as a friend and am damn glad I don't see him too often but would be upset if I never saw him at all). Actually Harry Reid's background was not all it seemed. Born in Busby, he moved to Aberdeen while a small child where his father was a bank manager, and his first secondary school was Aberdeen Grammar: Fettes was on an exchange and a scholarship, for Harry was very bright. I have taunted him for years that he went to a girls' college which infuriates him because he has corrected me for ever (he was at the somewhat sophisticated Worcester), and I pretend to have forgotten. For Harry the joke is wearing thin. For me that's the joke. But at the time that I was writing a fortnightly column for the *Times*

Ed. and had quite a lot of quite large articles under my belt, Harry was the *Scotsman's* Features Editor. Let Harry tell you a bit of the story in his own words.

'In those days, Jack was writing the odd piece for the *Times Scottish Educational Supplement.* These pieces were stupendously boring: there was no hint of the pyrotechnics to come. Jack seemed to be playing some refractory game, seeing if he could pen prose even more costive than the constipated stuff that appeared elsewhere in that most drab of journals.' This was quite true for I had ambitions as an academic still and, as I am a good parodist, it was easy to write in the didactic manner of scholars, especially Leftish ones. I am ashamed to say that I did it rather well. Harry became the Features Editor of the *Scotsman* and, as he says himself, had to wade through many submissions, some of them unspeakably turgid. Harry Reid again, from a foreword to one of my books: 'One day Jack appeared and with, for him, unusual timidity, asked if I could have a look at a couple of articles. I read the first piece, more out of duty than expectation, but halfway through it I started guffawing. It was the funniest thing I had read in years . . . We printed it and then another similar piece. The rest is, if not history, then the most remarkable success story in modern Scottish journalism.' Don't believe all you hear, not even from Harry Reid. Elsewhere in his foreword he describes me as having: 'an attractive personality, albeit somewhat louche and farouche, not to say crapulous and saturnine'. I think Harry just liked the shapes of the words. But what happened was largely as he described. The article he meant was about the debate on a Scottish Assembly and involved a critique of sentimental Scottish nationalism in the form of a wildly exaggerated diatribe about a ridiculous primary teacher who had distorted romantic episodes in Scottish history. I called it 'All Hail to Oor Wullie's Parliament'.

I remember writing the 'Oor Wullie' piece, the content of which, or at least the argument which it contained, I much regret. During the referendum for a Scottish Assembly I was one of those socialists who genuinely believed that the working class of England and Wales, and if it comes to that of anywhere else, were our brothers and sisters and should not be abandoned by we Scots. Also the Scot Nats pissed me off. It was a good argument and written with a certain verve. It was also written in longhand, meticulously legible longhand, as had every effort before. I had badgered Harry about the fate of this aricle and eventually, on the telephone, he revealed to me that he 'hadn't had time' to read it, and intimated that the longhand manuscript put him off. Don't give me or anybody else nonsense about typing courses and learning the keyboard and that stuff. It's certainly advisable, but it isn't absolutely neccessary. What is, though, is the yearning to be in print. My desiderata knew no bounds and I typed that article on my mother's portable that night and had it on Harry's desk by the next afternoon. I did the next article Harry describes as 'similar' which it was in a way and in another phone call from Glasgow Harry said something, in an off-hand manner, (you have to be careful about using the term 'off-hand' with Harry for he has lifted nonchalance to the heights of policy), that the *Scotsman* was thinking of getting me to do a 'Town Diary', a sort of counterpoint to Matt Mundell's Country Diary, which was, unusually for such an item then common to all newspapers, very popular and successful with the readership. I snatched at it, but demanded that it be called 'City Diary'. I didn't like the connotation of town in that context, like town and gown or townsfolk or that disparaging term our bucolic brothers sometimes invoke, 'townies'. Anyway I didn't come from any bloody town: I am a city boy, a city slicker, the Damon Runyon of Scotland I thought. So City Diary it was.

Mundell's pieces were about rabbits and stoats and the first stirrings of fluttery leaves on chestnut trees and were about five hundred words long. My first City Diary, titled 'The Metropolis Belongs to me', appeared on Saturday 8 July 1978, long before any Glasgow's Miles Better campaign was ever thought of, and long before Glasgow was better at all, and was over two thousand words of praise for city living. My next City Diary was about getting drunk in the city and I introduced Wee Tam who was based on a genuine Wee Tam – Tam Crockett, a wonderfully bibulous character, now no longer bibulous thank God, but still a character who was a close chum. I was the best man at his wedding, and nobody thought of Tam as anything other than The Wedding Guest for Tam was a boy who had shot a right few albatrosses in his time. It is difficult to believe this now but back then a celebration of fights and drink and satiety was not the stuff of newspapers and was rather designed to irritate the largely bourgeois readership of that Edinburgh-based newspaper, but also to glory a little in the vitality of city life, or at least my pals' vivacity. The article was also the first to appear which gave me the appellation I am still often given by many, from other journalists to people I meet for the first time – the Urban Voltaire. It was Harry Reid and Arnold Kemp, the then Deputy Editor of the *Scotsman*, who gave me the title, as both have explained in print before now, and I must say that I do get pissed off when sloppy journalists describe me as 'the self-styled Urban Voltaire'. I never self-styled that and my vanity, save that concerning my sartorial appearance, is greatly exaggerated. And for those illiterates who frequently question what it means – it is a reference to a character in a James Thurber story who is a backwoods cracker-barrel philosopher of breathtaking impudence who gets the better of Mr Thurber, a Rural Voltaire indeed.

The appellation was better than that which they'd originally considered, 'the thinking man's Billy Connolly', which is clearly both insulting to Connolly and to myself, and I suspect that the winning soubriquet lent me a certain imprimatur which I was quick to exploit. It rather gives a cheeky chappie air too. No matter how badly I behave in print I am more often than not seen as, to implicate a well-known hymn, a hobgoblin rather than a foul fiend. The hymn you either remember or you don't. But I'd rather be a hobgoblin than a pilgrim, I will tell you that.

A lot of people sometimes rather dismiss my work with the *Scotsman* but a great many former readers remind me of my days as that paper's City Diarist, and quite a goodly number of them switched their allegiance to the *Herald* when I moved there, which is certainly one of the reasons why the great rival to the newspaper from the east wanted me. The main reason was Arnold Kemp, but we will come to him at the proper time. Certainly the City Diary in the *Scotsman* ploughed new fields and about time too, because much of what passed for columnar features was tired tosh, the kind of bar-room drivel every tabloid punts, all ersatz controversy and drooling sycophancy towards established norms and culture, especially popular culture. Even the Scottish broadsheets had a strange lack of freshness at the time, though there were still those writers who gave delight, old-fashioned or not. the *Scotsman* had several well-known columnists in Tony Troon, Albert Morris, and Stanley Eveling, who did the television column (Stanley was also a fine playwright), and they were stylists in their own way. And of course the doyen of *Scotsman* writers, Wilfrid Taylor, whose equivalent across in the west was, I suppose, Alasdair Philips. And a new young one too, Julie Davidson, who later joined me in the *Herald*. Tony and Julie were the only ones I got to know and that was well after *Scotsman* days. In fact in those days Julie didn't like me, not one bit. I think she thought I was nothing but a sexist wee Glasgow bastard. But I drank quite often with Arnold Kemp, the Deputy Editor of the Edinburgh-based blatt, and Harry of course, and Michael Fry. But a few years back when Andrew Jaspan was editor of the paper, before he went off to his disaster of an editorship of the *Observer*, it is said that there was a policy that *Scotsman* employees were not permitted to drink during working hours and woe betide anyone shoving a few halfs down them in Jingling Geordie's or the Halfway House, both right opposite the employees' entrance in Fleshmarket Close. Back when I was a contributor such a ukase would have been considered absurd, Jesus: it wouldn't have been considered at all, and there were a lot of merry nights in these howffs and a lot of very volatile arguments. Highly intellectual too, for the *Scotsman* writers were, and it is to be hoped still are, unafraid of the charge of pseuds being laid against them.   Back then newspapers were very ancient in their technology and the smell of the hot metal yet permeated the building. The offices themselves were old, straight out of 'The Front Page', scarred and cigarette-burned desks, with scarred and cigarette-burned journos too. The front office in the paper where the public goes was and is magnificent, a Hollywood set, where you'd expect a cigar-clenching, tie-loosened, Fedora-rakish Clark Gable striding through intoning: 'So you wanna be a newspaperman?' Hughie Keevins of the sports desk was a drinking companion but I saw him more often in Glasgow because he himself came from Clydebank and based himself in the West.

There was a Glasgow office in Queen Street and I became friendly with a number of the writers there, especially the Glasgow editor, Kerry Gill. I would see them from time to time in the Rogano bar, then in the death throes of the Grant empire. (Donald and Val Grant oversaw this Art Deco palace and, as the last of many pubs that they had inherited, it was falling apart. It had been the haunt of many a prosperous businessman and Evelyn Waugh drank there when he was stationed in Glasgow during the War. Trimmer in the 'Sword of Honour' trilogy meets his lady loves there. W.H. Auden was a patron when he was briefly a schoolmaster in a prep school in Helensburgh, and I am told penned a poem set there, 'The Mermaids in the Oyster Bar'. Today the Rogano has long been restored to its original splendour and is one of the best restaurants in the country. And damned expensive.)

For some reason Kerry Gill took a knock to me and the last time I saw him, some years ago, he was drunk and swaying, standing in a downpour of rain outside the *Glasgow Herald* entrance in Albion Street, in retrospect rather symbolically, waiting for his wife, who arrived in time to see him shouting and gesticulating at me. 'McLean!' he cried several times. 'Why are you so aggressive?', and ironically, in a wild sweep of his arm, unintentionally struck me in the face with his folded umbrella. As it happens I had just come back from Edinburgh where I had made an abysmal recording for a programme on Radio Scotland, and I was soaked and tired, with work waiting for me upstairs. His wife remonstrated with her drunk husband and took him off in her taxi and I never saw him again. I have rarely felt so low as I did after that incident because I liked Kerry and I didn't know what I had done to cause such an outburst, even with himself in drink. I was having a lot of stick from my new colleagues in the *Herald* too, and it was a rather friendless time. A year or so later Kerry crossed swords with me in a letter he wrote to the letters page in the paper, and I never knew the reason for the animus which had clearly fuelled that either. I hope it wasn't the envy which I seem to have aroused in many other journalists because I want to think that Kerry wasn't like that. Maybe a misunderstanding: I hope so.

The incident with Kerry Gill was just one of many: it doesn't stand out or anything and I've only just remembered it, but I was always to find an animosity towards me in what is now, and has been for a long time, my profession, and I still encounter it a lot. In the *Scotsman* days it arose from the fact that I had another job, in fact that I had a job at all. For many years I couldn't get a union card, the NUJ card then as neccessary as the Equity card was, and damned nearly as difficult to obtain too. You weren't eligible for union membership because you hadn't any experience of journalism but you couldn't get experience because you needed a union card to work for the blatts in the first place: the vicious circle which bedevilled many a young stage hopeful's attempts to get the name in lights. Mind you there is no fucking problem if your name is Magnusson or Dimbleby or such, just the same way that there seems to be no end to the fucking innate talent of the progeny of every bloody ham actor. It is just amazing the way talent runs through families. Shite. And corroding shite at that. It makes me angry even now, this nepotism; so very, very angry. Nepotism in the media is probably even more rife today, when it is admittedly difficult for anybody to get work in the industry: that makes it worse when I see, time after time, some fucking spotty hopeful getting a wee start and sometimes a bloody big one and I discover who their mums and dads are. Don't listen, ever, to that ordure about 'the hardest thing is trying to get the job/part/role when they find out who my dad is' or when you read that 'Gemma' or 'Pippa' or fucking 'Roland' or whoever just wanted to be taken on for their own merits. Don't ever believe it because it will not be true. In the media all you have to do is scratch a little and you will discover a hell of a lot of the employees from clerkesses to bosses are nephews and nieces and sons and daughters. And don't be surprised at the undeniable talent and ability of a great many of them. Just think of the other potential talents, larger ones perhaps too, who didn't get any chances because some self-satisfied bratlet was given those they should have had. And think also of why so little changes there ever are in the soft pabulum you are fed by the media and entertainment industries because of nepotism, and then you'll be as angry as myself. I'm damned if I can understand the sort of youngster who simply wants to follow their dad anyway, even among visual artists, where it is common. If the parent is any good, the child is rarely likely to be better, and I should have thought any young man or woman would have considered something of their own to strive for. If I was a youth all over again I wouldn't have liked the notion of nepotism from my father either, and less the notion, absolutely real in my case, that he could not indulge in such a peccancy in the first place. I won't do it myself, even if I could, and damn any charge of sanctimoniousness which may be levelled against me. One of my nephews asked me once if I could help him get summer work in the press, perhaps helping out or doing a little spot as a temporary copy-boy, and I told him to write to the editor. I'll get him a job as a barman or in an hotel because I can vouch for him, which helps both him and the prospective employer, but I'll never pull a string for any of my relations in the business because of two things. One: it is a corrupt and vitiating practice which I hate and two: I think the press is too damned important to commit it.

Yet there was a reason for the difficulty in obtaining a card then: today union membership is increasingly not needed and employers love that. Low payments and short-term contracts, if contracts at all, are the order, and some organisations, such as the BBC, constrained so horribly by finance, and often headed by a new breed of Corporation galloping gauleiters, have become poor employers indeed. (In fact, the BBC, never a well-paying organisation, has been near-mortally wounding itself for some time now by the above. I've been paid more for a two-hour programme from time to time than the young researcher of the show was being paid for a week's work. There are plenty of people to blame for this in the Corporation but it isn't, believe me, the other employees.) Having all sorts of odds and sods coming into the media has undeniably weakened the bargaining power of journalists in general. Yet in some ways I think many journalists were a little unfair to myself in the years before I went full-time. After all it wasn't me who employed me as a columnist and they should have taken their grievances out on those who did. Sure I did another job at the time – as a teacher. Getting paid a lot less than journalists whose kids were taught by, well, teachers. But the hostility I experienced lasted many years and was often very intense. Don't worry: I was getting a lot of bollocks from teachers too. Bastards.

But all this time I was still teaching. The year at Jordanhill College was for me very pleasant and I must be one of the few who has ever uttered that, for almost every graduate hated it or professed to do so. It was a bit Mickey Mouse in the courses and the lecturers often thought they were teaching people who were the same as their primary school teacher students. Primary school teacher students were generally young shiny-haired girls from middle-class backgrounds who weren't considered bright enough to take enough Highers to get to a university, or worse, lacked sufficient confidence to go to one. They were babyish and babying in the main and often held a high regard for their own levels of education which were generally pretty low but they had been taught that they were the equals of the Yooni graduates, which was, and is, patently untrue for the overwhelming majority of students, no matter how inadequate many a university graduate might be. Their belief that a few texts in, say, psychology, or some kind of literature, qualified them as intellectuals

135

was breathtaking. After a few years teaching tots in primaries a great many of these students become authorities and there are few people whose occupations can be more easily recognised in restaurants or pubs or any public arena when they Simply Know Better than the ruck of common humanity. All of the above is painted with too big a brush, but many primary teachers will, with a rueful recognition, agree with what I have written. You can blame the teaching community itself for the phenomenon and for the lack of self-knowledge in teacher-training establishments, but it would be better for us all to admit it. Perhaps it might lead to doing something about the abysmal results in primary schools which are, however, invariably accompanied with blithe dismissals of any such criticism, and instead the trumpets blare shrilly in praise of the system. No wonder then that most graduate students training as teachers in the secondary sector were keen to dissociate themselves from teacher-training itself. Here's another unpalatable truth. Most graduates who went into teaching all those years ago, and probably most now, were the dullest, the least qualified, the most unimaginative and safe and security conscious.

Teaching was once an honourable profession – witness my experience of the old dominies in St John's Grammar in Hamilton – and was once reasonably well-paid too. I recollect one teacher there, Sam Leckie, who had both an arts and a law degree and could have gone into teaching or law. He chose education when he came back from the War because there was no difference in salary, no difference in status, and he was trying to Build a New World and thought education the very boy for that. Like the rest of his generation he continued to believe in education. He may have been sceptical, but he wasn't cynical until the lunacies of career-shaping teachers came in to dilute schools as much as they could. So I enjoyed Jordanhill College where I was – and I really don't know how this came about either – the student representative on the Governors Committee. I thought I had a glittering future in front of me.

My teaching practice had been at a school in Castlemilk, a huge council housing estate in Glasgow which had attracted the usual level of criticism and had above the usual level of problems though Glenwood was not what one would have expected. It was the first comprehensive school in Glasgow and its first headmaster was a unique character called Hamish Gardener, a Communist, and a bit of an authoritarian. He had every child in that school, from first year to sixth, in smart school uniforms, and every pupil had homework diaries to be signed by every parent. Not surprisingly Glenwood achieved quite remarkable academic results because of Hamish's regime. When I went there the headmaster was a chap called John Jardine, and he carried on much as Hamish but to a little less effect. It was still a damned good school though and I learned a lot in my teaching practice there. So I thought. In reality I learned fuck-all, for real reality was waiting for me, waiting to strike.

I'd finished Jordanhill with a bit of a flourish: had done well in the exams, and had published a lot of material in the education papers. I have a suspicion that I was thought a touch insufferable in my earnestness: I think I was a bit. But nothing I thought, or wanted to do, worked at the school I was sent to, a very large one in a mixed social area, with a headmaster who went on to become the chairman of a major educational report and be knighted for it, Sir James Munn. Sir James was a highly cultured man who had started not in education but in the Indian Civil Service, and was one of the last examples of people of high calibre who opted for a career in school education at all. Unfortunately he had a principal teacher of art who had no calibre at all, and, rookie as I was despite my more mature years, I couldn't get on with him, or the school either. I left at the end of the year which concluded with an incident concerning the principal teacher, a man called Smith who must have been the only art teacher in the country who habitually sported a rugby club blazer. My next school was nearer to me, in Toryglen, a 'scheme' once up-market, but quickly spiralling down. Here I was to spend eight years.

The problem I faced with schools was that a greater change in them had occurred in the five brief years I had been away from them than had ever happened since the Butler Act of 1944, or maybe even the Fisher Act of 1918. Practically none of you readers out there will have a scooby what I'm writing about here but you really should because probably the only other legislation which has had as big an impact on your lives this century is that emanating from the Beveridge Report. They were to do with compulsory education and schools and laid the basis for both. And in my five years away there had been the raising of school leaving age which invited thousands of resentful and ill-prepared youths to stay on at schools which had nothing for them to do. In some schools we gave them the equivalent of the old National Service painting the coal white,in which task, I may say, the bulk of pupils resolutely refused to acquiesce. The other feature had been the strange business of thinking up Comprehensive schools. It reminded one a bit of the old joke about Lenin, Stalin and Trotsky in which all three had been marooned on a desert island with nothing but a tin of beans to eat but with no tin-opener. Lenin attempts to open it with a small sharp stone. Stalin gets a bloody great boulder and tries to smash it open. All to no avail. Trotsky demands the tin. 'I'll soon open this,' he says confidently. 'Now,' he says, 'imagine a tin-opener.' The great changes in education were largely at that level, with more phantoms o' air than anything else. Five years away and now I was presented with an educational system I hardly recognised. I didn't like it either, and never truly came to grips with what had been a profession I had chosen on the basis of a circumstance which no longer existed. Thinking now, much of the problem I faced was that I didn't like the look of it, of anything in it. In fact – and this is going to sound horribly odd – it was the way things looked which had allowed me to enjoy my first stint in schoolteaching and it was the way things looked which eventually made my teaching life a misery.

In Hamilton I liked the look of the buildings for heaven's sake. They looked the way schools should, I thought, with tall ceilings and tiled walls, and big, blackened red sandstone exteriors. Not the flimsy concrete boxes that the modern schools were. The pupils looked different too. Somehow even the largest and roughest-looking youths can't look menacing in a school blazer and a pair of ink-stained grey flannel trousers. And the girls looked, if not pretty, at least young. The new schools were filled with brutes in Levis, I know, I know, that was just the girls. In fact few girls dressed up much then in the sump schools, they just looked dirty. Instead of the shambles of an appearance one naturally expects from adolescents there was actual grime, and a sticky and angular look which was faintly discordant, like patients in borrowed clothes. The first time around in schools I had enjoyed such ceremonies as school assembly and school choirs, and had, for the first time in my life, felt part of it all. I didn't have to believe it, but I knew that as rites of passage for schoolchildren it made a sort of sense and gave plenty of opportunities for rejection later on, and stability of a kind after that. What exactly was it which stirred me when the children at St John's came into the assembly hall in their Persil-washed shirts and blouses; the eerily affecting sound of children singing, the hymns themselves, so redolent of my own childhood? 'Courage brother, do not stumble/Though thy path be dark as night . . . Some will hate thee, some will love thee/ Some will flatter, some will slight . . . Perish policy and cunning/Perish all that fears the light . . . ' What was it in these hymns, in these strictures, which caught me like raiment snagged in the barbed wire fence, what was the fence? The wire? the barb? Why did I long for that, and was it another time, a kind of *Grand Meaulnes* fantasy? Why, indeed did I then rather like being an adult amidst childhood? I hadn't much enjoyed my own. And at the same time also relish the *trahison des clercs* in which I expected to continue to indulge, especially as an art teacher. It was, I admit, due to lots of people like me that the changes in the way we saw schoolchildren, in the way they saw themselves, came about and I have regretted my small part in it since.

Eight years in Queen's Park. There were some good years. The year for instance that I took a sixth year form class for the first time. I remember all of them, a little as that idjit Mr Chips remembered his charges on his deathbed. ('Pity he never had any children ('Oh but I have, you know, I have. Potter, Pollet, Porson, Potts . . . ') I too remember the names. Elaine Lister, Elaine Brown. Ian Chambers and Alan Croall and Israr Chaudry. Michael McCurry who went on to do Law and Isoble Aitken who became a policewoman. Twenty-two of them and I remember every name. It was the first time I'd had much of a chance to work with older pupils, for art was a subject which the bulk of children gave up, especially if they were academic, at the end of third year. I organised the register and the system as a kind of tutorial group. I had regular interviews with every one of them, based on reports from their teachers, many of whom thought me off my head. Others, especially the principals, resented anything which smacked of a usurpation of their imagined authority. If they were falling in a subject, I asked them what the problem was and told them I'd speak to their teachers and see if they could help. Most of the teachers went ape-shit and cracked up. What I had always suspected turned out to be the case. The teachers who told the bosses to stick their new just-thought-up time-consuming drivel up their arses sidie-ways had no problem with helping the kids out in a scheme which had sense and decency to it and, as we weren't being po-faced wee bastards with the weans, we didn't get any resentment from them either. I told the kids that they could do, basically, what the fuck they wanted. A few of them will probably remember what I told them: 'It's sod all to me,' I would say when they hadn't done their home-work or dogged off school or class, or came in with hangovers, 'I've got my Highers.' Well, the bulk of them got theirs. Out of that class of twenty-two, sixteen went on to college or university or into nursing or a similar profession. I remember the buggers got me a Christmas card which they all signed, and a bottle of Black Label. In the summer they got me pissed in the Albert Bar. Good boys and girls they were. But I'll bet very few of you out there would ever have thought I'd do such a thing. Or hold such a sentiment. Or tell you about it. But I'll tell you this: all these bleeding heart bastards you used to hear talking great gobs of drivel about what they were doing for the 'young people', with all their bloody reports and implementations and their grovelling to education chiefs, never did a thing. It was the so-called cynics, ones like me, who did the work.

15

A lot of bile spilling out in the last chapter, I think. But there you are, even Our Lord cracked up with the publicans in the temple as I have said often enough to Mrs Heraghty in my little south-side club. You can see that I have returned to the sunny side of myself, and thanks be it is so. If my years teaching art at Queen's Park School were to end with such disillusion on education there were indeed sunny times at the start. Queen's Park had been a school with a long tradition but the school had been moved, physically, from the old area of Battlefield to the housing estate of Toryglen in a bout of municipal chicanery and the new Queen's Park was bound to subside into a shuddering end. A few years after I had taken my leave I passed by the place. It had been razed to the ground and nothing of it remained, obliterated like an Alexandrine city. They should have done that while the weans were in it. And the staff.

When I arrived there, at the start of a new term I had taken over in the Art department from an old chum from Party days, Shug Fletcher. The headmaster was Peter Bell, who had taught me all those years ago in Allan Glen's. Glasgow is, after all, a homogenous city. If you put yourself about a bit you will soon discover that Scotland's a village. And Glasgow's a street. Sooner or later you will bump into everyone. Well I have anyway which is how I was eventually to earn a bob or two in my business when less gregarious colleagues have made, er, less. In fact, there were a lot of contacts in the new school, and I enjoyed the Art department which consisted of a bloke about my age, or only a bit younger, called Barry Blair, and Betty Galt, the principal teacher, a lady in late-ish middle age who was a distant kinswoman of John Galt and whose architect father had left her, among a few other possessions, a genuine Charles Rennie Macintosh table and chairs which must be worth a bloody fortune by now. Betty retired some years ago but still keeps in touch, sending postcards from some dreadfully exotic spots of the world. The other member of the Art department, Barry, was a strikingly handsome fellow in a slightly girlish way but if the schoolgirls had ever fancied him they soon didn't because Barry could be very caustic with them, though he was a keen and secretive womaniser in his private life before he got married for the second time. He was a very fine draughtsman though, and a good teacher. Other young chaps I soon palled up with were Drever, yet another Party member, Gerry Burns, a laconic mustachioed ex-Trotskyite, and a big, loose-limbed English teacher called John Cairnduff. He was known as The Student because another teacher, a late entrant to teaching, Commander Ralph Pounder, had woken up one day in the staffroom, spied Cairnduff, and cried. 'How long is that fucking student going to be in this fucking place?' Cairnduff had been a member of staff for three years.

It was a merry little band and we soon became drinking chums. Cairnduff was the callow youth incarnate. He had a mass of shocking red hair, a pair of bright blue eyes, a long upper lip, and hands too big to fit a normal pocket. In short if anybody had cast him as a typical Irishman he would have been considered ludicrously overdone. He was bright and well-read but a bit wild and there may have been some Irish in him, though he was most certainly a lapsed, and very lapsed, Catholic, an ex-pupil of the nearby Holyrood Secondary. Once, when Queen's Park had a group of dissenting children from a Catholic secondary in the Gorbals, Cairnduff was detailed to be their register teacher on the basis that, as a sort of a Romanist or so the bosses thought, he would be more knowledgeable about the Catholic children. Cairnduff promptly named his class '1 P'. The 'P' was for 'papes'.

For quite a while the merry band stuck together, much to the horror of the dreary little bourgeois in their herring-bone tweed sports jackets and Newton Mearns accents who were going places in the world of schooling, but eventually we all split up into other schools. A few years later Gerry Burns, another heavily lapsed Catholic who set up an Orange flute and mouth organ band with myself to annoy the Presbyterians in the staffroom, organised the Nardini Adventure. This was the merry jape we had been planning for years. On Friday lunchtimes we'd all go out to a local boozer and on the way back in Drever's car we all suggested just going straight on all the way off to Largs and have ice cream in Nardini's Cafe there, and then get rat-arsed with drink. Well, some years after the diaspora of the tribe, Gerry sent us all invitations to our various schools so we each truanted from work that day and presented ourselves at nine in the morning in Glasgow Central station, dressed in disguise, false beards, dark glasses, that sort of thing. We were all in our

141

thirties for God's sake. The Nardini Adventure took place and we ended up sending out an alarm signal on a ferry to Millport when we were convinced that Barry Blair had fallen overboard. Each of us had consumed several pints and at least a bottle of whisky during the jaunt . Only myself made work the next day.

It was that kind of a life, not boring but, except for myself, stupendously aimless. Myself, I was still at the writing. And the union activity. The writing first. I had made a fair reputation with the *Scotsman* and had, in the East, a minor sort of cult-following. I doubt whether I'd ever have been able to make a break with the teaching life in that paper, and would, perhaps, have ended up an occasional writer, with my columns a kind of hobby which made my pedagogical efforts bearable. But then things changed at the top of the *Scotsman* steps. There was a strike. It didn't last long but it had a devastating effect on the paper with the best title in Scotland. A spate of departures took place, the most important of which was that of the Deputy Editor, Arnold Kemp. In March 1981 Arnold took over top spot in the *Glasgow Herald*, the editor's job itself.

It was, as Arnold himself says, perhaps the greatest move any Scot can make in his own country – moving from the picture-postcard capital to the real one, and was, I suppose, rather unexpected, though any of the Kemp family can be expected to do the unexpected at that. But Arnold should have been the quintessentially Edinburgh establishment figure. Educated at Edinburgh Academy, an institution among many such Edinburgh institutions so august that boys were not accepted on the basis of money in the background or anything as crass as that but in the background itself. It was, after all, Sir Walter Scott's old school. Edinburgh University afterwards. His father was Robert Kemp, the dramatist (his most famous work was his version of Lyndsay's 'Three Estaites', but he is also remembered for setting up Edinburgh's Gateway theatre), novelist, pioneering radio producer, and for many years contributor to the 'Editorial Notebook' in the *Glasgow Herald.* Arnold's background was therefore cultured, democratic, liberal towards the Left, enquiring, artistic, and, in fact, immensely patrician in a civilised manner and very much Scottish. Arnold was all of the things mentioned above: an intellectual. This was in marked contrast to the *Herald* traditions which were commercial, if not a bit money-grubbing in fact, business orientated, hard-headed, and with a tendency towards bluff philistinism. Arnold is never bluff, though he can be amazingly off-hand. If he gets bored with you halfway through a sentence, he will simply up and off. Curiously this does not offend, it merely disconcerts. But he can also be very bloody-minded and determined which was important, as it happened, for me. For, as

Harry Reid wrote some time back, I was the first *Scotsman* writer he took with him to his new blatt. (And Harry was soon to join us as Deputy Editor, after a stint as Sports Editor at the *Sunday Standard*.) It caused grievous offence in some quarters.

Actually I had a year before proferred my services as a columnist to the *Herald* in a letter to the then editor, Alan Jenkins, after Willie McIlvanney had jouked off in what was described as a fit of pique at the time but which turned out to be a very justifiable temper indeed. I received a letter of rejection from the then Deputy Executive Editor, the late Tony Finlay, which I found profoundly annoying. I sent a reply in which I roundly condemned the *Herald* decision, ending up by informing them that they would regret this because I was practically the Messiah they had been waiting for really – a reply which went, cyclostyled, around the building because of the very last line in my letter. It stated: 'What is more, my mum agrees with me.'

What is more, my mum did, because she and I lived together in a small flat in a high rise in Pollokshaws which is where she was moved to after my father died. Had he lived long enough to see retirement he would, as a school janitor, have been given a better house in one of the most coveted areas, probably in Merrylee housing scheme itself. But the flat in Pollockshaws was decent enough and there were good tenants. The next door neighbour turned out to be another bachelor and his mother, the bachelor being, it also turned out, an ex-fellow student of my brother Brian, a wee couthy chap called Alex Dimeo. (It gets worse. I had known his uncle down in The Great Wen all those years ago, a famous London gangster called 'Italian Albert' Dimes, who had been implicated in the murder of Jack 'The Hat' McVittie.) My mother continued working as a school secretary until she retired at sixty, actually and it's true, to look after me which she did and which she, and I may say me as well, much enjoyed for a good many years. She also enjoyed what success I had achieved in journalism and during my time at the *Scotsman* and *Times Ed* she would sometimes go through to Edinburgh by train to hand my copy in when I was late with a deadline. The people on both publications may well have found this odd but they were always very nice to my mother on such occasions and gave her coffee. It's not as bad as it sounds: my mother got a pleasant day out going round the Edinburgh shops and she liked that, coming back with socks or a shirt or tie from Jenners for me. Certainly my mother did damned near everything for me, wakening me in the morning with a cup of tea and enquiring what shoes I intended wearing that day. I'd still have my head on the pillow as I replied 'the black brogues' or 'the toney-red slip-ons' or whatever, and be just sipping my tea as I heard her giving the brogans a good polish through in the kitchen. Every boy's best friend is his mother, believe me. Mind you it wasn't all one way. I did after all pay for everything, and often had a job convincing her that she needed more money, or that we should get a new washing machine or whatever, and altogether we lived together perfectly happily. After my father died I had taken her around a lot, to films and the theatre, to shows and exhibitions, railway trips around Scotland, and she liked seeing my friends in the house. It can be a very pleasant life, living as mother and bachelor son, and my mother had friends and relations she saw a lot, as well as her other two sons and her grandchildren and there was a great deal of companionship. I used to talk to her a lot, late at night, sitting on the edge of her bed when I had come back from the pub, talking often about my father, and about her own early life, and what it was like during the War, and before it when she was little girl. I got to know a great fund of history about my family, and her family, into many generations for my mother had that Celtic – she was Cornish after all, though she had been brought up in Stevenston – that Celtic love of ancestral lore. My mother was a very shy wee girl and could never quite believe she could do things well enough but she could, she could. After she died I found that out quick enough. I couldn't and can't do half the household things she managed like looking after all the finance, the rent, insurance, energy bills, all that stuff. I remember when she was persuaded by my father to apply for a job as a school secretary – she had gone back to work only when my younger brother was eight years of age, working first in Fullers confectioners as a cashier and then in a sub-post office – she spent the first week in tears at night because she was convinced that the job was too much for her. She was wrong there too because she spent nearly twenty years as a highly competent school secretary in Balornock Primary school, and was a well-kent figure in Bath Street, the education offices of Glasgow Corporation, because she was rather a favourite of Dr MacIntosh, the legendary director of education we have met in this narrative before. But then she was a great favourite of all my pals because when we dropped back late at night with a carry-out and loaded for fun she would get up and dress and dance with all the lads and lassies to the records I had blaring out, well into the night. Fed a lot of us too. There are a lot of people out there who remember my mother with much affection. Yes, some of these times were good, and the times with my mother were very happy for me, and I think, for her.

'The Editor regrets to announce that in a moment of inattention he made an agreement for Jack McLean to contribute regular articles to the *Glasgow Herald*. The Urban Voltaire has, however, been given stringent warnings on questions of taste etc.' Arnold continued, ' . . . although readers of an irritable or genteel disposition are advised to give him a miss . . . ' That was how I was introduced to the readers back on 1 May 1981 – May Day was probably a coincidence – and it shows how my talents were perceived: a cheeky wee droll who pushed the barriers out a bit. I don't think I've ever entirely, if at all, lost that reputation, which rather irritates me sometimes but it is probably true enough and I shouldn't greet anyway. I've earned a damned good living out of that persona.

Arnold wanted me for his new paper because he thought that his new paper should have me anyway, but also because he wanted to put lots more Glasgow in the Glasgow of the title of the blatt. Clearly I was a Glaswegian working for an Edinburgh publication – and though the *Scotsman* has a marvellous title and one of the best mastheads anywhere it is by no means Glaswegian, in fact, it often pursues a mean-spirited show of indifference towards Glasgow, and occasionally a spite, and always a callow superciliousness towards the city. Just rarely, the Edinburgh paper unintentionally lets slip an envy for Glasgow and its denizens. This is an attitude probably long gone among the bulk of Edinburgh's citizenry though it does indeed continue to be revealed by the more mentally challenged element of the capital's upper class. Glasgow doesn't have this affectation about Edinburgh, I am glad to say, and the *Herald* would be unwise to adopt an uncivil policy towards our sister over there. But though there are enlightened spirits in the Edinburgh paper there was no doubt that a Glaswegian writing mainly of his city and the West of Scotland part of the central industrial belt was a little odd. Odd too that the *Glasgow Herald* didn't have, well, me. So Arnold wanted me. But a lot of others didn't and made it very clear. I have said all I want about the union difficulties, and the justifications which were used, but whether just justifications they were or not I certainly encountered a rare hostility, an disapprobation which veered close to a social ostracism in my new colleagues.

I encountered much the same in Edinburgh with the *Scotsman* of course and in both cases the feeling that I should not be there at all was exacerbated by the fact that any change is fraught with anxieties and I was a very cheap scapegoat for people's chagrin in both papers. After I went to the *Herald* I was given rather short shrift by some of the *Scotsman* people. One of them was Jim Seaton, who had taken over from Harry Reid as Features Editor, and who is now, in fact, Editor of the Edinburgh paper. Why I had a problem with Jim Seaton I'll never know but he firmly told me that I was not welcome to submit anything at all to his blatt ever again. I pointed out that this may well be the case but actually, his paper still owed me money, which was true, and it still does for it never paid for one of my columns. Seaton was very curt and went on about how I should never be working for any paper and if it was up to him I'd never have got taken on at all. It was just after the strike, that's true, but I had made damned sure that I never submitted a thing during the dispute. I left the office after a short argument, and a short two words. A few days later I heard that Seaton was going about telling people that he had physically thrown me out of his office. He couldnae have thrown Shirley Temple out of his office, and I was bloody sure he wasn't going to swan around telling a foul lie like that about me so I went through to Edinburgh and searched high and low seeking him out with a view to kicking the shit out of him. I was a bit impulsive in those days, but I'm glad I never found him for I understand that Seaton is quite a decent chap and anyway it doesn't do to act quite so robustly.

Robustly is the euphemism for another early adversary's actions that first year in Albion Street at Arnold's Editor's Christmas Party held in his office. This was a jamboree which was much looked forward to by the chaps and quite a lot of the chapesses too for there was a not inconsiderable relaxation between the sexes on such occasions. This was the first time I had met most of the *Herald* people, apart from the bosses really, and I was enjoying myself because I felt for the first time that I was actually a part of the newspaper business. Perhaps that was what made the incident with our Defence Correspondent so sickening for myself, though it was to turn out a lot more sickening for our Defence Correspondent. There was a short exchange of words between us in the middle of the party and then a very brief flurry of blows in which the Defence Correspondent revealed that he had no defence personally and in which he unintentionally kicked Jimmy Reid, who was talking to me about jazz (he used to talk to me in those days), on the leg. For the sake of some kind of harmony I was asked to leave while the rest of the party tried to remonstrate with their errant but by now livid Defence Correspondent. To little avail because while I was standing, bemused by recent events, in the pub downstairs, Ian Bruce – for it was he – was breaking his fingers upstairs in the Editor's room by punching the wall. Brucie kept up his animosity for some months after that, including refusing a drink which I sent across to him in the Press Bar until one day his pal, Iain Gray, (Iggy), prevailed upon him to admit that I wasn't a bad bloke really. Ian had just come back from covering the Falklands War in which he had been one of only two journalists to yomp across the entire bloody thing and who earned the universal respect of the troops and the envy of Max Hastings, now editor of the *London Evening Standard* but then the King Bee of the war correspondents. (More than envy, a certain justifiable fear because Iain was indeed the Scottish journo Hastings wrote about in his account of the Falklands conflict: the one who threatened him with certain death with a

146

fighting knife.) In short Brucie was a bit buggered after the Falklands and justifiably so. It is just as well that he never caught me with a wallop because he was commando-trained and in top physical condition and would have knocked the shit out of me. This was a long time ago. He's been a good friend to me these last fourteen years or so and I won't hear a word against him. He and Iggy are still the colleagues I look for first in McEntee's, the *Herald* pub (the Press Bar), which the journos and inkies use as their NAFFI.

Both the incidents I've described sound a bit petty really, playground stuff, but there was a hell of a lot of it to begin with and though I could hardly be considered an especially sensitive soul in my dealings with work mates a constant diet of slights began to pall. Iain Gray was recalling recently the time when he came up to congratulate me on winning one of the British Press awards. I recoiled a little and, as Iain says 'It was obvious you thought this was another trick, another piss-take you'd come to expect. Made me feel lousy about some of the others.' It was true as well. Some of 'some of the others' are still about and, even after fifteen years I am still uneasy in the 'their' company. Once, a few years ago, I finally cracked with them after I had been very publicly snubbed and told the entire crowd that I couldn't give a fuck about what they thought of me but I thought them boorish and cruel to be so obvious. I must have said it with some dignity because they apologised and today there is a nervous and suspicious sort of politeness in whatever casual exchanges now take place between us.

Certainly I do have a difficulty with some fellow journalists. Often there is so little common ground. I'm not there in the office doing shifts day after day, party to the daily round of boredom and excitement you will find in a newspaper. Nor do I have the sort of dealings with superiors which most journalists have to work at for, outside of, I suppose, the Editor himself, and the lawyer, columnists and feature writers like myself are largely responsible to no-one. It is a pleasant situation to be in, in some ways, but it is also a lonely one at times, and can be very insecure. You do have a tendency to be so outwith your colleagues' lives, lives which are very internalised and cabalistic as well, that you find little to talk about and the only damned subject you can come up with is yourself and your own doings. Sure, it could be made a little easier by some of my more judgemental colleagues, but there are times when I can't entirely blame them for their coolness towards me. I don't know if all other features writers who live so much in their own heads find the same though I suspect a lot do. I know that so-called 'personality journalists' all feel a definite comradeship towards each other, regardless of age, gender, background, or subject area. Everybody has to have a herd to belong to after all.

But back in 1981 when I joined the *Herald* I was running with another pack as well. For I was a schoolteacher, (among them I was in a distinct group too: art teachers stick together against all the rest), and it is a large, and often distressingly vocal, pack. At the start of the Eighties teachers had fallen well behind in the salary stakes from the days of the Houghton agreement. (At the conclusion of that salary increase the dominies, gorged with lucre, went off in their droves to purchase the then fashionable check sports jackets. The pattern became known as 'Houghton Tartan'.) And the teachers' main union, the Educational Institute of Scotland, had become absurdly supine, stuffed with headmasters and greasy-pole candidates for such posts. In fact a great many EIS Council people were in open cahoots with the management and some indeed were stool-pigeons. Keir Bloomer, one of the leading union activists during the Houghton campaign, had turned gamekeeper and allowed himself to become management as an education official. I never blamed Keir for this volte-face, surprising as it then was, for I knew him to be an honourable man who, for a start, was personally wealthy enough not to have to be a bloody schoolteacher in the first place; and anyway, I liked Keir, whom I had known when he was a history teacher at Glenwood in Castlemilk, and I still do. In recent years, however, I have seen many a union activist, including a few of the 'Mad Trotskyites' – the Infantile Left Disorder brigade – take up the cushy numbers out of the classroom and in management.

(If you want to know how these promotion-seeking quislings acted then just have a good read at the series of splendidly revelatory books written by a chap called John Mitchell. John had been a teacher himself and now works as a sales director for Houghton Educational Press. In that position he had an ideal opportunity for listening to all sorts of conversations in staffrooms and beyond. He also had a wonderful ear for dialogue and a keenly attuned sense of the absurd. The five books he has published about schools are based on an imagined diary kept by an imagined, but horribly realistic, character called Morris Simpson and the diaries which chronicle his career through the Eighties and Nineties from his first probationary year to, at the end of the last book, a kind of promotion, should be read by everybody who has any kind of interest in schools and schooling. I'm not the only one who thought that. Frank Pigniatelli, the charismatic Director of Education for Strathclyde Regional Council, the largest local government position at the time in Europe, actually bought several hundred of his last two books for distribution to every school in his constituency. It caused a right furore at the time because John's books aren't only scathing, but are very funny indeed and why nobody bothered to dramatise them on television one can never know. Frank Pigniatelli, whom I first met many years ago when he was a bus conductor, was a very surprising man and he still is. When his post disappeared on the local authority reorganisation he, after knocking back several jobs including the Education Director for New York, was appointed as a supremo of Associated Newspapers. But anyway, read John Mitchell's books all the same. Also I wrote all the forewords to them. Come to think of it, I wrote all the glowing reviews of them in the blatt too.)

It was in this context, with the EIS packed with management yes-men, that myself and a late entrant to teaching, Kenny McLaughlin, an ex-heating engineer and ex-Party member and a life-long trades union activist, decided to stand as EIS Vice-President and President respectively. On Kenny's part it was simply that he'd had enough of the vacillating nonentities who generally got themselves paraded before the faithful at conference. On mine it was outrage that the only candidates for any kind of office that the Left could put up were from the Trots and the bananas who supported them. There was horror at this piece of impertinence and the EIS itself disseminated a press hand-out with a wee bit extra innuendo shoved in quiet ears in the right places. Kenny McLaughlin was, he says in his book, *One Great Vision*, used to this kind of dirty tricks strategy, but so was I and I was outraged at the less than subtle implication that we were mindless militants out to poison the young minds of our little charges. I was all for legal action against the Institute and its officials, an act in which we would not only have been justified but one which would undoubtedly have won us, I think, significant damages. We did get the press to publish editorial rebuttals of the coverage which they had quite innocently printed, and several of them drew attention to the distinctly odd and heavily biased EIS press hand-outs. Despite a strong campaign from Kenny and myself, when we went on the stump throughout the country we lost, but did so creditably, and it put the Left into a position of strength in the Institute which it has not quite relinquished to this day. Anyway, Kenneth became President two years later in a final rout of the Rightist forces.

All during this spat we could detect the hand of the EIS General Secretary, the great John Pollock himself, the 'wily John' as I correctly dubbed him in many an article. No matter what he did, and what a great many very inferior critics said of him, John Pollock was indeed a great man, or he certainly could and should have been as Kenny McLaughlin himself says, despite his long disagreement with him. Pollock was an Ayrshire man and a great Burnsian, with an extremely sharp mind and a mastery of political wiles. Twice chairman of the Labour Party and President of the STUC, as well as President of the World Council of Teachers, among many other posts, John had been a brilliant student, and then one of the youngest headmasters ever, in a large and august Ayrshire secondary, and if there was ever a man marked out for the highest of offices in the land it was he. Few in the political world will disagree that he could have been a very great Secretary of State for Scotland, and perhaps a great Prime Minister. Largely unknown to the public at large, certainly until the last teachers' strike which he was to lead, Pollock was a major power-broker within the Labour Movement and Party for many years. At his funeral (John died in 1996), many of the mighty turned out, genuinely, to pay their last respects. I spoke to one of the cameramen from STV who was there. 'Who was this guy anyway?' he asked. I told him he was the guy who had put film in his camera and his arse behind a school desk. It was a bit of a sound-bite but I meant it. The one politician who rather stuck out as inappropriate was Helen Liddell who was there as Labour Scottish Education spokesman because Pollock would have had no time for her educational rhetoric.

I had many disagreements with John. I once rebuked him by stating that 'my employee should refrain from expressing personal criticism of his employer, i.e. me,' and his response was to congratulate me 'for drawing this inescapable if tense relationship' to his attention. And once, I disgracefully appeared with him on television in a debate in which I was very pissed. I wrote later to him and included an appropriate Burns, I think.

The friend whom, wiled from Wisdom's way,
the fumes of wine infuriate send,
(Not moony madness more astray),
who but deplores the hapless friend.

Mine was th' insensate frenzied part,
Ah! Why should I such scenes outlive?
Scenes so abhorrent to my heart!
– 'Tis thine to pity and forgive.

I'm quite good with quotations and I wish to Jesus I was as good at behaving myself. The televising of the debate, which was on St Andrew's Day and was chaired by, I think, Lord MacAuley, had started late and I'd had a great deal too much in the company of the late Charlie Graham of the *Glasgow Evening Times*, a lovely cordial man who, unknown to many of his colleagues, had been a teacher himself, and the Reverend Stewart Lamont of my own paper. On the way out I offered to fill in the snotty commissionaire of the Royal College of Surgeons as well as the BBC Producer. On the train home I drank a half-bottle of whisky with an old chum, BBC reporter Stewart McIntosh, and sang to a young and shocked family. I had never behaved so badly before nor have I since, and to this day cannot understand it and blame the spirit of self-destructiveness. I had to do it on telly. Actually the senior producer, Dave Bachelor, with whom I was to work some years later, cut my appearance down to a few seconds and no viewer was sullied by my appalling performance. There was talk of 'He'll never work again' up and down Queen Margaret Drive, but the sometimes quixotic Scottish Controller, Pat Chalmers, liked me and in less than a week I was doing a Saturday broadcast. This outcome of my degenerate behaviour notwithstanding I still occasionally wake up in bed sweating, and in a foetal position, moaning 'Jesus? Sweet Jesus', and wishing I was somebody else.

16

During the early 1980s I may not have been somebody else but there was a lot of myself going about. I was still doing my teaching job, in fact worse, because for a year I was the acting Principal Teacher of Art. I was also writing my column for the *Herald* and as many features as I could get, and running a Radio Clyde show twice a week, one on the Arts, on Sunday nights, and another on Thursdays, a phone-in programme which was repeated three times again and became an amazing success. Amazing because it went out at less than prime time, on the Thursday, live, at 6.15 in the evening. The original brief was for me to take the calls and give the callers a rough time of it to the point of near-insulting them. We got the idea from some of the American radio shows. But my bad intentions didn't last because I couldn't sustain it, especially when the callers showed good sense. I remember when one caller gave my argument – it was about motor cars or something – a good roasting, he concluded by asking me in triumph: 'What d'you make of that, Mr Smarty McLean?' I told him what I made of it. 'You're right, Mr whatever-ye-are, and I am wrong, nae danger of that. Next on the line we have . . . ' Afterwards Alex Dickson, the Clyde chief controller took me to task. 'Alex,' I said, 'When we're wrang, we're wrang. It'll be good for us: you'll see". He did. Our audiences soared.

Another time Alex, an extremely affable, but decidedly cunning fellow with the sort of bonhomie which has you buying shares in non-existent gold mines, grabbed hold of me accusing me of left-wing bias on a programme. 'Look, Alex,' I said, 'for a hundred and fifty a week I'll tell the punters to vote for the National fucking Front. For the twenty-five quid you pay me,' I said, 'I'll keep ma ain politics.' Alex considered. 'You know best, Jack, you know best,' he conceded lamely.

The programme, which was chaired by Mike Riddoch, a total professional who had much to do with the success of the show, was perhaps the first 'shock-jock' show in Britain and was very popular indeed. We took every news item of the day and I pronounced upon it and then we opened the phone lines. Little Hazel Irvine was the production assistant for Clyde at the time and manned the phones and stuff. 'The listeners would harangue Jack on any subject and he would harangue them right back. It was less a production exercise,' she says, 'more a case of holding him in check. I listened from the control room, terrified . . .' And it was a bit like that. I've rarely had so much fun in my life. I'd emerge at the close of the session bathed in joy and ready for a right few drams and any more arguments you could come up with, stimulated to a dialectical fever. I doubt Hazel was the only one who caught the buzz. Hazel was and is a smashing girl who, to this day, I ever think of as a particularly nice very young sister. But Clyde, parsimonious as always, wouldn't pay her a decent wage when she asked one day. Two weeks later she was the link for the Winter Olympics on ITV. But it was like that with Clyde. It's started a lot of real talents but their bosses are awffy fond of a pound, and it's lost a lot of stars too. I left Clyde eventually because they'd paid me well enough for a show I did on education and when it folded and I was going back to my call-in programme they offered me the old rate which was £25 a week. I had just started full-time as a journalist and was embarking on a decent income so in the circumstances I was right to stop working for Clyde. But despite the fact that my, admittedly fitful, career in broadcasting has often been very successful, and that I enjoy a fair amount of work from the BBC, I had a great time, perhaps my best in radio, with Clyde, and will always regard people like Mike Riddoch and Paul Cooney, Paul Coia and Alex Dickson, and a lot of others as well, as among the best people I've ever worked with.

I was, though I didn't know it at the time, coming to the end of my teaching career. My year as the acting Art Principal was a good year though. It was and is the only time in my life in which I have ever been a boss and it proved what I had long suspected: it is a bloody sight better being a boss. For a start those who are real principal teachers invest you with the status, however mythic it might be in reality, of being a boss. I had a phrase for it at the time. What's the collective noun for a group of principal teachers? Answer: a lack of them. Some of the more halfwitted now listened to what I said at principal teachers meetings as well. But there was one of those strange phenomena which every teacher and ex-teacher can tell you about – an inexplicably good year of weans. The Higher class, and the 'O'Grade Art classes were bloody wonderful, not just potential artists but nice kids as well. One of them was a wee blonde slender girl called Lesley Roberts who had told me in her very first year that she wanted to be a journalist. She was a talented young artist as well. She told me she wanted to be a journalist when she was in Sixth Year and when she was at university and when she left it, and all that time she was asking me for references which I gladly gave. And then also for journalism school. And again for her first job with a PR company, and her start at a local newssheet. I even remember phoning guys saying they have a very clever determined young woman whom they must take on or they'd regret it. If they didn't they would have regretted it till their last days for Lesley ended up winning the Scottish Young Journalist of the Year Award in 1995. I only hope she remembers her old dominie when I am old and in my dotage and needing a turn. A very nice and sweet girl as well is Lesley.

It was a very pleasant year that, though admittedly I was a bit of a trial for Norman Love, the heedie. For a start, if I had 'free' periods, especially if they were after or before lunch, I buggered off to Heraghty's Bar for a few halfs. To this purpose I had a taxi waiting outside my classroom, which butted onto the back playground, just before the bell went. I always got back in time to take my class afterwards and only occasionally had a wee glaze on me. Today it would doubtless be a sacking offence, but back then it wasn't even an offence at all, though a little unusual. All the same I remember many grand afternoons teaching, for once real teaching at that, the boys and girls in my certificate classes. Teaching them how to draw and paint, how to work in clay and, once, glass. It was a good year. When the SCE results came out the Art ones were the highest in the school. Better. It was eventually revealed that they were among the highest in the whole bloody Region. There you are then.

At this time, as well as other things I was also the Teacher Representative on Strathclyde Regional Council. There were only two of us, myself and Katherine Finn, a long time activist who had started as a Trot militant and gradually learned sense – a bit too much if you ask me because she became a pillar of the Labour and EIS edifice. She was an EIS-sanctioned candidate, and the other had been a bloke called Iain something, I forget what. He too was a Trot, but both had been endorsed by the teachers union and indeed by the ruling Labour Group in Strathclyde. A few of my chums thought this rather an outrage. Unopposed candidates? Jesus, we were in the middle of a strike, the big teachers strike which they went on to win in money and lose in reality. So the small group of politically motivated men put me forward as a rival candidate, largely because I was undeniably, through my column which often criticised the education bosses and their satraps, the best-known teacher in Strathclyde. The EIS and the Labour Party went berserk with anger and frustration. I won by a landslide and the welcome I got in the chambers of the Strathclyde Regional Council Education Committee, probably the most important, and certainly then the most highly profiled, group in the Strathclyde juggernaut, was wondrous to behold. The Councillors snubbed me, walked about talking of 'a bad smell in here', sometimes boo-ed me, organised pre-meetings behind my back, and generally treated me like shit. They even made sure that out of the four committees which the teachers' representatives split between them I would get the two less important ones while Kathy, by now a Labour Party member, would have the major areas (including the Discipline Committee). Even the Tories were enemies, for I was on the Left, but one they didn't understand. And Dr Christopher Mason of the SDP was no friend. He wasn't even polite. Early on he came up to me in the Councillors coffee room and told me blithely that I was a fool. 'Nothing but a clown. You're a clown.' he told me. He was, gloriously, to regret that a year or so later for after one debate in which I had stitched him up and rather left him floundering, his normal urbanity dashed to the floor, he approached me saying: 'You're a bastard, McLean. You're a bastard.' It was a lovely reply to get to make. 'No, Dr Mason, a clown, surely,' I replied, 'nothing but a clown.'

It didn't bother me, any of it, because, for a start, not all the Labour Councillors were agin me at all. In fact a number of the cleverer ones were making themselves practically comrades in arms, for whatever reasons best known to themselves, though not a few for the best of reasons entirely, because a number of these Councillors were true democrats and if there is one thing which it was difficult to be in the largest local government authority in Europe it was a democrat. I had the goodwill and support of a surprisingly large group of these councillors, headed by that thoroughly decent and clever fellow, Gerry McGrath, a councillor of long standing and a power in himself. And more, I had the covert support of a number of key education officials, some of whom I'd known and been friendly with for years. One of them, of course, was to be the Director of Education himself Frank Pigniatelli. And the final triumph was when I eventually became, I suppose, a chum of a one-time bitter adversary, the King of Strathclyde, the Mayor Daley of them all (without the corruption I hasten to add) – the foxiest, the most powerful, the leader of the Labour Group, Charlie Gray.

We had exchanged many insults over the years and Gray had done his Machiavellian best to have me out on my ear. But there were two things which were important here. One was that I supported, some thought quixotically, the large-scale closure of schools which Gray had proposed. The other was that Gray was and remains an exceptionally intelligent man, though a classic working class auto-didact, and a man of extraordinary self-will. There is no doubt the inhabitants have a great deal to thank Gray for, because his courage and tenacity, tempered remarkably with the kind of municipal pragmatism which could be found in the old Tammany Hall bosses, achieved a great deal even under a Tory government hell-bent on crippling Labour local authorities. Like his neighbour in Glasgow's City Chambers, Pat Lally, another old adversary I like and admire, Gray was capable of extreme charm, and dreadful brutality in his political dealings. He once told the firefighters' union, the FBU, that he would have them 'crawling back on their knees within a week.' When they won every demand within that same week he praised them for their good sense and said he'd been with them all the way, 'if they but knew it.' Neither the FBU nor myself have ever wavered in our respect for Charles Gray but, Christ, he was very hard to get round.

The question of the school closures was dreadfully fudged though at the time there was an extraordinary amount of heat about it. I knew, as did Charlie Gray and anybody else with any sense, that there had to be a major programme of school closures because many schools which had the capacity for over two thousand pupils had actual school rolls of a few hundred, even allowing for the amazing distortions which many headmasters tried to make of the real figures. This meant entire staffs, including janitorial and cleaning, who could have been deployed in other areas, and maintenance costs, and other levels of expenditure which could have gone into the proper business of education. It was crazy, but of course no local councillor would agree to schools in his own ward getting the axe. Some of them reached wee agreements with other councillors too, scratching backs till they bled. It also led to all sorts of nonsense with horribly middle-class schools such as the Catholic girls Notre Dame suddenly claiming to be 'just ordinary schools' and boasting of the number of their pupils who were on free school meals. You'd have thought weans were ragged urchins the way they told it. I went out on a visit to Notre Dame. The children sported a school uniform which would have done credit to a Hessian Field Marshal. In some of the 'sump' schools the local parents and the teachers tried to tell you they were practically bloody Eton. One casualty which should not have been was the little girls' school, the famous Charlotte Street. Our Lady and St Francis, set in the area round the Barras. It was a school with an enviable academic record but, unlike bourgeois Notre Dame, its pupils were traditionally drawn from the poorer families.

I wrote a column about their plight, in which I referred to the largely working-class girls in their brown and blue-edged uniforms, a sight known to everybody in the area of Townhead in which I had been brought up, a sight of these wee princesses to gladden the most misanthropic heart. I wrote of 'the diamonds in the glaur' and it was a most affecting piece. Not that it did any good though, for the priests, the Catholic males, negotiated it away in a deal which saved Notre Dame and gave St Mungo's boys' school a lease of life. Grand doubtless for the boys of the Mungo but a damned disgrace for the wee working class girls for whom Charlotte Street had afforded many a chance. I went to the Mass in the school which took place on the Sunday before it closed its doors for good and was rewarded with a mention from the retired but still legendary headmistress, Sister Felicity. 'It took one not of our Faith' she said, 'to stand up for us . . .' Ach, maybe there was an ulterior motive on my part: the girls had been my Estellas when I was a child, in my blacking factory.

My stand over Our Lady and St Francis school was practically my last act. I resigned from my teacher's post shortly afterwards. It had been rather brewing up for many reasons. I hadn't got the official Principal's job, despite our department's success in the SCE exams. A chap called Hector MacLean was promoted over me. He and others activated what was – which years later came to light – a campaign of constructive dismissal. I can't say I blame the Education Department for I'd been a considerable thorn in their side for many years. I don't think much of Hector MacLean though. My mother's death some time before was surely the real reason why I decided to give up teaching after all these years.

I wrote once about my mother; when she died. She died from Alzheimer's Disease and I don't want to tell you much about it really. She had lucid moments sometimes when she knew what was happening to her and it made her terribly distressed. I used to pretend to her that nothing was wrong at all to stem that but she did know sometimes. And people were very kind. When she forgot everything, where she was, what she was doing, she'd always remember my telephone number at the school and I'd go and collect her in some shop, in the bank, wherever she was and always find some young assistants sitting with her, making her a cup of tea, while she happily talked about her son, me. One Christmas I found a note written on a piece of cardboard torn from a breakfast cereal box. On it she'd written: 'Sorry Jack, I have made a mess of Christmas.' I can't cope with this. I'm stopping now.

Two actual events ended my teaching job in fact. One was caused by a pupil called Charles McCall. I'd taken him out of Miss Paterson's class and Mrs Connolly's because he kept on telling them – when he was at school, which was infrequent – that he was 'going to ride them'. Believe me, women teachers get that rubbish a lot and are used to it, but I took McCall in anyway. He rarely came to the class, which was a certificate class though not a particularly good one. One fateful day he turned up, to noise up really. I gave him paper and pencils and started him off on a drawing, telling him that there was no reason why he shouldn't even, if he wanted, do the 'O' Grade in Art himself. I showed him how to go about the drawing. He told me he wasn't doing 'any of that shite' and tore up the paper. He did that three times, breaking the pencil on the last occasion and throwing the two stumps away. God knows how I kept patience, but I gave him another piece of paper and he promptly spat on me. All the years of rubbish from little turds like him welled up in me but, truth to tell, I think I'd have reacted the way I did just for him spitting on me. I practically pulled him through the fucking ink-well on the desk, and started clubbing the little bastard as hard as I could, with him trying to defend himself, shouting: 'Ah'm gettin' ma Social! Ah'm gettin' ma fuckin' Social!' as I laid into him. (For of course Charlie had a social worker of his own, also a psychologist, and special teachers, and in fact we were spending more on the bloody little toe-rag than it would have cost to send him to Eton, I mean it.) I was dragged off by the two women in the department. That afternoon, true to his word, there was his Social. She wanted me charged with assault. I wanted her charged with lunacy. On Friday I was to receive my full, official, warning. On Friday morning I went into school, took one look at the classroom, thought 'What the fuck am I doing here?' and strolled down to the Jannies box and gave him my keys. 'Ta Ta, Bill' I remember saying gaily, 'I'm off.' And I was.

Then Endell Laird, the then editor of the *Daily Record* and the *Sunday Mail*, offered me a job. He wanted to steal me away from the *Herald*, and he wanted it badly enough to make me a very sizeable offer which he did over a good lunch in a favourite Italian restaurant of mine on the south side, La Bussola (which is a measure of Laird's thoroughness, finding out where I liked to eat). I told my blatt. It was seconds later when they came up with an offer. At first, it wasn't as good an offer either, but it was the first offer they had ever given me which would allow me a living as a full-time journalist. And then they started making me bigger offers though they admitted that they couldn't pay me the much larger sums I could get as a tabloid journalist but then, said Harry Reid and Arnold Kemp (with a few others joining in), you have a great career ahead of you. You'll never be the same if you go to the tabloids, they'll never let you write the way you do with us. They went on for days. There was a fair bit of intellectual snobbery, always likely to sway me, flying around. 'Look what happened,' they warned darkly, 'to Jimmy Reid when he left us.' Reid had ended up writing for the *Sun*.

(Reid's stock was pretty low at the time among many journalists and indeed among most of his former comrades in the Labour Movement, who felt that his frequently intemperate outpourings in the Tory gutter press against Arthur Scargill was nothing short of Government propaganda during the strike. This was not in fact entirely true but it could well be said that he did the miners' cause no good and some harm by his personal antipathy to the Barnsley ranter. I might as well record here my disapproval of Jimmy Reid. He was allowed a while back there to have a go at me in print while I was dissuaded from a reply, but that is not the reason for the opprobrium in which I hold the former Communist Party organiser. Despite Reid's genuine gifts as a popular journalist and broadcaster, I still think of him as a bar-room pundit, an I-happen-to-believe finger-prodding, bit of a blowhard. Just what the tabloids want. But there you are then. We cannae all be pals.) By a strange twist of fate Jimmy Reid is now back as a columnist in the *Herald*, in which he is permitted to pronounce mightily on any matter which takes his fancy, him knowing all about anything, so to speak, like. Anyway the look-what-happened-to-Jimmy Reid was perhaps the point which swayed me. We celebrated my new contract with my blatt in The Buttery, a famous establishment and one of the best, certainly the most atmospheric, restaurants in Scotland. I have celebrated many triumphs in there, though it was the sadly gone Fountain in which myself and the editors toasted another new contract, offered after the *Independent* had tried to snatch me. It is sometimes a bit like footy players in journalism, though not nearly as lucrative or as illiterate as one imagines. (I remember once taking my mother to The Buttery for her birthday. At the end of the meal she wanted to clear up the plates and help in the kitchen.)

We got off to a good start in full-time journalism, the *Herald* and I. Mind, we'd been doing well before it anyway, because I had actually won a British Press Award before I chucked the pedagogy. But I started doing a lot more features and there was a great deal of puffing me in the blatt. It should have become embarrassing, those photographs of me every week in the paper, but it didn't cause me any blushes. I knew it came with the work, and, of course, the income, and, especially I suppose, with the chance to be a bit of a pundit myself. I took the chance with every hand I had.

At first I wasn't sure I'd know how to go about getting material. I found out though, and very quickly. You just went there. You talked to everybody, and listened to everybody and hoped to God you could remember enough of it. You also worked to your strengths and realised what you couldn't do. In my case I couldn't be a reporter, ever. I was too old to learn that craft; how to ask the right questions, what the right questions are. I'm not sure I'd ever have been able to do that. But I've got a good eye and an ear for dialogue, and an imagination to go with both. They have to make up for my inability to handle facts in a straightforward, factual way. So I embarked on features which were interpretations of what facts I could discover; the same dichotomy all over, ever since school and before. I can understand the science of imagination, but not the art of convergent logic. What the hell, there wasn't any logic about one of my first features. I went down to the Oxford and Cambridge Boat Race on the Thames and we won a watch. Talking of winning; I don't think I gave the result. I certainly can't remember it.

But I remember the piece very well. Myself and our rowing correspondent, Mike Haggarty, a world referee, international coach and universal rowing luminary, one of the inner circle of rowing, and he rather surprised one. He turned out to be a chap about my size in a M&S sweater who hadn't seen a razor for twenty-four hours or more, and who spoke in the tones of a St Aloysius old boy down on his luck. I'm quoting, I think, from the damned article I wrote. But Mike knew everybody there was to know, and the photographer, an ex-pat Glaswegian called Arthur Foster, was just the man to show me the ropes of how to go about cornering fellows. I met Daniel Topolski, who had juicy stories of the scandals the year before when the Yanks had caused mayhem, and scandals of the day, because the Yanks were trying to do it again. I liked Dan immediately and he liked me because I talked to him at first of his father's work which I much admired, and knew, as an ex-illustrator, quite a lot about. (Dan's father was of course the famed artist, Felix Topolski). Then I had an encounter with a rather pissed Denis Thatcher after his minders had tried to bar me from slurring words with him, and the Prime Minister's bibulous hubby spoke at length about how much he liked Glasgow and 'Come and have a drink, old chap' with every other journo wanting to kill with resentful envy. Everything went right. I visited all the rowing clubs, and ended the night in my club, the Cheslea Arts, talking to Spike Milligan, a member, though he didn't remember me charring for him over twenty years before. During the weekend I met up with an old chum, the journalist Neal Ascherson, whom I had known in *Scotsman* days and who is one of the finest writers in newspapers. I had meetings with girls dressed in Beefeater dresses who were the PR models for the gin company sponsoring the whole event. I met pals later in a variety of Establishment clubs. In short, in one brief feature assignment I had found out two things. One:put yourself about. The other is: be lucky. I was more than lucky: the feature, with a glorious front-page spread for the weekend supplement and wonderful and flattering photographs, helped to win me another Press Award later on, and it established me as a feature writer in the eyes and minds of the Boys on the Blatt. Another reason why I mentioned this particular piece is that I consolidated my increasing confidence that I could go anywhere, and nobody could stop me. Gentleman's clubs, the inner sanctums of the Establishment, even them. Anywhere.

(There is sadly a corollary to the statement above. As a member of the Glasgow Arts Club I was entitled to reciprocity with all the London clubs. The reason why I am no longer a member of the Glasgow Arts Club is because I was expelled from it some years ago after I had written a piece which mentioned an insufferable Anglo-Scot I'd encountered in one of the clubs which, I suppose, I shouldn't have done. One of the Glasgow members accused me of not being a gentleman, and I thoroughly agreed with him, pointing out that my antecedents weren't gentlemen either. The Anglo-Scot in question had relations who were gentlemen. But at least none of my family were convicted thieves either. The Anglo-Scot was a relation of George Pottinger. Yes, the Scottish Office mandarin who did a wee bit of mailbag technology at HM's request for his gentlemanly part in the Poulson Affair. I refused to apologise on the basis that if I did that every time I'd insulted somebody in print I wouldnae have a column at all. I regret this stance now. Actually, I just want back in the Arts Club where I used to while away many a happy hangover.)

There were a great many other features after that. My visit to the Police Federation's annual bash at Crieff Hydro – the first time any journalist had been invited to penetrate the very core of this august, but necessarily secretive group because I was invited to the Executive dinner. The Federation, who had employed George as their PRO were deeply suspicious. As it turned out they were very pleased, not to say, surprised, by the resulting main feature, because, though I didn't tee-hee to the polis, I was there to see what these shop stewards of gendarmes were like. I gave them a jolly, a bit, and was right to do so. I'd still rather have the Forces of the State outside my door than the feral Falangists of delinquency.

I started to write features which were all about going away too. I mean they were about being someplace outside of Glasgow, just because it was. One of my first jobs with this mission in mind was an overnight stay at the most exclusive hotel in Scotland, Inverlochy Castle. This was when I discovered how much I like working with photographers. A lot of writers don't. In fact, some photographers try to avoid writers, for often the best of reasons. My colleague, William Hunter, was regarded as something of a nightmare for the snappers (a term considered by the photographers as one of abuse), not because he wasn't a nice fellow, which he is, but simply because nobody, least of all himself, ever knew what he was going to write and his idiosyncratic musings were impossible to anticipate. But from the first I like being out with photographers. For a start I liked them anyway. I've often, and I mean it with considerable regard and admiration, described them as 'trombone players in jazz bands, drummers in rock groups, and goalkeepers in fitba teams', in short, not quite all there really.

On the Inverlochy Castle escapade the photographer was James Galloway, now *The Herald* chief sports photographer and a good pal. We hit it off immediately on the trip and I listened to the moans Jim had which were quite considerable and rightly so because he was getting messed about a bit by the bosses at the time. A pretty fair gripe all the same was that while I was booked into the amazing Inverlochy, Jim was in a cheap guest house down the road nearer Fort William. This was due, we were told, to there only being one room available, which is probably true because this hotel is fully booked years in advance. I've stayed in many hotels, many of the best five star because I'm a sybaritic little bastard and, even if I'm paying, it is always the best and most exclusive places I'll lay the weary head. It may well be thought a form of compensation for the many years I earned sod-all, but it isn't: I just like the look and the feeling of the best of gear and I enjoy hotels, restaurants, pubs, tea-shops, anywhere public, and I like them when they look splendid. I don't throw money away on holidays, (I haven't taken a holiday in sixteen years), or cars or any of that, I spend my money on proper luxury and to hell with it. But of all the hotels I've ever been in the Inverlochy stands with the best.

I remember there was an American family called Cocks staying there at the time. The head of it was a Chicago canning millionaire and he brought his entire family across to the hotel every year for his birthday. He had a splendid party and everybody enjoyed him enjoying himself. He got slightly and happily tipsy. The last I saw of him was himself toddling up the staircase with his wife, off to bed. He gave us all a diurnal benediction and then his toupee slowly slipped down his face.

Myself and Jim got talking to a pair of well-dressed couples, clearly wealthy, (you'd have to be to eat there), who were local and been having dinner. It is an enormous advantage when you're out on a job to have somebody else with you because people will talk to two guys but not to one. One of the blokes we were talking to owned what he described as a 'nightclub' in Fort William. Would we like to go? It was late but, hell, yes, we would. Jim, reminded me that we had an early shoot the next day because he wanted early morning shots round the hotel's vast estate, (it has a full golf course, and horse-riding, fishing, and deer-stalking for heaven's sake), but I was fired up with a night-is-still-young flush of, well, lust really. So off we went to Fort William.

The town is set in the most beautiful scenery damn-near in Britain, and I know it very well, because I've covered a few shinty games there and Highland games and stuff, but the town itself was built by what must have been East German architects for the buildings all look like fucking DHSS offices in Gogol's day. But the 'nightclub' turned out to be a disco for youngsters upstairs and a pleasant wee bar below. Jim had a few beers below and I tried my luck in the discotheque. The girls you would get the jail for, the boys were adverts for Clearasil. I joined James for a whisky or so and chatted to the young barman who was a Glasgow DJ two nights a week, till the young fellow had to eject a Fort William major tearaway, a youth in stubble and black biker's jacket. The Wild One shouted horribly and issued blood-curdling threats which I took very seriously indeed because he was a fair lump of a boy, but he was put out quietly enough, and the place was emptied save for myself, Jim, a couple of members of staff, and a few desultory girls who had been allowed to stay and I wonder why. We'd settled down with a few drinks when the door burst open and here was the errant youth with all the threats of half an hour before. 'Take that, you bastards!' he cried savagely in his soft Gaelic accent, a contradiction itself it sounded, and threw an object at the mirrored gantry. Me and Jim, Glasgow men and experienced enough, hit the deck instantly. We knew the shards of glass and other debris could rip right through you. Things are gentler in the Highlands though. Fort William's Marlon Brando, the dastard, had thrown his empty chip wrapper.

It was a good night for me though. I nipped a wee bird and we drove Jim home to his guest house en route to the hotel, Jim telling me all the while, like a boxer's manager to his protegee, about the early start in the morning. It was a devil of a job getting the lassie out the hotel early in the morning, I can tell you. When Galloway arrived to take the snaps of me I looked like Caligula after a meths session in a Govan air raid shelter. I never wrote about the bird.

They were paying me for this too.

17

If the previous chapter read, towards the end of it at any rate, like a footy player's biography written by his ghost then the reason is that my new life as a full-time scribe was really rather like a footy player's at that. The column was still, and remains, the most important part of my work, that's the league games I play, the weekly encounter in the mud and glaur when the crowds expect me to score at least one goal, even if the team doesn't win. But the features are all European matches; sometimes I get a Cup Final. Sometimes the venue is splendidly exotic and full of foreign magic, occasionally it is a little-known opposition in a drab country, but they are all show-games, the features. From time to time I get asked to do something purely as almost a representative of the newspaper: that's an International, and, just as in football, rarely pays as well. These days I seem to get less Internationals. I suspect I'm a bit out of favour with the selectors. My sports columns are probably the most fun of all for me: they're the five-a-side tournaments my club truly wants to win. Arnold Kemp once described me almost in those soccer terms. He said I wasn't a Billy McNeill: 'He's the *Herald*'s Jimmy Johnstone,' he said. I was very pleased with that, even if I did know that he was referring to my waywardness. (Arnold also once vigorously defended me from an attack mounted on me by a chap in the Glasgow Art Club by informing the lieges that I would 'come to be seen as Scotland's Flann O'Brien'. I was touched but gently reminded Arnold that Brian O'Noilan, alias Myles na Gopaleen, alias Flann O'Brien, died skint and naked having been fired by the *Irish Times* in the last few years of his life.) But it was a starry time all the same, very like anybody else in the entertainment business, especially football.

I had the ball at my feet right enough. Then there was a great deal of goodwill about, and I don't mean that cynically. Why the change came I don't know but I'm damned glad it did, though there are still enemies around, and are there not in any job? I have my allies yet. The goodwill though started me on a lot of lovely jobs to do. Sometimes Arnold would suggest an idea. He once asked me, over a glass of especially old vintage port, if I would do an article which had suggested itself to him while he was reading Tacitus the night before. A glass of vintage port? Tacitus? It could have been the eighteenth century for God's sake. Another time he told me that 'Lanarkshire, m'boy, is a bloody awful county.' When I expostulated that it was not, that it was a lovely county, even the wee grimy towns, he told me to do Lanarkshire. 'Prove it, m'boy, prove it.' Myself and Angela Caitlin, the photographer, did. We went up to the Falls of the Clyde, up at Kirkfieldbank and Rosebank and Biggar and Strathaven, places like that, and Angie took some idyllic photographs. I wanted to do the grimy towns as well so I hit Larkhall first, and then Coatbridge. A bar in Larkhall I visited had the usual Protestant icons on the wall, for Larkhall is of course a by-word for being staunch, loyal, and true, the photos and prints of HM the Queen and the Duke of Edinburgh and so on. I asked the punters, after a few drinks, what they thought of Paul McStay, the Scottish and Celtic captain and a local lad. 'Keeps himsel tae himsel, aye,' they said sagely, 'Himsel tae himsel,' they agreed. 'Jist as well,' came a far-away voice, 'the Fenian bastard.' I was a bit taken aback by the force of this dreadful small-town bigotry. In Coatbridge I went into another pub, much the same as the one in Larkhall, with exactly the same punters almost – wee bunnets, mauve bri-nylon semmits, the lot, though with portraits of John F. Kennedy and about eight pontiffs on the amber smoke-darkened walls – and told them of the response to McStay, whom I would have imagined would be thought rather a hero even in bluenose Larkhall. The response in the Coatbridge bar was muted on McStay too. 'Aye, a' very weel but whit's the bastard daein' in Lark-ha'?' A nice touch though was Motherwell. We'd been looking for a photograph which summed up the industrial part of Lanarkshire, a nice rough-ish central industrial belt kind of picture, because Angie already had all that Arcadian beauty of the Clyde Valley in the can. We had almost given up when Angie spied the photie which set it exactly right. It was by the monstrosity of the town's Civic Centre, a great, beached dead mammal, grey and concrete, and municipally depressing. Outside was a wedding party with the groom and friends in full Highland dress, the bride in glorious ivory satin with a train damn-near stretching to the station on it, a proud set of mums and dads, everybody with fags going, and a massive, gleaming unbelievably expensive – even to hire – white Rolls-Royce standing just by them. Industrial Lanarkshire to the life.

But other senior editors – back-room boys and girls they are to you out there but important figures in their own right, Ronnie Anderson, and Bob Sutter, and Anne Simpson – kept pouring in ideas for features for me, as did reporters and subs and I was never short of inspiration. Alf Young, an old pal who actually taught me at Jordanhill though he is younger than I (he was a very young lecturer in education and we go a long way back), was always good for a notion. The most fecund of all in the ideas was Harry Reid who liked me to do big prestige things which reflected well on the *Herald*, and, of course, me. (I've never understood why Harry, a fine writer himself, with plenty of published work to his credit including a fine book on England, always prefers a back-seat, but then I don't know why anybody wants to be an editor when he could be out there writing all the time instead.) And a fair few ideas came from me.

There were two pieces I wrote, however, which made me at last think of myself as a journalist rather than simply a writer who wrote for newspapers. One was early days: an interview with Michael Forsyth, who had just recently been appointed as Under Secretary of State for Scotland. The interview was in Dover House, which is perhaps the most magnificent of any of the Whitehall offices, though it is in The Mall in fact, and was once lived in by Lord Byron. (Michael seems to get all the best shops for the official residence of the Scottish Secretary. Bute House – which is splendidly next door to Ivory & Syme, the fund managers, and Dawson International the knitwear people – is the most lavishly beautiful of all the government properties.) The interview concerned Scottish education and though the Minister had the usual brace of officials with him he never had to consult them once for a figure or a statistic. He looked to them to confirm what he knew, which was impressive. I found him then suitably distant and very polite and calm and I liked him, I don't know why, but I did. It was a good interview too, and I was rather amazed I'd done it so well. Later meetings with Forsyth have not changed my mind: I still like him. He has a self-deprecatory wit – a sharp wit though – and an amazingly clear grasp of his brief. His politics may be different from my own, though in some matters they vary surprisingly little. For instance, education and the bogeyman myth is mainly newspaper hype, perhaps sometimes fuelled by Conservative clodhoppers' antipathy. And a great many Labourites loathe him because they are much afraid of him and have every right to be so. He doesn't fudge unless he has to, and is most certainly not quite a gentleman. He'd have got on well with John Wilkes.

The other piece which let me know that I was a journalist proper instead of the dilettante I am oft regarded as was a three-day full-page piece on Scotrail. I wrote the entire thing in five days, which included four days travelling throughout Scotland. Once again Jim Galloway was the photographer, and we were being shown about by John Sheridan, then a Scotrail PRO and the voice for some years of Railcheck on the wireless. He now has a successful PR company. A lovely chap, John Sheridan, and we had, for what is after all meant to be a rivetingly boring subject, a damned good time doing the piece. It meant though that I had to get facts and get them absolutely right for there is no animal like a railway buff for insisting on the most pedantic veracity. And I got it right, interesting enough for the average reader to take three days of it, and factual enough to get praise from the railway anoraks. As it happens the rail bosses, locked in struggle with the Government and other power-brokers, liked the series too for it opened out some of the points they wished to make themselves but couldn't say in public. It didn't take Arnold Kemp to say it for me to know but when he told me at a *Herald* function just before the series went to print that I 'was a damned good journalist' it was the first time that anybody in the profession had called me a journalist at all.

There was naturally a number of spin-offs from the name I had made for myself among readers and even non-readers: I became rather well-known, certainly for a journalist in Scotland – the great days of newspaper-people being household names were well over of course – but I got quite famous all the same. There was a lot of radio work, and I was also the BBC Scotland visual arts chap, going through to Edinburgh every week to do my stuff. Neville Garden was the presenter and the arts programme was eponymously titled 'Queen Street Garden'. The show ended a few years back and Neville was somewhat retired from the Beeb which upset him quite a lot. Most of us though were secretly glad because Neville has had God knows how many heart attacks and there's no many decent men left: we cannae afford to lose another. I did television too, which I don't like because although I've a grand face for the wireless I don't look good on telly. It's an irritating medium too, all that waiting about for the bloody sound men and lighting people. One particular series I did was my own chat show, after midnight on STV, the early days of late night TV. The 'Jack McLean Talk Show' it was titled, and was produced by Paul Murricane. It never worked, partly because we were using a set which had been designed originally for Rosemary Long and looked like a cross between a French *fin de siècle* bordello and a funeral parlour. It didn't help our first programme that I had to use a right ear-piece in my left ear and it kept slipping out. Nor did the shows work entirely, especially one of them in which we realised that the guests were a little too disparate. In it Andy Cameron was the only one who came across well. Iain McLaughlin (Scottish rugby's 'Mighty Mouse') hardly spoke; Brian Wilson MP turned up halfway through having missed his London train; and the Rangers' old full-back, wee

Bobby Shearer, was a trifle, well, couthy. We had a smashing night out later though with Bobby taking us round Edinburgh boozers which were owned by former football chums from a past but well-remembered era, by me anyway. We ended up drinking in a bar owned by Harry Hood in the company of fellow publicans Lawrie Lesley and Jimmy Millar. If you don't know who they are it's your fault, but they were legends in my childhood.

The only TV thing I've ever done which I really enjoyed was filmed by Hal Duncan and his sidekick Robin Segar, and it won a European award. They were very pleased with the result but have never asked me to do anything for them again and I am not surprised. The scenario was that there was this pub regarded as the most difficult to get to in the United Kingdom and I had just been warned off the drink and was going to have my last one in this pub, which was in Knoydart. We filmed me coming out of my own wee Glasgow pub, getting into the car, travelling by car and then by ferry, and all sorts of places were scenically filmed, and then the night in the pub on the return journey. Aff the drink? I was pissed throughout, stopping off wildly at God knows how many hostelries for another dram. And it wasn't only me: the rest of them were howling throughout too. I remember filming on the ferry-boat back. The cameramen were so ill with the efforts of the night before I ended up re-writing the script. We finished in Glasgow, filming what was to be, in the film, the beginning: me setting off on my epic journey. I couldn't stick to the script I'd written easily – it was a three-minute monologue to camera after all, and that's a job for a professional actor. We had take after take, and I fluffed it every time, even with the idiot boards. Eventually I turned to Hal. 'Can I just busk this crap?' I asked, 'I can do it if I busk it.' Few directors allow this for it usually goes wrong. I extemporised the thing and it was done in one take. The last shot we made was mute – one of myself striding out of the doors of Heraghty's Bar and getting into the car which was to whisk me off to the Highlands. This was impossible too because we had lorries, buses, ambulances, and eventually three bloody fire-engines zooming right across the camera which was filming the incident from across the street. Then the schoolweans came out of the nearby primary and pranced in front of the cameras, giving 'V' signs, and cheery hellos to their mums. It was myself who solved the problem. I selected the biggest child and showed her a fiver. 'This is for Tony Ventre in the Classic Cafe,' I said – Tony's shop was round the corner, 'tae get Mars Bars for the lot o' youse if ye can keep these bloody urchins quiet till we finish filming.' It worked and we got our shot and the kids their Mars Bars. A damned fine bevvying three days it was. The film was called by us all, what else? 'Moydart in Knoydart'. It won the award and Gus MacDonald of Scottish (another Allan Glen's boy incidentally), sent me a bottle of their own whisky and a wee note saying I'd been great and he'd heard how entertaining I had been and the boys were still not well.

I continue to do television and the occasional bit of filming but generally I don't enjoy the long hours of it, nor does anybody need the dreadful months and more of street recognition just because you've been on the bloody cathode ray machine.

One series of films I did do was during Glasgow's Year of Culture when English and world TV were beating the path to the portals of every Glaswegian sound-biter they could get their mikes on. It was a wonderful year that Culture time, ruined of course by the kill-joy temperance-led Calvinism of the City Fathers who rewarded the Glasgow populace and beyond for their tireless efforts to make Glasgow look and sound one of the most vibrant cities on earth by closing every fucking thing down at the end of it. What the idjits were thinking of doing when they introduced curfews and broadcast unsubstantiated stories of dreadful violence and drunkenness on the streets just after perhaps one of the greatest municipal PR coups since the Great Exhibition of 1851 I cannot imagine, but a few weeks after the world press had gone home with marvellous reports of how Glasgow was the in-place to be, they were all back giving it 'No Mean City'.

But for myself and a lot of others that year was one of the longest and most enjoyable parties ever. In fact a terribly sad coda came from out of the mouth of a young pal of mine after it. He'd been eighteen when the Year of Culture happened, and old enough to get into the pubs and clubs. 'I thought it was like that all the time, Jack,' he told me a year or so later, 'when you got to be eighteen, all the adults behaved like that with pubs and restaurants and fun and everything.' Well, ye were wrang, son, Glasgow can always find a way to make you pay for your pleasure in regrets.

My colleague and friend for nearly twenty years, the *Herald* diarist Tom Shields, had set up a magazine a year or so earlier titled 'Culture City', a title which the Glasgow City Fathers wanted for themselves but hadn't thought of. It was a damn good magazine too, glossy and beautifully produced, with a large number of fine writers, old and absolutely brand new. I did the art reviews, which wasn't difficult because I already went round a great many galleries in Scotland, partly for the Beeb, but mainly for myself anyway. There was an explosion of galleries and artists, and the same in theatre, music, festivals: a charivari itself. I don't know how I lasted the pace really for I rarely got to bed before four in the morning and I was up early for more excitement. I was playing blues harp with a lot of bands, writing a lot of copy, meeting a lot of people, doing in a lot of the amber fluid, and sleeping with more women than I could cope with. By the end, so to speak, I was red-raw.

There wasn't much time for any reaction to set in, however, because I brought out my first book, an anthology of articles of mine called *The Bedside Urban Voltaire* with Lochar Publishing, followed a year and a half later by a second anthology. They went very well indeed though they made very little money for me. Incidentally I don't think they made anything much for Lochar either because it went bust. Myself and Iain Hamilton were having a drink in Babbity Bowsters of a lunchtime when we heard that Lochar was to close. 'Stone' Hamilton, so called not merely because he was one of the band who snatched the Stone of Destiny back in 1952, but because those who know him reckon he is stone mad at that tried to get legal contact quickly enough to squeeze ourselves into the creditor line but we didn't get there in time. We both had two books out with Neil Wilson and Mike De Luca who made up the Lochar Publishing firm but to no avail. Neither of us really blamed the two boys and indeed both of us went on to publish again with Neil in his new company. The creditors who come first of course are the banks and the Inland Revenue and the printers and really important chaps. The last to be considered by the law is the idjit without whom there are no profits, let alone losses – the writers. It is said that Chuck Berry never plays a concert unless the money is in cash and up-front. Writers are bloody ding-a-lings right enough. (I first met Stone, another ex-Allan Glen's boy, in a pub when we had a wee debate in which he fiercely informed me that I was the most argumentative man he had ever met, the worst case of pot-calling I have ever encountered. Later, I wrote a profile on him which, oddly, he liked. Iain is a strange melancholic man who, if I believed in a deity, has been touched by the hand of God. Don't forget how that marks you. A melancholy man who cheers one: a paradox that; like the rest of Iain Hamilton. I am very glad I know him. We are friends, I think. Anyway, the books coming out were good for me and my business in the end, and it's nice to have your own work on your bookshelves. I wish I had mine. I ended up giving all my copies away.

In 1993 I brought out two books. One was the text for a book of photographs by Colin Baxter. He paid me outright but didn't put my name on the cover, though it appeared on the flyleaf. Frankly I didn't care for the photographs. It was my nephew David who pointed out what was wrong with them. There was only one photograph with people in it, and they were blurred and intentionally out of focus, just like Colin Baxter's idea of Glasgow really. But, despite the appalling lack of proper proof-reading, the text was all right. The other book that year was another anthology of my work, this time about sport, my sporting columns. I'd been asked to write on sport I think because the paper needed to get me more money somehow to stem another offer which had been made by a metropolitan newspaper. Certainly the

Editor took Eddie Rodger, the then Sports Editor, and myself out to lunch to assuage Eddie's fears. Eddie and I got on very well but Eddie thought of me as a bit of a flim-flam merchant, for which perception he has a certain justification, but start as a sports writer I did. My first assignment achieved a lasting donkey laugh for myself. I got the name of a player who'd been sent off wrong, the scoreline wrong as well. In a magnificent burst of lunacy I got the name of one of the teams wrong too. How the boys laughed. But we got over that and I began to write on so-called minority sports. Nowadays other blatts try to copy us, as do the broadcast media, but so far they haven't found a writer idiosyncratic enough or indeed a sports desk indulgent enough either to make a go of it.

By the end of 1993 I was, when I think of it now, exhausted. I had three weekly features in the *Weekender* supplement. One of them was a piece on whisky distilleries which involved a lot of travelling (along with Harry Turner the photographer and our head of marketing, Abigail Pritchard). Another was a day in the life of a supermarket, say, or an hotel, or a sporran-maker – a diverse array of occupations, trades, and sometimes scams. The other piece is one the demise of which I regret dreadfully, a shortish weekly question and answer column entitled 'The Department of Useless Information'. I enjoyed this very much because it was a lot of fun and even if I did make many of the letters up to *encourager les autres*, see the French, I liked the daftness of it all, and enjoyed the orotund Augustan prose in which I couched it all. There was one correspondent from Skye, who had cloaked himself in a pseudonym to no avail because I have friends in Skye and we discovered he was the local polisman; he had wondrous questions of a daftness so sublime I looked forward to his weekly postcard in the mail. One of the questions was about why, if a mirror had you back to front, it didn't reflect your image upside down. With the above and two books that year, the broadcasts and other features I would write from week to week, and my column to boot, no wonder I was tired and needed a break. For once, I should have taken a holiday. But I didn't. I was eventually to get a holiday I didn't bargain for though.

It was at the end of November that I had dinner with Arnold, in the Buttery it was. Arnold had arranged this, for what reason, be it whim or intent I know not. It was a good dinner. I had wild duck with coriander and a tarragon cream sauce and Arnold had oysters and then lobster I remember, and drank whisky, as I always did because I don't like wine, throughout. We talked of, oddly, my future. Oddly because Arnold generally only talked of my future when he thought I was going to exercise it elsewhere. What Arnold had asked me to dinner to talk about was, it emerged, me. He told me that he wanted me to adopt more gravitas. That my days of being the *enfant terrible* were, if not over, to be gradually phased out. The wee scamp, the jackanapes, was to go, though I was to retain my position as a satirist and humourist. But, said Arnold, 'You can write with a great deal of power and persuasion, and I want you to make these changes over the next while: we're going to make you more than an entertainer.' I didn't receive all that many jollies and much appreciated them when I did, set me chirpy for a while, buoyed me up because, like most people with a great deal of self-confidence and chutzpah, such insecurity in one's persona as exists can be very unsettling, not being used to the evidence of it. Less than a week later Arnold was bounced out of his editorial chair. I had worked with Arnold for eighteen years. The day before Christmas I met him in the Uisgebha pub in Glasgow's Woodlands Road and gave him an engraved silver quaich for old times sake. Later I damn-near needed the silver back too.

The new editor came across from our sister paper the *Evening Times* and there seemed no point in making any conclusions about him but take him as I found him. I found him straightforward and down-to-earth (which is not shorthand for philistine), though – and this is going to sound odd – strangely shy of me. Certainly he knows I am considered an asset to the paper by the readers and so he will consider me as such too, for he is, I am told, a newspaperman to his fingertips, though that, frankly, sometimes sounds a touch pejorative to me. Twenty years ago I was taking the piss out of showbiz dreadfuls like Nicholas Parsons, say, or Bob Monkhouse, and all the rest of the false-consciousness which people were fed then. Orwell's prolefeed it is. They are still there, bigger than ever and just as crappy. Newspapers promote drivel like them and I hold so-called 'real newspapers' often in contempt for doing so. So giving me the old olive about 'newspapermen' doesn't wash.

I just hope George lets me write. I've not been used well this last year or so, but whose fault that is I hesitate to say, maybe a little bit of mine, though there are perhaps signs of George putting me back in the spotlights. I suspect he thinks I've got some brand new sparkly outfits for the show, though I think the spangles were always there myself.

There are those who would have me out in seconds, and newspapers are a fickle business, especially in these times in which a lot of young men and women are knocking at the door, with raw knuckles, and hungry throats and very sharp teeth. I know I'm at the luxury end of newspapers, even if I am a favourite with readers. Newspapers didn't like my brand of writing when I first started in this business and there's enough people out there who hanker for the good old days and certainties of the *Express* and Godfrey Winn or Douglas Fairey and all that shite. A bit like those tired old greeters forever telling you about the great days of Scottish variety and the old comics. Younger people don't know this but take my word: it was unremitting drivel. These are the people who fondly recall insults to you like Arthur Askey.

I lost a lot of money with the changes in the business, an income of over twenty-five grand. This is because the features dried up. In fact the features editor, Jackie McGlone, had scarcely used me, perhaps once or twice. What imagined slight was the original source of this I do not know but it has deprived me of a lot of fun as well as poppy, and the readers of a lot of me. There can be as many as thirty-odd pieces in my own personal 'queue' which will not be used, and God knows how many ideas for features I simply abandon at birth because I know there is little chance of it being published in the newspaper I work for, (by the terms of my contract I am not permitted to work for another newspaper and quite right too, though I note that some of the other younger people seem to be bound by no such constraints). Not a few of the younger people who are printed instead of myself are pretty pleased with that I suppose though one, not so young at that, told me that my day was over. I was simply no longer the fashion she implied. Well, she's not doing so well herself, perhaps as a result of thinking there should be a fashion in writing in the first place.

18

Heraghty's Bar is on the south-side of Glasgow and I started drinking there a couple of years after I'd returned to Glasgow from art college in Auld Reekie and it's my pub, where I drink. A wee base of operations all these years, over twenty of them. Every time the reader finds my column starting: 'As I was just saying, Mrs Heraghty . . .' you should know that it was almost true and I was trying out the weekly piece a little on Anna. It hasn't only been my column which Anna Heraghty has helped me with: a bed in heaven to her for the help she gave me when my mother died and later when I moved house. But that's a long time away. Anna's husband was Michael Heraghty, a fine-looking man, always immaculately dressed. I'm not saying he didn't take a drink, for he did, but he was a bright cheery gentleman, with fun bursting out of him. He was a very gregarious man, very popular, and well known and quoted in Glasgow and in his native Donegal. One of my favourite stories is of the time he was confronted with a brand new electronic till, and had a wee amber or two in him. It was when he started pressing all the keys that John Strange, the part-time barman who has been part-time for fifteen years, asked Mickey Joe what he was doing with the new-fangled cash register. 'Can't a man,' said an indignant Michael, 'phone his own wife?' A great character Michael, and his ghost still lingers in Heraghty's yet.

But it is an office and a ballroom, and a confessional, and a community centre, like all real pubs. It is, as I have often called it in my column, my little club. A lot of organisations use it as a contact number for myself – the BBC, even in England, rings up Heraghty's when it wants to find me and I'm not at home or in the office. Certainly the pub has, occasionally annoyingly, a fair number of the media and Glaswegerati as sometime customers. They are

174

mostly treated very well, even Gerry McNee who upsets some of the Celtic FC hordes who imagine that Heraghty's is a partisan pub. It is not, but idjits think it is. The more moronic Celtic fans get upset at Gerry because he says honest things about the football team which alone seems to make their sad wee lives bearable. I just wish they'd have their sad wee lives somewhere else.

But Heraghty's, while a base for lots of my chums as well as myself, was and is by no means the only pub I ever go into. I have been drinking in public houses since before the legal age to do so, and never regretted the many thousands of hours, or at least not many of them, I've spent in pubs, or the thousands of whiskies I've shoved down my throat. I think you should know that it has been some half a year or so since I stopped drinking alcohol, or at least any more than an occasional toddy or a wee sherry. I did this, not because, as popular stories in my parish seem to have it, I have 'been warned off by the doctors', but because I became ill with a serious lung infection and couldn't bloody eat, let alone drink whisky. As prosaic as that; no sudden Damascus enlightenment. The way some have it I was Dylan Thomas in New York: the Last Days. Well, that's shite and you can take that from me. Pert and faintly sanctimonious congratulations on my sudden temperance do not please me one bit, but I'm as astounded at the ludicrous importance Scots attach to alcohol, whether it be drinking it or disapproving of it. I drank because I liked it and the company was grand, and if I want to I'll drink again, and whenever I think it a fine idea. Drinking is another sad pleasure the Scots have made of a blessing to us.

But one thing is certain, you meet a lot of people in pubs. One of the reasons why I know as many people as I do is pubs. And of course a bachelor existence. I haven't cluttered up my life with women and weans, or got myself snug in a cave-dwelling with the boulder rolled in front of it every night. I prefer to pick my scabs in public and in the company of others than sit in a suburban hovel night after night teaching my children to despise me. I am by no means a family chap. I've no regrets on that score either.

Desi McEntee, one of the family who owns the Press Bar, once bemoaned to me, and Desi is not a man who often bemoans either, about pubs and his part as a publican. 'Ye see, Jack, ninety-five per cent of decent men go to a pub for a drink,' he dolefully pointed out, 'but a hundred per cent of arseholes do as well'. And of course he's right; I've worked long enough in the spirit trade to know it. But it is only on bad nights that Desi and myself should worry about the hundred per cent. Concentrate yourself on the ninety-five souls out of the hundred, and you will realise why Will Fyfe had it that a teetotaller was a dead loss. 'Ach when ye're a teetotaller, ye've a nasty feelin' that everybody's yer boss'. But there's nothing like the *bonhomie* of a nice wee pub, preferably a wee dark one with the winter coming in, (another thing Desi once vouchsafed to me on a sun-splitting summer evening was that, 'Scotland's no the place for good weather; it disnae sit right on it.' He like myself rather looks forward to huddling in dark bars on a cold night. Winter's braw, in short.) If Lewis Grassic Gibbon found the Scots as unpleasant as he did Jews, 'endlessly picking away at their scabs in their dark caves' as he wrote in his anti-Semitic vein, while he found the Philistines 'a healthy and cleanly race', with their healthy and cleanly sing-songs round their camp fires, as he wrote in his pro-Fascist vein – it was an essay on Glasgow from which these illuminations are drawn – then he wasn't alone for it has been the cry of the bourgeois since long before Poujade opened up his particular philosophic shop. I will tell you this: I have met a lot of people in pubs.

Or anyway through drink. The old phrase 'we are related through drink' is true enough and I am fortunate to have a great many relations at that. It was not long ago that I found myself at some august press function and looked along the entire top table, to discover that I knew damn near every one of them, some better than others. I knew Cardinal Winning and the Reverend Bill Morris of Glasgow Cathedral, and Lord MacFarlane of Beardsen, and Gus MacDonald of Scottish Television, and Pat Lally the Lord Provost and just about the only one I hadn't in one way or another passed the time of day with was the Prime Minister, John Major. There are two reasons for this. To grasp them you have to realise that I knew Billy Dewar, the head waiter, and Joe Cantley the head barman (with whom I worked and whom I called the Cantleyville Ghost because he was never around when you needed him: Joe never understood what I was bloody talking about), and I knew the taxi driver who took myself, Willie McIlvanney who talks to me these days, Jimmy Reid, who sometimes does, and the Prince of Darkness, Alan Davidson, the sports writer, back to the Press Bar where – who else? – Desi McEntee served us and we all knew Desi and he knew us. The taxi driver was Biff Connor, whose dad, Jackie, is a well-known veteran cyclist and even better known as a bookies writer on the racetracks, both dog and horse. Later that night I dined with just about my oldest pal, John Nicholas, whose cousin is Charlie Nicholas of the Celtic, in Tony Matteo's restaurant, the City Merchant, and Bernard Corrigan, the fish merchant was talking to Tony because they both know each other not just through the trade but also because Tony once owned The Duke of Tourane where the Celtic players ate. I often meet Bernard in The Scotia which is just round the corner from his headquarters shop and is leased by him to Brendan McLaughlin who also owns the Clutha Bar. Brendan I first met through Alex Dimeo whose uncle was Italian Albert

Dimes, but I know Brendan better through Billy Connolly and the old days of the Marland Bar. Brendan used to work with Gus MacDonald of Scottish Television. There's the reason why I know all these people and a lot more besides. A second reason? I mean the reason why I don't know John Major. The reason for that is that Major wasn't brought up in Glasgow.

Ach, the real second reason is that Scotland is a very democratic country, and is so through Calvinism, in its real and actual sense, with which the country in I was born is shot through. The Calvinism which focuses on the essential disputatiousness of the Scots and other Celtic groups. This culturally innate sense of the democratic intellect is doubtless what fuels my hatred of nepotism. Like the weather nepotism doesn't sit right on Scotland. There has got to be something good about Scotland, for, as I wrote once in an essay for, I think, *The Glasgow Herald Book of Scotland*, it is no joke being a Scot. I wrote for a similar *Herald* book on Glasgow as well (I've lost count of how many anthologies I've written pieces for on my city; you get a reputation for that genre and the late Jack House made a living damn-near out of it with my Glaswegian comrade wee Cliff Hanley doing a bit supplementing his income too), and the piece I wrote for Glasgow wasn't melancholic at all. It wasn't cheery either, though I can write cheery Glesca pieces to order: it was apocalyptic. But the essentials of Glasgow lie in the sense of democracy. If you take the nabobs of the top table I mentioned earlier you will discover that none of them talk in the Anglo-Scots one would find in Edinburgh. Glasgow toffs talk in their city's demotic and often live in it too. Certainly Tom Winning and Bill Morris would find little difficulty talking to a punter. What's much better is that a punter would make bloody sure he could say his piece to both prelates, in a pub if need be.

It was in Heraghty's that I met my chums and made new ones, and in lots of other pubs too. Indeed when I first came back from Edinburgh I had started a wee club first in a rather beautiful, if then badly run-down, public house called The Corunna. Myself and Tam Crockett were the leaders-aff really. Tam was then a stupendously larger than life character and now that he is of good repute too, much cannot be revealed except to tell you that his exploits are now of mythic proportions. Tam it was who, when terribly pissed, would throw his glasses at the gantry in whichever pub he was in and repair to the gents, emerging shortly with a pair of specs drawn on his features in felt-tip pen. Tam was one of those widely read chaps (he had studied under Walter Allen at Coleraine University), who lived the Runyonesque life to the hilt, including spending, as well as making, large sums on the horses. He had an extremely stable background, but half lumpen prole, half solid middle class. He'd been expelled from Hutchie Grammar, but his two brothers had been school duxes. A very wild boy indeed, Tam was. It was as though he had decided to become a character. Truth to tell he didn't have to try anyway. But I learned much from Tam. He could be astoundingly old-fashioned and at the same time he embraced Punk Rock with a fervour. He liked it because it fucked things up really, though a more orderly man than Tam Crockett I have rarely met. For a wee stout man he had enormous presence. He still has.

Tam had a salon about him though, and this also included eventually a seraglio as well and although we didn't drift apart we began to do the same things as each other but in different places, which is the best way when friends have to go in separate directions. For a while I inhabited another pub called the Bay Horse. And then Heraghty's. I brought some of the chums from place to place, perhaps by force of personality, though I am hardly the one to judge, but certainly because an experienced bachelor is always a focus for other lads' forays into merriment. And concerning merriment, Tam is one of a band of friends who, however loosely, know each other from all over. Jim Mowat, whom you have met before, used to invite myself and Tam and other actors in the movie down to Liverpool where Jim then worked. He also invited big Martin Currie and Iain Reekie, who we had both met in Edinburgh. Nowadays Martin and Iain are pals with the chaps in Heraghty's and Anna Heraghty's nephew, John, the theatre director, often works with Iain Reekie junior who is the director of the Traverse Theatre. Big Martin is a close pal too. We'd met in Edinburgh when I was a student and Martin was a building worker. Later Martin became a mature student and in fact eventually the Scottish Chairman of the National Union of Students. I did a profile on him because Martin Currie is one of the best known characters in Edinburgh. Much had been made in the tabloid press of this student leader who had been better known as a trades union agitator. True as it was that Currie had spent most of his life as a workie I determined that the truth would out. I wrote that, 'If he'd laid as many bricks as he had panel lines he'd have built the bloody Taj Mahal by now'. It was a good line and untrue enough to get a laugh. Martin and Reekie were ex-Communist Party of course, but very much of the Good Time branch. Martin was a sizeable figure in the Labour Movement as well and gently used to take the piss out of people like Abe Moffat and, in the past, Willie Gallagher, and such CP stalwarts. In the pursuit of pleasure and contiguous responsibility it could take decades for such socialists as remain to catch up with people like Currie and Reekie, and Mowat. Oh and Tam Crockett as well because, of course, Tam was an ex-Party member as well. And the thing we learned from each other was that you could move about in any circles you liked if you liked.

Thus all of the above are as at home in artistic cliques as they are in sporting circles. A building site or the Assembly Rooms they can all manage muster. This is going to appear crass and somewhat jejune but it helped that we could all fight a bit, though I suspect we will all half-heartedly try to deny it.

I mentioned earlier Anna Heraghty's help when I moved house. Shouldn't mean much that but it did because I moved background, persona, ideology almost, and certainly what magazines call lifestyle. I moved all that when I flitted from the council flat in Pollokshaws which I had shared with my mother. When my mother had moved in there following my father's death it was a decent high-rise flat, set in a decent enough area. Pollokshaws had been a very odd district in itself though, its denizens known for generations as 'the Queer Folk of the Shaws'. This was simply because originally the village had been settled by Huguenot weavers. (Surnames like Lamont, De'Ath, Venters, Roger or Rodger, and Morton, all corruptions of French titles, were common.) Pollokshaws I remembered because my father in his fine madness had once booked a week's holiday there despite the fact that it is perhaps a fifteen-minute bus ride away from Glasgow Cross for heaven's sake. He'd even had the hamper containing the family clothing and necessities delivered by lorry to the holiday home. It was, as it turned out, quite a sensible idea because the area was a small village with a few pleasant Georgian buildings and cobbled streets set in the parkland of Pollok estate when I was a child, and we children thought we were in the middle of the country, while my father wasn't too far away from the Glasgow streets he felt at home in. But the building of the high-rise flats had changed the area's vistas, and later its character. By the time of my moving it had become infested with low-lifes and the odd pusher: it is a lot worse now, ten years later on. I was urged to get out of it by the house being broken into three times in my last year there. Working class vitality had taken a new turn for the worse.

The first break-in the thieves took all the electrical goods, including a rented video recorder. Only the rent bothered me about that. I hardly knew how to operate it and had got it in for my mother to see the TV programmes she liked. Naturally being an idjit of working class background I was not insured. The next time the robbers took everything including my mother's jewellery which I'd set aside in little parcels ready to send off to female relatives. They took her wedding ring. Cheap at the time of purchase it had been and the gold had worn through at the back. It would have been thrown away later this symbol of a war-time marriage, awffy nice that. The third time there was sod all to take so the miscreants 'beasted' the joint, which is to say they slashed all my clothes and beat up the furniture and smashed crockery. They also pissed on my bed and crapped on the hallway floor. The police told me that the housebreakers soil the floors and so on because they get nervous. You wonder why they can't get nervous on the lavvy like anybody else. If I were ever to find out who the bastards were they will have every right to be nervous because I remember taking the mattress off my bed downstairs as urine flowed down my arms and chest and I remember taking my clothes off and binning them and then having a three-hour bath, scrubbing, scrubbing, to take the filth of their piss and ordure from me, the stain of their foulness. And they have every right to be nervous indeed for, as I say if I find them, they will be breaking into houses in the future very, very slowly and with the most terrible limps because I will have their legs broken in as many places as I can think up. That's not just for me: that's for all the people who find the visitation of these maleficent urban locusts as vile as I did. Ach, I don't think I could do the above but somewhere inside I wish I had the vengeance in me. And perhaps I don't wish that at all. What I wish really is that they didn't exist.

By now such a thing as a house hardly mattered. I'd even managed a kitchen fire. (Started by taking my eye off a sauté pan with sunflower oil in it. I didn't have usual lumpen chip-pan fire, nothing but a nice wee bourgeois sauté pan for yer Urban V. here. I remember that the firefighters who put out the inferno were all chums of mine from Heraghty's. 'No you, Jack?' they cried, as they stomped into the house: Alan Campbell and John-Paul MacDonald, and big Davy Paton and all their mates. Today all three of them are prominent full-time officials of the Fire Brigade Union and I taunt them by claiming that the last fire they've seen was at the end of a Havana cigar for Chrissake. They taunt me back by insisting that the little gold FBU badge with the numbers 2 and 5 on it isn't the twenty-five year service badge they presented me with for doing a bit of PR work for their union but actually the number of times I've called them out for chip-pan fires which is a damned calumny. But by now I didn't really have a house, I had an address. Time to do what I had never considered in my life before – which was to buy property.

This may not seem much to most of my readers but it was drastically radical to me. I'd never really had a domicile, just somewhere I slept at night, kept my clothes, and shaved in first thing in the morning. I never thought of my house; more: I thought property other than that of the most transient kind, clothes, books, records, that's it: I thought of property as theft. I don't mean other people's property. I considered property as the theft of your own soul, the way Red Indians thought a photograph was that. Property was something outside of you, and a burden, often paid for by others through tax relief or some other bloody scam. I was not a houseowner, anymore than I was (or remain) a car driver. (In fact I tried driving lessons once and the very first day out I killed a dog. It was a wee dog, a little Jack Russell, and it died in my arms in Newlands Road. I wept, for heaven's sake for I am very, very, fond of wee dogs and cats and any animal with four legs and fur if it comes to that.) But there I was sticking a right few quid under my oxter and living like something out of *The Fugitive*. All the same, I don't think I'd ever have got round to buying a house if it hadn't been that a house, a block of tenements actually, came on to the market.

I'd always wanted to live in that house, a boyhood dream it was. This block of flats opposite a park. As a child when we took the 107 trolley bus across to the south-side to Cathcart, to the picture houses – the George, the Kingsway, the Toledo – we had to pass by this elegent sweep of a terrace with its statuary encrusted facia, its Parisienne fenestration, the mansard roofs and attic skylights, an almost feline delicacy about it: I'd always wanted to live there. The terrace block of apartments was built in 1896; a grand age for myself the *fin de siècle*, and one in which I rather think I would have felt at home. Shades of a faintly precious aestheticism. Proust could have crumbled a madeleine here, or sipped a strangely rose-coloured tisane or a queerly yellow absinthe.

I instructed my lawyer to put a bid in for eight houses on the basis that I would get at least one of the buggers. I like that phrase: 'I instructed my lawyer.' Now I didn't only have a lawyer, I had a bought house. Refurbished the entire block was because it had been falling down for years. Part of the frontage had been replaced because a fire had gutted one entire house, from basement to attic; and the terrace had fallen prey to the ravages of sub-letting. This had once held a smart hotel, the Parkview, which had quickly descended into a sub-bordello. In the early 1960s it had been a venue for Sunday jazz. (Ralph Slater, the man who founded what is now the largest men's outfitters in the world, according to *The Guinness Book of Records*, was once a musician and he had in fact played there: Ralph is an old friend.) This, one of the most beautiful tenemental structures, certainly in Britain, was very nearly demolished but refurbished it was, and today it can be seen at its best at night with the curve tracked by large Edwardian lamps, and floodlit. I am amazingly proud of it.

I moved in with nothing: left damn-near everything in the old council house in Pollokshaws, including all the delft. (Black beetles had colonised in every dish and cup and saucer. I am ashamed to say I am frightened of beetles; doutless there is a psycho-sexual reason underlying my horror of insects but up front all I can say is that they look so alien that I have a near-phobia about creepy-crawlies.) I left everything really, the old life too. Free at last, Dear God, free at last. I moved in to my apartment with the help of the chums.

Chums like Benny McGowan (his father was the legendary Govan bookmaker Corrie McGowan; 'Don't be sorry; Bet with Corrie'), gave me chairs to sit on and sticks of furniture and the odd pot. Friends from Heraghty's helped me move everything. Big Arthur Kerr, the boxer, got the fright of his bloody life when carrying, for God's sake, the bloody great heavy washing machine and spin dryer up the stairs all by himself, the door to it swung open and the washing tumbled out along with three basinfuls of suds. I'm not too good at organisation myself. This was shortly after I had chucked teaching and had taken a bit of a chance as a result of which I was lacking in fiscal confidence. At first I bought cheaply but later I was to learn that error, not that I am especially extravagant in such matters. Apart from the paintings that is. And clothes. And drink, food, hotels, books, almost everything really, except that I do not get into debt. Now there's a touch of Calvinism. But it was starting out in my forties, the way most people do in their early twenties, and it was one of the happiest times in my life. It really was.

Over the last few years this house of mine, this flat, has become like a child to me. Why did I write that? Why not a wife or a mistress? I suppose because I made this and this is mine. I've read of this rather absurd anthropomorphism of houses in novels. *Howards End* didn't seem all that odd to me all the same, even if the characters did. Well this house of mine I have lavished fine clothes upon. I remember my pal Jim Mowat seeing the apartment for the first time for God's sake. I'd been there about three years. He sat, drink taken I know, on the sofa in that large bay-windowed room with all the exquisite things in it, so far away from the nomadic out-of-a-suitcase existence I had always led before, and wept like Dorothy Buchanan seeing the flowing array of Jay Gatsby's shirts. I know it's only a house but it's not, anymore than friends are only friends or times past forgotten. And of the times I don't forget, one of them is that long first winter when I moved into where I live.

It was a cold winter we had of it. The snow lay across the landscape like the hands of a virgin lady; the brittle branches of the trees across the way were garlanded with skeins of silver silk. The birds spread wide across the pewter-coloured skies squawking for food out of the shriven ground. Gelid pools gleamed like moonlight in the hard white tundra of the park's vista across the way. I could go on like this for pages. The pale rim of the moon cleft into the golden sands islanding a few last figures in distant pools and stretched far away. Nothing like a jewelled prose to describe what there was that cold winter, outside my window, for it was true. I was doing something I had never embarked upon before and one day I will do it again, making a domicile. It was a wonderful time. The apartment had been refurbished and all was new but it was dreadful. The workmanship was so bad I could have easily sued those concerned for the disaster, except that the bloody company of cowboys who had made such a botch of what should have been a lovely job, one to take pride in, went out of business before any of we owners could do anything about it. The outside of the building was done by another firm entirely and was splendid, and remains so. At first I didn't care; it was my abode. Then friends came in. Billy Kelly was the main man. It was Billy who did the painting and decorating, all the carpentry, the electrics, the plumbing of the cooker and washer and fridge, the lot. The plasterwork as well. The magnificent bookshelves which guests to my house imagine have been there, richly refulgent, since last century, Billy built them. Looking back there was a sort of unseen invisible committee overseeing this transformation. Billy Kelly of course, and his pal, Tony Gallagher, the coach boss who transports so many off to Ireland throughout the year, including the *Herald's* own Anne Simpson, and Anna, an Irishwoman who looks after the house. (She once, rather shyly, told me she had something to tell me. I urged her to speak. 'It's a bit embarrassing' she said, 'I don't know how to start'. I insisted she come out with it and thought of every possible horror, condoms in the bed or worse. 'Have you seen the state of your underpants?' she said, 'You could read a magazine through them'. Jesus. Today my underwear would bring gasps of unsolicited admiration from any ambulance crew.) They were all Irish if it comes to that. Thus it was that they brought to my house all the flair, imagination, bloody mindedness, erratic tenacity, and astounding generosity which I have found characterises the best of the people who live or come from the island across the way.

Anna and Tony are from Donegal, a place I have been going to for many years, ever since I lived in Ireland briefly in the 1960s. Tony's from Kincasslagh, not far away from his next-door neighbours, the singer Daniel O'Donnell and the goalie Packy Bonner, but he has lived in Scotland since childhood, though his links, through his business and members of his family, are still strong in Ireland. Tony and myself have taken many trips across the water, once I sort of remember, on a kind of world tour of Ireland. I was gloriously drunk from the start to finish and had a great time, visiting old friends and making new ones the way you do in Ireland. Tony put up with me and drove me all over the country in his sleek dark-blue Jag, and I had enough of a jag in me for a fortnight myself. Known everywhere as Tony Mai, (after his mother, the Irish custom of naming people thus due to the number of them sharing the same surnames, a practice common to all Celts), he is a great friend to me though we frequently fall out, to the divertissement of our chums, because I have a terrible intemperance in my speech and would hang myself for a good phrase, and caused too by Tony Mai's readiness to go into a huff. But Tony is sharp and clever and I wish I had half his savvy. As a huff though the time he pronounced to me that I was barred from Ireland has got to be his best. I was going on a press-tourism trip to West Donegal for the paper and Tony Mai was bristling over some imagined slight I had made about his native heath. Also, he said, I would only be jarred throughout. So he barred me from Ireland. I went anyway, with a young colleague from the blatt, Keith Sinclair, and we had a grand time of it because, as I was more or less the spokesman for the entire group being older and having a great many friends in West Donegal, I didn't get jarred at all and Tony got the most encouraging reports of my demeanour. Including the fact that I had visited his mother's grave and laid flowers there as well as making a wee personal and godless prayer. All I was doing was what Tony had done for my own mother, but the Donegalies lauded me for my condign gesture and I was treated like a visiting Prince of my People. But anyway, Tony and myself are close, and share an interest in good times and fine things, as well as a searing detestation of the West of Scotland diseases of religion and bigotry. And it was Tony who scoured the land, including the Emerald Isle, for fitting furnishings for my house, and somehow oversaw what was happening there.

Billy Kelly is the Celtic genius incarnate with a sense of awesomely lateral logic. He it was who, fulminating in a melodramatic philippic against the Irish – 'Murderous, venal to a man, wid steal the ee'ye out of yer socket . . .' – was confronted with the irrefragable fact that he himself was, in fact, Irish and from Enniskillen, replied, with a thump on the bar-counter to go with it: 'Thet's how I know!' But Billy could make an imperial palace out of a bower of trees, and he did. Each morning we would sit on the armchairs at the bay window and sip coffee, smoke fags, and discuss the plans for the day. Truth to tell, often the discussions ended smartly in the Queen's Park Cafe, and often Ann would castigate Billy for leading me astray. Any idea you might have here that I was rather like a young princeling having a new *palazzo* built by faithful retainers and dependent craftsmen should be dismissed from your minds immediately: Billy referred to the flat as 'Our House'. I only get to live in it.

It doesn't surprise me that Tony and Billy and Ann were all originally from Ireland for I've had a lot of fun there over the years, especially in Dublin. The most, perhaps the only, European city in the British islands is a cause of many a recollection starting on my first visit thirty years ago when I was with a girl and got caught *in flagrante delicto* on top of a hill near Ballsbridge, and where I met Brendan Behan who deliberately soiled himself to show Paddy Kavanagh, he said, how disgusting humanity could be if it tries. He was disgusting in Davy Byrnes, of all places, and they barred him for the afternoon. (It was the girl, a dark-eyed siren called Juliette who had attracted such literati.) My pal John Nicholas once asked me if Ireland was my bolt hole, because I have spent enough time there. Ireland a bolt-hole? The way I've behaved there for thirty years Glasgow is instead. Simply I like Ireland because it is a very literate and articulate culture with writers marvellously well regarded and I am ever well treated there. A lot of friends in Ireland and I have not a single drop of Irish blood for centuries in me.

But there have been a sizeable amount of enemies in my own country. In my own trade especially. I hardly help matters for myself. Mind you I'm ever surprised when a victim of one of my lampoons is upset for I have to take a deal of that myself. One such lampoon has cost me dear. That was when I wrote a wee impertinent column in which I referred to three prominent Scottish journos, each of them famed for their own iconoclasm. I thought they would take it the way they handed it out but I was wrong with two of them at that. One was Ruth Wishart. She has never forgiven me and even refused a bottle of pink champagne I sent across to her once in Babbity Bowsters Hotel. I invited her out to dinner to try to make amends for what was after all merely a somewhat waspish joke. But Wishart refuses to speak to me. I wish I hadn't written it because in this country you can't speak out about women journalists.

The other target was a broadcaster I much admire as being a veritable polymath and one of the sharpest minds in Scotland, and a man with whom I got on well at one time, Colin Bell. I'd actually been his first guest on two separate radio series of his, 'Taking Issue' and the later 'Head On with Colin Bell'. It was the latter to which I referred when I wrote that the reason for the title was that, 'Sooner or later someone is going to put the head on Colin Bell, and a good thing too'. A joke, for Chrissake. But Colin snubbed me in the BBC club rather flagrantly and showily so I wrote the next week that he was behaving like a Big Girl's Blouse, and so the next week he behaved like a Big Girl's Blouse all over again and denounced me wherever he could find anybody to listen. I have a real regret that Bell should have so misunderstood my motives for the original line. I wasn't being malicious but mischievous. I was just being smart. Today I am cast as a pariah by most of Colin's coterie, and I have never been asked on to any of his programmes, which is a bloody shame because he is still one of the best broadcasters in Britain and I'd dearly like to have Colin bury the hatchet. The third writer I insulted in that one column was with my own paper, Joyce MacMillan, and Joyce was the brightest of the lot because she didn't bridle at all when I said she 'had a certainty of opinion which would do credit to Wittgenstein she was that sure of herself'. The other insult was that I said she was pretty and Joyce is a very articulate feminist indeed. Joyce found no problem with that and just bided her time till she got me back in a column in the Other Scottish Broadsheet. I don't remember the insult, though I recollect enjoying it. But anyway the above is an example of rather egregious people handing it out but not taking it back. And of being a lot more spiteful than ever my calumnies had been. I don't understand such sensitivities myself. People who are in the business of putting themselves forward shouldnae greet when somebody gives them a wee sherricking. Trabb's boy should ever be remembered.

Among the characters I have jostled with often in Dickens' streets it is this bane of Pip's life I perhaps admire the most. 'I beheld Trabb's boy approaching. Deeming that a serene and unconscious contemplation of him would best beseem me and be most likely to quell his evil mind, I advanced with that expression of countenance . . .' It was not to be, for Trabb's boy indulged in a series of histrionics feigning paroxysms of terror and contrition, occasioned by the dignity of Pip's appearance. (Yes, *Great Expectations* again.) 'As I passed him, his teeth chattered in his head, and with every mark of extreme humiliation, he prostrated himself in the dust. This was a hard thing to bear but this was nothing. I had not advanced another two hundred yards when to my inexpressible terror, amazement, and indignation, I again beheld Trabb's boy approaching . . .' Another round of the merchant's boy's melodramatics occurs, this time hailed with the greatest joy by a knot of spectators. Thence follows one of the most comic episodes in the English novel with Trabb's boy exacting a glorious revenge on Pip's stuck-up ways, ending with putting the once haughty Pip more or less to flight. But it is Pip's response as chronicled by his author which delights most of all. 'But unless I had taken the life of Trabb's boy on that occasion, I really do not see what I could have done, save endure. He was a boy whom no man could hurt; an invulnerable and dodging serpent who, when chased into a corner, flew out again between his captor's legs scornfully yelping. I wrote, however, to Mr Trabb, to say that Mr Pip must decline to deal further with one who could so far forget what he owed to the best interests of society, as to employ a boy who excited loathing in every respectable mind.' I bow to the very dust of the ground to Trabb's boy, a master in my art, one to whom all in my trade should defer.

Anybody who leaps on to centre stage and shouts Look at Me Mammy, I'm Dancin' should bear the Great Trabb's boy in mind a while. Dear heavens I've insulted enough people over the years who have taken it well enough. The best really are politicians. I once said that George Robertson had a mouth so small you wondered how he got the meal in it. (I also said, horribly crudely, that his mouth was the size of a three-year-old's vagina. A dormouse's at that.) Another occasion I remember I wrote that the trouble with Donald Dewar was that he contrived to be boring and passionate at the same time. Jim Sillars I described as having the political judgement of Tsar Nicholas, the compassion of Stalin, and the good luck of Leon Trotsky. And the looks of a Kilmarnock kulak. All three of them continue to bandy words and no hard feelings. There have never been any on my part. I just like a smart remark, and expect no quarter in return. But only in words. Deeds are another matter entirely. Was not Pope said to be a kindly man in his acts towards others? But even that poison dwarf occasionally regretted his words.

Curst be the verse, how well soe'er it flow
that tends to make one worthy man my foe.

19

Trabb's boy is not the only hero I have gathered up from literature. Like most writers I have perhaps lived too much in the realm of letters. In fact I remember my father once, exasperated, berating me for reading. 'That boy's always got his nose in a book, he is dreaming.' My father generally approved of noses in books, especially if you were working a loom at the time – in common with many of his generation he much approved of David Livingstone – but only when it 'led to' something concrete. Dreaming he considered to be a sort of masturbation. Which it is of course. 'You'll never earn a bloody living,' he said, 'just reading.' A dissertation on the superiority of 'practical experience', a favourite topic, usually followed. In fact, this thesis, so horribly often expressed by so many working-class men, has of course a basis in truth, not the least of it being that many intelligent craftsmen who should have gone far in their profession to the advantage of both themselves and industry were constantly superseded by those with the scrawniest of qualifications. But my father was wrong about all that reading not earning a living. I have done very well out of the business of reading. Certainly other people shoving the beadies from one end of a sentence to the other. Much of the motivation behind writing is wanting to read something you agree with yourself.

I don't say I live my life in books for I don't though Arnold Kemp once wrote that I 'lived life as though it were a movie' and I am rather afraid that I might do at that. I do like to dress up. Yet I don't think I emphasised enough in a previous chapter my obsession with books when I was a teenager. I spent a huge part of my life in bookstores, particularly second hand bookshops of which there were many in my adolescence. And the book barrows. A favourite photograph, one I have framed myself in my dining-room, (I have a long wall

188

frescoed with framed photographs in the splendid dining-room, which I never use for dining in fact), shows a book barrow *circa* 1952. The personnel around the book barrow consists of a Bearsden-type of female in her Jaeger pleated skirt and seamed stockings, an old duffer in a pork-pie hat, a healthy and sonsie schoolgirl, a wee foreign-looking woman in a white raincoat and a French beret. She looks East-European, and I should be surprised if she wasn't Jewish, and a lean young bus conductor with, for the times, too-long hair. The reason why I know he is a bus conductor is a recondite piece of arcana I much enjoyed recognising. He has a chain from his lapel to his pocket. A whistle that chain was for, and only conductors, not drivers, had a whistle. Intellectuals all, in their differing ways. The only character missing in the picture is me. Perhaps I took the snap.

Such barrows held a plethora of old long-out-of-print books, and always a goodly number of stirring pamphlets from the prolific pen of the anarchist Guy A. Aldred, books by people like Theophile Gautier or Henry Harland or Willa Cather to name but three from different eras. Today such writers belong to a distant and dusty corner of academe, more's the pity and the shame. There is scarcely a magazine article in which the interviewee does not claim to have 'read voraciously' – in interviewese 'voraciously' always goes with 'read' just as the bastards always 'curl' their bloody legs under themselves on the 'big comfy Victorian sofa' and always 'sip thoughtfully' their Italian bloody Lavazzo coffee as they tell you their wild days are over. 'These days I live simply, for the open air, nights in round the fire, a vegetarian pasta – I can eat anything with pasta – as you get older you un-learn . . . ' I could write that shite with a frontal lobotomy on me. But 'voracious reading' comes into that category of humbug except that in my case it was true and I read as one demented. Books, thousands of them, were my models and I learned much of what I pretend to be out them.

One model I didn't take out of literature at all was that of a seducer. Indeed I didn't bother with anything anybody had to say about relationships with the other sex. Thus I am sometimes misunderstood about my attitudes to women and girls. I remember Kenneth Roy, that indefatigable journalist, editor, sometime entrepreneur, and a good, though by no means uncritical, friend, once doing an interview for *Scotland on Sunday* with me (which won a Press Award and five hundred or so quid), and that was one of the things I felt he got wrong. He got a lot right, I think, too. He caught the melancholy, and a great deal of the sulphurous vituperation which often chokes me. Two things were off-beam though. One was when he wrote that I had 'done badly at school'. I have always been a touch embarrassed that I did well. It was by no means the image one wished to project in my youth or even yet, rather like no husband alive wanting their wives to know that they were quiet and well-behaved in the classroom. Husbands lay it on that they were practically Lord George Hell. But the other assertion which Ken made was when he suggested that I didn't like women. I protested that I did and Ken quoted the next remark. 'What is more, women like me.' And it's true that I said it. And the statement is, I think, true as well. But in the *SOS* piece Ken just about had me leering. It looked very nasty, very lascivious. I know Roy the journalist didn't mean it that way, but readers saw it so. Especially as I have a reputation for misogyny anyway.

It is a reputation I hardly deserve surely. It's true that though I admire a great many women, I often express little respect for most female members of my trade (entire careers pronouncing on yoghurt and sanitary towels), and it's true that I find a lot of womanish prejudices irksome, and it is most certainly true that I have no serious relationships with women. A confirmed bachelor doesn't always mean a woman-hater or a homosexual though, and I have chosen a solitary life when it comes to women. The old-fashioned Spanish aristocrat had a splendid custom of keeping two houses, one for himself, and another for his spouse. On such an occasion as the wish to meet with the lady for whatever purpose, including conjugation, he would send a little *billet doux* and the household would suitably prepare for the chap's visit. I can think of no better means of keeping a marriage happy. And unbroken. Sadly I cannot afford such a *ménage*: the next best thing is to live on your own and hope you can slake the desires of the flesh without too great a frustration in your life.

But the truth is that I like women's company, often more than men's, and most women who know me will confirm that they like mine. I am flirtatious with women, and attracted to pretty or vivacious women. I don't like ugly women, that's true, and ignore plain ones. I just don't think they have a gender really I suppose, and the idea of them possessing a sexuality seems inappropriate to me. All this is quite dreadful of course but it's what I feel, and thank heavens that very few women are either plain or ugly. Ach it's no so dreadful at that: it's what human beings think mostly. It's just a bugger that ordinary-looking fellows with very little poppy have to settle for a bit of a dog. An awful bloody sacrifice just for a momentary excitement and a wee tickly bit at the end of it if you ask me.

My own sexual relationships are hardly interesting to readers and scarcely more so to myself. They are healthy enough and I suppose a little unadventurous. I don't much like talking about sex unless it is sheer bawdiness, and I am embarrassed by talk which veers into the emotions. As for the sex act itself, my needs are simple enough. I can't for the life of me see why anyone would want to stray any further than genital sex, and on the few occasions I've been persuaded into an attempt at an oral sex act I have not enjoyed it nor have I been sexually stimulated, rather the opposite in fact. The Latin word 'vagina' incidentally, was a very vulgar word to the Romans, and means 'little purse', a bit like the modern 'honeypot'. What are today's vulgarisms were perfectly respectable to the old Romans, and indeed the word 'Queen' itself derives from the word considered the most coarse in the English language. Myself I've always thought of the vagina as a little silk purse, and welcomed it as, and this must be Freudian, a place of comfort at last. In any case, what has always attracted me towards girls, and my prose on this subject has ever seemed to upset feminists, is their soft limbs, the way they walk and sit and hold their hands, the soft sibilant of the hem of a skirt on their legs, the shadow of an eyelash on the bloom of a cheek. I like pretty, rather then glamorous, girls. I like nice rather than well-read girls. Ach, I just like girls.

But there are lots of women I like for lots of things. Let it not be forgotten that I profiled a number of women journalists when they were starting out because I found them impressive. I profiled the young Kirsty Scott because of a programme she did for Radio Scotland called 'School's Out': she had splendid control and a lovely dark voice. And Lesley Riddoch when she kicked off what is now Ruth Wishart's programme 'Speaking Out'. Lesley is a big girl who could be awful wild when younger but great company. By big I mean a lot taller than me. I remember once going into a pub with Lesley and her towering above me. There was just this wee barman behind the bar, and a little guy in a hooker-doon bunnet in front of it, and myself and Big Lesley strolled in, just after opening time. The little fellow in the bunnet turned and looked at us, me the small fellow, Lesley six inches taller than me. 'Jesus Christ,' the wee guy said, 'Simon and Garfunkel . . .' Lesley incidentally told me more lies of omission for that profile than you can imagine. She got through it all without telling me that she had been head girl at Glasgow's Girls High, and the first female President of Oxford University Students Union. She's a lovely and formidable woman who doesn't think I'm a wee sexist bastard after all, though I must say I don't give a rat's arse if anybody thinks that of me anyway, including Lesley.

The only reason I've told you anything about myself and women is to put you out of your misery. My romantic dealings with girls have been generally cheap and cheerful and I see no cause for changing that. I have no desire for such an anchor or such shackles as a woman permanently about the house. In any case my once considerable appetite for sexual conquest has thankfully subsided. I used to get myself in a lot of trouble over it. I still find girls fascinating but the days of unbridled concupiscence are hopefully long gone since the dreadful tangles of the past which carnality can bring – I recollect one appalling interlude when I was sleeping with two sisters and their mother without any of them knowing about the others: it made any George Segal sex comedy look prosaic and has long been a source of recounted mirth for my chums. I yet fall in love with young women but worry when they fancy me: I would worry about any pretty young girl who made a pass at a fifty-odd aged roué like myself. I would suspect them of a kind of 'Play Misty For Me' neurosis. I'd probably be right.

The other area I know readers of mine always wish to know results in a question I somehow find boring, or at least I find my answer boring. It's about the people I've met. This is shorthand for Famous People. Why people want to hear about famous people I have met or they have met or anybody else has met. My old colleague, Jack Webster, for instance, has a touching regard for fame or at least he adores being touched, however fleetingly, by it, and he is hardly alone in this. People write books all the time about that lick of flame around their hand as they stretch it out to taste the fire of fame. Mind you there are circumstances in which one cannot help but be impressed. I recollect a fair old rodomontade I was giving out to a few cronies in Heraghty's one night, of my twenty-first birthday when I mounted this little French girl round the back of the casino in St Valery. (I remember I withdrew myself in the manner usual then, that primitive form of contraception, coitus interruptus, and ejaculated all over her. I had turned away to adjust my dress when the girl called to me, in English. Pointing to the evidence of my seed all over the panties around her knees she asked me, innocently, ' What ees thees, Jacques?' and then, I swear it, 'Did eet come out your noze?' I wish I'd have thought of it then, an aphorism truly fitting for such a suggestion. I wish I'd replied 'Fuck nose!' Incidentally, I sweated for days afterwards because the girl was eighteen and unbelievably the age of consent in France then was nineteen, or so my so-called pals said. Anyway I told the story. Archie Hind, the novelist and playwright, upped the tale. He'd spent his twenty-first as an orderly in a field hospital in the Malaysian jungle during the Insurgency. But George Quar, the telly chef for Scottish TV, twirled his splendid moustaches into his marvellous Fernando Rey beard, and upstaged everybody. 'I spent my twenty-first birthday,' he reminisced, 'hiding under a bed in an hotel in Havana while Fidel Castro was having his revolution. It was a wee bit hairy for a while . . .' You cannae top that. Nor the fact that George, as First Class Passenger head steward on the *Queen Elizabeth*, had danced with a slightly tipsy Grace Kelly because she'd asked him. I don't care if Archie did write a seminal Scottish novel, he comes way behind wee George at that.

I don't count famous people I've met if I did so only in the course of my work, have seen them at some press conference – have been, if you like, a tourist. There is a wee, harmless, vanity of mine displayed upon my bookshelves. Signed books. The lowest category are books signed by authors I haven't heard of before. After that comes the group of writers who don't know me. Then it's books by writers who do know me. The top group are books by writers who write little dedications to me. I have much the same approach to Famous People, though my attitude is a lot less deferential than I possess with books. But some people whom I suppose are famous I am glad to know. A lot of them are perhaps only really famous to me. Some of them, like Iain Hamilton, of whom I have written earlier, have a curious edge, a strange eerie attraction for me, a touch, perhaps, of Olympus. Sir Fitzroy MacLean was one such. A hero for me, for many years, ever since I was a child and first read *Eastern Approaches*. Oddly the wives of Iain Hamilton and Sir Fitzroy, Jeanette and Lady Veronica respectively, have that peculiar evanescence too.

Among performers I can think of, few politicians have much beyond that certain sense of overpowering velleity which belongs to most politicians and all power-seekers. Tony Benn certainly, but I always thought there lurked behind those dreadfully reasonable tones, that air of if-we-simply-sit-down-and-think-about-it rationally, the verdicts of the zealot. Michael Forsyth I have mentioned before, but the present Scottish Secretary impressed me and no doubt there is a measure of the boy from the other side of the tracks which appeals there too, but he has a presence all the same. The late George Middleton, one-time STUC supremo, and acknowledged to be the ugliest man in Britain, had an undeniable power with him, but that was when I was a boy and I can make a recollection. John Smith came across as cheerfully normal, odd in a politician, Neil Kinnock as depressingly so, not odd in a politician at all. I have yet to find that unique sense of statesmanship in other authority figures which three educationists, and politicians in their own way too, displayed, John Pollock, the teachers' leader, and H. Stewart Macintosh and W.S. McEwan, Directors of Education for Glasgow and Lanarkshire respectively. Nor, incidentally, in clerics, though Father Anthony Ross, the students' chaplain at Edinburgh, had an air of beatitude about him. He certainly looked the part.

The only member of the Royal Family I have met is Princess Anne and on one occasion she did impress. It was at a gymkhana event in Culzean, near Ayr. I'd been shoving down a few goldies with the posh ladies who were running the Riding for the Disabled stall, and a few more with the Irish grooms across with their horses, when the *gendarmes* appeared and detectives and dogs and a battery of press photographers and hacks. And then of course, Princess Anne. She's no looker, that's for sure, and very homely but then we never got to elect our Royals so what do you expect? The Princess Royal had The Path laid down for her by the advisers and other horsey lackeys but moved ever so slightly away from it and into my orbit. I'm not a Monarchist, and hardly care about this German family of lumpy bourgeois, but suddenly there was Princess Anne talking to me as I was washing down a dod of clootie dumpling with a wee half. 'Ah, Mr. McLean,' she said sweetly, 'so good to see you. And All is Well at the *Glasgow Herald*?' I was impressed. That she should remember me at all let alone the paper I represented. (I'd met the Princess a year or so before at a Save the Children Fund launch of a book they'd published which had a short story of mine in it.) The other journos were positively viridian with envy because there is a chance of front page with this kind of crap, and our snapper was, well, snapping. A smart woman, I thought, to remember me, and doubtless well-briefed. It was then I realised that if she wasn't smart I was at least thick. Looking down I saw that I had a bloody great identification badge on my lapel. It read: 'Jack McLean, *Glasgow Herald*'.

Artists and musicians I have met over the years are invariably impressive anyway because they are wonderful actors (actually a great many actors are a bit shadowy, for all their stagecraft), but for that feeling of being in the company of somebody extraordinary I can think of only two painters, Elizabeth Blackadder and David Hockney, the latter whom I have only encountered once, who had that special air about them. Most painters have an éclat of their own anyway, not all of it put on for your benefit. Of musicians I have encountered two stand out that way. One was Eric Clapton who was very quiet and well-spoken, and very, very sad. He had been an only child and it shows. The other was a remarkable bluesman, Buddy Guy. I met him after his show at a Glasgow theatre. He had changed out of his stage clothes and was sitting back after a beer with the rest of his band when he decided to open out the guitars again and had a wee jam session just for us till two in the morning. But I have met a great many musicians. Kinky Friedman, who is a crime novelist as well as a Country and Western performer, is grandly outrageous. For a start his band is called The Texas Jewboys, and one of his songs is titled 'There's been no good Jews Since Jesus'. He won the Sexist Songwriter of the Year Award in the States a few years back for a song called 'Get Your Biscuits in the Oven and Your Buns in Bed'. When Friedman visited Glasgow the first time he was sporting a large Stetson and dark glasses and upsetting the staff in the bookshop where he was signing copies of his latest book by smoking a massive Havana cigar. By utter chance I had a cigar in my breast pocket where I had secreted it after some press dinner so I gave him it and we have been friends ever since.

Writers are generally a bit boring though an encounter with three at a literary lunch in Glasgow's Hutcheson's Hall was a little startling. The three were John Mortimer, Anthony Burgess and Alasdair Gray, as likely a bunch of lads as ever put quill to parchment. It was one of those lunches in which book-minded ladies worth a bob or two pay to consume chicken and watercress with a spinach compote and listen to the literary giants slurring incomprehensibilities after the liqueurs. (I once took Lesley Riddoch to one of them through in Edinburgh and Lesley catcalled Lady Antonia Fraser. She laughed herself sick at John Julius Norwich. Lord Longford was the last speaker and Lesley behaved herself and took to making exotic faces at me throughout Pakenham's drooling drivel.) But I escorted the three authors of Hutcheson's Hall to a nearby pub. All three were very pissed. Burgess left with what looked like a very young Italian waiter; John Mortimer, a lovely man, took to groping his very young PR lady; and Alasdair crowned the late afternoon when the safety pin which was fastening his corduroys snapped and he revealed to a batch of girl students from Strathclyde University's Philosophy Department that Scotland's greatest living novelist did not in fact wear any type of underpants. The barstaff were well used to Alasdair's eccentricities and carried him to a taxi. The taxi driver knew him too. 'You'd better use the lavvy, Alasdair,' he told the Savant of the West, 'Ah'm no stopping in Woodlands Road again.' Don't talk to me about writers.

Nor can I tell you much about sportsmen and footy players and the like because I don't want to. With very few exceptions most athletes are muscle-bound in the head, especially footy players. When you meet exceptions like, say Tony Higgins, the grossly articulate boss of the Professional Footballers Association, or Packy Bonner of Celtic, you are conscious that they know they're exceptions. In fact I get on well with sportsmen, once again especially footballers, because I don't tee-hee to them: just being a professional sportsman doesn't impress me very much.

In fact I'm not really very easy to impress anyway which might be a form of egotism on my part, though it is often just ignorance. More often than not I haven't a scooby who half of the celebrities I ever meet are, because I hardly ever read the tabloids and went without a television set for years. It is no affectation on my part when I come out with questions worthy of a High Court judge. Scotland is such a small country that if you are anywhere near the public eye you are bound to come across damn near everybody who has risen to any prominence at all. For all their stardom few celebs manage to convey that quality when the audience goes home. Some of them don't want to anyway. One of them was Burt Lancaster and I didn't meet him in the course of work at all. I was standing in a wee pub on the south side owned by a lovely lady and a friend of mine for years, Evelyn Sexton. It is quite a smart bar now called Kelly's, but still a wee man's bar. Back when Lancaster strolled in, it was very much a wee howff and nothing wrong with that. It was a Sunday afternoon, just after opening, and there were a few regulars in, not many. In comes this big fellow we all recognised. I also recognised the company he was keeping because it was Charlie Gormley the film director and a few of his pals. Charlie bought a round of drinks. Nobody said anything to the film star, just continued drinking away. Lancaster bought a round. Still he was ignored, in a gentle fashion of course. It turned out that the actor was across here to film 'Local Hero' and had asked to go to a Turkish bath-house so Charlie had taken him to the Pollokshaws public baths where, paradoxically, he would be less likely to be accosted than in, say, the private Western Baths. Lancaster had then demanded to be taken to 'a tavern'. So here he was, along with some of the film crew. And nobody said a bloody thing for at least half an hour. Suddenly a punter leaned across and picked up the jug on the counter. 'Gonny no' hog the fuckin' watter, Burt,' he scolded, 'therr's merr o' us besides yerself.' Lancaster, who I once heard talking socialism on a TV chat show, didn't turn a hair. But he stopped hogging the water too.

Meeting celebrities isn't the interesting part of what I do anyway, anymore than travelling abroad is any kind of spur for myself. In Huysman's novel *A Rebours* (the book by Dorian Gray's bedside in which 'the sins of all the world were passing in dumb show before him' according to Wilde), the protagonist doesn't need to visit the actual places he wishes to encounter, he simply invokes the locations by means of scents and foods, and, basically, his imagination. The character, Des Esseintes, was modelled on an aristocratic dandy called Robert, Comte de Montesquiou. The *Herald* once ran a portrait of the French aristo in a Christmas weekend supplement spoof, with the caption 'Jack McLean: It is thus that I shall vote Tory'. I shan't be voting Tory but I do dress a little like your man the Comte, on a good day anyway. What I have in common with Des Esseintes is that I like travel in my mind, and eschew it, when I can, in the body. I don't like travelling, though I do enough of it. In the years after I started full time in this business I have travelled all over the country writing features, perhaps as much or more than other journalists. If I didn't like the travelling, I liked the writing jobs and I am quite good at travel pieces anyway. An art school training is good for many things, and one of them is an eye for silly details, the sort you can spin prose from. But I don't like the discomfort of travel and the obsession many people have with being somewhere else strikes me as a bit trite and suspect too. Escapism, I suppose I think it: there's a deal of my father's Calvinism in me yet.

Nor for my part shall I go far
As travellers do, who oft do roam
But make my strengths, such as they are
Here in my bosom – and at home.

Good old Alfred Lord Tennyson, for he it was who penned those lines. Couldn't agree with the chap more.

But it isn't merely the discomfort of travel I dislike; I mean I put up with it no bother at all if it's for a purpose, or at least to write. I like that. But travel for its own sake is absurd and I despise it. It makes you a tourist. Doubtless few of you out there can understand the extent of my withering contempt, or my reasons for such an emotion, for tourists and tourism. It's because it's worse than being an outsider, a tourist is. It means you don't mind being one, your stupid mouth agape, your brain content with adding nothing, just watching to no purpose other than voyeurism. Thus I have never been inside Notre Dame or climbed the steps at Saint Michel. Nor have I gone anywhere near the Tresi Fountain or seen Leonardo's Last Supper. But I've dined in Maxim's and slept with a girl studying at the Sorbonne; have talked with Alberto Moravia in a *bottiglieria* in Roma, and given out leaflets of support for the FIAT strikers in the Galleria di Vittoria D'Emannuelle in Milano. Ah, see the boasts, the braggadocio of it. Fair enough though when you think about it. Only a turd would go with a tour party to the Martello towers in Dublin to recreate Joyce's Dublin in his mind, when a glass of Guinness could do that in any pub in the world. There may be a kind of snobbery lurking there: there most certainly is a certain fastidiousness. And a dislike of being one of the suckers out there. I've spent a long time and long hours in being an insider but, though I know most people think I am one, you never are if you start off your life as an outsider looking in. You're merely an insider saying to yourself: 'Is this it? It can't be.' A silly thing, Pride. Designed for a fall, hitched for hubris, Pride is. Yet I admit that I am proud of the fact that I know such huge numbers of the taxi-drivers, barmen and barmaids, publicans, bookies, villains, flymen, artists, businessmen, lawyers, all-round mountebanks and sand-dancers of my city and a bit beyond. I like the gypsies; I like the caravans, as I like the caravanseri. I like the noise and the lamps still lit. I don't want to go home in the dark.

20

The dark valleys are out there of course, ahead of me. I've always rather liked the idea of Death's Dark Vale, at least the notion that you passed through it and got out at the other end, like the sunny, happy endings in a *ciné noir* film, out of the shadows of travail. But recently in fact I passed through the dark glen myself, with the great threatening mountains on both sides, the way unlit, as I have perhaps hinted in a previous chapter. But courage, brother, do not stumble. Through that penumbra of a few months ago I stumbled enough but truth to tell, I wasnae caring very much at the time: there didn't seem much I could do anyway and I had no gods to bother at a time like that.

But the sun is peeping out a bit now, a little pale and watery perhaps, a little wan, and wabbit, a lovely word that. At least I'm back in business and alive. And there's a lot of knaves and hypocrites and dissemblers and Mr Bliffells out there yet to annoy and needing it. And many a reader to tease a little or divert a touch. And myself to be pleased with the results of it. Most enjoyable that. And in truth I like it when I know I've said what the readers wanted said, and, often irrationally, think they cannot say for themselves. I have no objection to being a tribune: even if I like a hob-nob with the patricians there are times when I damn-near want to get the piano-wire squads working flat-out. In any case, what would I do without that burst of spleen or whoop of delight I get to draw for you each Friday in the blatt?

My newspaper, like all papers, knows the value of an unbridled commentator like myself. A while back, George McKechnie was speaking at the retirement presentation of a colleague, who has figured before in this narrative. He pointed out that the columnist had recently featured in a reader's survey as the top draw among the writers in the paper. I was listening, characteristically outside the room, along with Gillian, one of the *Herald* lawyers, when I heard this preposterous statement. I looked at our lawyer. 'That's what's wrong with bloody Scotland. They want to hear Jack Webster's homilies about the good old bloody days, and quines and effing loons, and all that sweetie-wife stuff. Readers bloody surveys indeed. That's why I'm pissing off out of this benighted land with its warm tales of cheery inconsequence and . . .' It was just then that I heard George continue with: 'And Jack McLean was the second top of the favoured writers thereby showing the diversity of . . .' I turned to the lovely Gillian. 'There are certain features of readers surveys, however, which . . .'

Readers are important of course, but generally letter-writers aren't. The ones who approve of you write to yourself. The ones who don't write to the Editor, often demanding you get the old P45 – they rarely think of asking such a sacrifice from the Editor himself. Myself I don't much care what people, including close chums, say about my columns. Some will love thee, some will hate thee, as the hymn goes. You get people whose judgement you respect in many matters telling you they thought such and such a column was poor that week, and others, equally deserving of respect, saying of the same article that it was great. I don't listen much to readers' views. It's not my job. It's their job to listen to me. Or not. But I don't listen to critics, benificent or otherwise. That apposite hymn again. 'Some will flatter, some will slight . . .' But every newspaper writer has got to consider the feedback from the readers in the street or pub, particularly the pub. Myself I usually like it, enjoy the contact. I even answer the questions when I can though often the enquiries couldn't be answered by King bloody Solomon.

The most common question of all, as every columnist will tell you, is: 'How Do You Think Up Your Column Every Week?' Enquirers with questions like that ever ask questions in capital letters, an oral form of writing in green ink. Part of the reason why I never have any difficulty thinking up what to write for my column is that it isn't like that: thinking up things. I have an opinion for everything for heaven's sake. Yet to consider your job, your work as a writer, as simply something to think up and fill spaces, that would be dreadful. It would certainly be no fun. Sadly I think a lot of writers do that, and have no fun at all. A lot of them are newspaper writers to boot. In any branch of the arts and entertainment if it's just a job you shouldnae be in it, if you ask me, which you didn't of course. Some of these writers are said to be 'trained'. Like horses. Circus animals. If I never went to any school of journalism I don't think I am all that much the worse for it, but I suspect many of the younger writers are; very much the worse. At any good art college, for example, the drawing and painting lecturers are artists. The silversmiths and jewellers are silversmiths and jewellers. They are workers in their own fields. But as far as I can see the journalism schools are packed full of people who couldn't earn their living on any newspaper, and couldnae write a message line. Who are they to teach the young men and women hopeful of this industry to which I belong? But how hopeful are the neophytes anyway? Such musing in public is not doing me any good; it will do me harm, for the young journalists will not like what I am saying and it sounds like Age creaking. A great many of the young journos sound to me like Jack Webster though, but not as good. (I have to tell you here that actually myself and Jack get on well. We have an amicable and convivial disparity to enjoy in each other. I just think he's a bit of a Merry Mac: we are of different times.) A lot of the young entrants seem to be well out of their time, though, old-fashioned somehow.

Many of the older newpaper writers though, of an older tradition, I suspect see myself as yet an upstart, one of the newer fellas, a bit the way the old Tin Pan Alley songwriters considered people like Bob Dylan. (Quote: 'Methinks the young songsters have got a bit above themselves. All this protest. We wrote songs about boy-girl love and it was good enough for us.' *Melody Maker*, 1967.); or the way the Merry Macs are forever tilting their reedy little lances at, say Billy Connolly or the newer stand-up comedians even. 'We never had to use bad language to get laughs. Why Arthur Askey and Ken Platt and . . .' It wasn't true in any case. Those comedians used filthy language and enough racism to give half the nation jobs in the Equality Commission for life. Even yet. But Dylan is a genius and Connolly could be said to have been much of the thrusting influence on more recent, less anodyne and perhaps more realistic comedy. And both have been around a long time. The real reason why both were so ill-regarded is because they were talking about something other than meaningless twaddle and inconsequential quips.

I have friends among many of the older hands and cause to be grateful to them. And many I admire. People on my own paper who do things I can't, such as Murray Ritchie, a friend I value very much despite the fact that, as is the way with the Scottish male, we almost never spend a civil moment with each other. He's been in Europe four years now and I miss him much. Or Alf Young, a delight to read even on economic or industrial arcana usually beyond my capacities. Writers elsewhere too. I rate Ian Bell, once a *Herald* writer. Don't ask for light-heartedness from Ian for this is a dark foreboding toll of a Bell, but I believe he will be a truly major journalist in years to come for he has a gravitas to go with his intellect. The days are probably past when the James Camerons will have the same opportunities but there are those out there who can take on a fold or two of the mantle. True, it is difficult to see where the comic stylists are, the Thurbers, or Leacocks before them. (A budding cartoonist once approached Thurber's editor on the *New Yorker*, Harold Ross, complaining that he was being ignored in favour of 'that tenth-rate cartoonist, Thurber'. Ross pulled on his cigar and quietly put the hopeful supplicant right. 'Third rate,' he corrected.) But yet, there are newspaper writers around surely, and more to come.

But too many journalists, despite the long traditions stretching back to Hazlitt and Addison and Steele and before, have always simply wanted a by-line, or some spurious glamour, or even only money and many of the young ones coming through, to my surprise, seem to me old-fashioned in their ambitions. Mocking useful toil really, but paltry ambitions always do. I cannot bring myself to heap blame on many younger people for they have grown up in a paltry age. With leaders who resemble more than anything The Hard Faced Men Who Did So Well Out of the War. There is that powerful smell of something more awful than mendacity about – the reek of mediocrity. The same aroma of the gaberdine coats and the greasepaint of the Fabulous Yana, the tawdry yearnings of the under-educated, the vulgar ostentation of New Money, the exhaustion of the ethics of democracy, the unyielding towers of class and privilege, the sleaze and slander, in short, the Fifties before Elvis.

That's the stuff. I like a bit of purple prose; in fact, gentian voilet really, just the stuff to clear the impetigo scabs of a shabby, unwashed age. I like it anyway because it is words which earn me, after all, a living, but of course they do more than that, which is why I worry about most tabloid papers and much of television. They are either innocuous, or they are worse and employ the high moral tone of the Pharisee in the temple. But recently one of the Scottish tabloids blazoned its pages with a feature on a favourite theme, part of the hysteria whipped up over concerns about child abuse, and the consequent confusion over the realities of it. This, for a tabloid, lengthy piece was an exegesis of outrage over a new film of Nabokov's novel *Lolita*. The writer described it as a dirty, a perverted, book. Either the writer was philistine to believe that was true of this beautiful and haunting novel, which possesses not one single erotic scene, or the writer knew damn well it wasn't, in which case he was a liar and a humbug. Either way he shouldn't be in his job and if I had my way he'd be wearing his arse for a hat.

I am sermonising here of course, and I have to stop it. There is probably a touch of the dominie in me still: I don't suppose the homiletic urge has ever quite disappeared. All the same it is a grand thing to be allowed to go on such a rostrum as a newspaper. I like to think that a decent columnist can amuse while practising his or her objurgations on the wicked or panygyrics on the glories of the angels. It has unfortunately become rather more difficult within the last decade or so for lampoonists and satirists: so much of what Dean Swift, for instance, would have passed as the most unlikely absurdities have come to pass as realities. It's a grand life the writing is. I've had happy times in it, perhaps some of the happiest, and there's been lots of them over all. Happy times? I think of them as little vignettes I take out from time to time, as you might take out a favourite film from the video shop. I remember them so vividly, in pictures, remember them as they happened, times when I knew I'd remember them all my life. My mother in Linn Park when I was a little child, and the auburn floor of the wood; my mother in tweeds and a tiger-claw brooch when she was young, I remember that. My father in the prefab on a Sunday, telling us about Monty, a story when he himself had comrades. Once we asked him what the difference was between pancakes and crumpets. He promptly put a pancake through the adjacent kitchen-sink wringer and feverishly stabbed it with a fork. 'There's a crumpet,' he said, and laughed and we all did. Yes, I remember that too, a good time with my father. Once – it was in the sunshine in Lauriston Place in Edinburgh, down from the art college, late spring – I was a young man, and handsome too I think. There were girls and I was doing what I wanted to do and the future lay ahead of me, from the far-off peaks of Darien. The sun shone in the cracks of the dusty pavement. Suddenly I thought to myself: 'This is a good time I'll remember, years later on. Remember it as a time when I knew that the world wasn't wide enough for me and it was there to be conquered by myself.' It was, I knew even then, self-conscious enough but true, and a thrill ran through me like liquid flame. Oh, a great many happinesses among the merriment and the melancholy. I knew it then, on that spring day, over a quarter of a century ago, that I had been blessed with many blessings, and many talents.

I have been a little profligate with them I know and self-indulgent too, but anybody who has ever experienced that buzz out of work and play, knows that indulgence is part of it. When I get up to play blues harp in a little R&B band, anybody who's ever seen and heard me play can see the volts going through me. I get that same tingling feeling after writing a line or more that's right, just right, in the way a sudden stroke of a pencil or a brush does when you draw. The opposite: when you have set what you saw and heard and felt inside yourself, when you have set that free into the wide eternal skies. Many blessings too. I have two brothers among my friends. I had a mother and father. One was an emperor, and one was a mother. And if I have sought with too great a vigour the approbation of them all I have been largely rewarded. I talk too much at that.

21

S HOULD any local authority want schools closed down in the near future they should send for me. I'm your man for the closing, especially in the pedagogical establishments. When myself and award-winning *Herald* snapper Angie Catlin zoomed off on a mission to trawl a bit of my childhood for photographs to illustrate the pages serialising this book we discovered that a lot of things change in fifty years; a lot of things just disappear. Schools for a start. It took a bit of doing, photographing the spaces I have wreaked upon the world, but Angela is a brick. I just haven't left many of them standing in my wake on my erratic way though life. I should have wrote an autobiography that was realistic for the start of the Twentieth century: an open book; an empty one.

That disappearing trick of the locations of childhood is probably common to all those of my age. The same thing would have been true of anybody born a century before me. A mid-Victorian would see much the same demolitions of his childhood places and the creation of new habitats as anyone of my generation would find in his time. For both ages were new ages. Just as the mid-Victorians saw their old slums and rural villages swept away, did that post-War generation of mine see the swift disappearance of the works and pomps of those Victorian improvers. All the same it is discomfiting to discover just how little of my childhood remains. An occasional trunkless leg of stone here and there. A lot of desert stretching far away.

Mind, the first stop Angie and myself made on the day for returning to old haunts was not only still there, but very nearly unchanged. It was a school. It was Holmlea Primary School. The teachers were as cheery as the ladies I remembered, though a lot younger and I may say better looking. A lot more sceptical and, well, street-wise, or maybe avenue-wise would be putting it more accurately for Holmlea is a nice, rather middle-class, establishment, and I don't think anybody could complain about that description. The children were well-dressed and healthy, and well-behaved too. Usually in classrooms of the modern school there is bloody mayhem when the weans realise that there's a stranger in the classroom: a time to wind up the teacher in front of visitors. In Marlene Anderson's Primary 7 class the children were responsive, polite, quiet, and that was while they were being photographed during their playtime and kept in for the photies.

So Holmlea was still the little haven I remembered. And so was Cathcart, that douce little village, (the locals actually call it The Village at that), on the banks of the River Cart. True, the first home I remembered, one of the pre-fabs among a small cluster of them, had long since gone, replaced in the 1960s by pleasant small private houses. But yards away was the Linn Park, open again after a few years of work needing done. Beside the babbling river was the Snuff Mill, just by the bridge of that name. The mill has been turned into a series of lovely buildings, dwellings, an idyll. I speak to the only resident so far, Peter Crolla, and his wife. They use the same word. Idyllic. Pastoral. Cathcart hardly seems any more like Glasgow, the black Glasgow I was brought up in when I left this Sleepy Hollow as a seven year-old, than it ever did.

The Linn Park itself is old, older than it was, not just fifty years older for that is true of course, but elderly. A little arthritic and hard of hearing. That grassy slope I remember rolling painted eggs down on Easter Day, is grassier and rougher, still neat enough but not as springy to the touch. The park is clearly yet well enough looked after but it seems in its very grass and trees very sedate, an aged lady wiser but no longer the head of the house. Then you realise why this is. It is hardly used, that's why. In my childhood Linn Park was mobbed all summer. With children, old people out for walks with dogs, courting couples, teenagers showing off their new ice-blue jeans, the boys pulling the girls' ponytails in an attempt to pull the girls, whole families on Sundays. These many years of emptiness has left a miasma of desuetude, a pall lying over it. The park is not merely empty: it only holds her memories now. Sad.

Across the river we find one of my other old schools. This is where the trunkless legs of stone emerge, like the stubs of broken teeth in the rictus of a skull, bones strewn everywhere. Townhead Primary School was set in the district it was named after, an entire area now gone, replaced by the tendrils of the motorway interchange, though there are some new housing developments and very smart and perjink they look too. Nearby is the Strathclyde University campus where was once the Richmond Street row of huge Georgian mansions which housed the Cruelty Man and his family, the Somervilles, now gone too. The swimming baths, the deep end of which was inhabited by large, wicked water spiders, the cubicles with the cast-iron bathtubs for the weekly wash, never existed, or don't seem to have. Morrin Square, Parly Road, what was once Cathedral Street, nothing there. The Barony Church stands still. The school itself has been razed to the ground though the entrances are still there. I am photographed at its portals, talking to two big polis, for the Duke of Edinburgh is attending a service next door in the Barony, a service commemmorating the life of John Logie Baird, the centenary of whose birth this day is. An irony this. Baird was a former pupil of my other old school, the secondary one I toiled five years in, Allan Glen's. We wander up to John Logie and my alma mater to see if there is a picture in it.

The old hothouse of my youth has long been swept away and the modernish building in its place is now part of the Caledonian so-called University. This is ironic as Strathclyde and Caledonian now both make a pretence to John Logie Baird as a former student. The intrepid pioneer of telly attended lectures at the Royal Technilogical Institute after obtaining his leaving certificate at Glen's. But there is nothing left of the old school. Except a little outpost now blackened with years and disuse where Allan Glen's Science and Art departments shared premises with St David's Primary. In a room at a corner of this derelict structure, I was taught art by my old teachers, Ralph Cowan and James McGill. The building moulders now; looks rather like these old war-time gerry-built blocks you find on old RAF aerodromes. Is there nothing but ruins left out of my life?

What do I expect? After all, I didn't go to Eton or Charterhouse for Christ's sake or the dreaming spires of Oxford either if it comes to that. None of the buildings in which I was tutored were prepossessing; designed for demolition they were. Even Edinburgh College of Art, where I was a mature, in years anyway, student has a new-ish dreadful edifice built on to it and the original red sandstone horror would have passed for the head offices of the Cheka. The new building – all right it's twenty years old but it's new to me and I was never in it – would do for the Stasi. We didn't bother photographing either. It would have been an insult to Angie and any other photographers. A contumely to Mr Fox Talbot and Monsieur bloody Daguerre. In fact, the building is so unimpressive it would be a bloody waste of the invention of silver nitrate itself.

We dismissed London locales where I had spent some years of my young manhood. The Kilburn in which I lived is unchanged and the house itself still resembles No 10 Rillington Place. Actually that's not far off a reality. The mass murderer Denis Neilson committed his grisly slayings a few houses up from my lodgings, and buried his victims in a back garden very similar to the one where I once tried to bury over 200 milk bottles. But anyway this blatt would doubtless think a London soujourn a trifle exotic for myself, well, anyway expensive.

But if you want something cheap you can look no further than the ailing towns of the Ayrshire coastline. Thus we arrived in Stevenston, that Ardeer-factory town, now with no factory or anything else. As even its sister, Saltcoats, has given up any idea of being a holiday resort, Stevenston would be unwise to attempt tourism. Its lonely wind-swept beach was never up to scratch anyway. Even in the Saltcoats heyday the sand dunes at Stevenston always looked as though they had been used as practice for the D-Day landings. You used to find oily parts of tanks in the grey grit they called sand. A picnic at Stevenston was a punishment for naughty children.

We found my Grandma's house, the bungalow I remember dreaming about when I lay in the dark cellars of the Blacking Factory of my childhood, with its pebble-dash exterior, and the splendid rockery in the front garden, the crazy-paving snaking round from the large back garden, and the diamond-paned windows, with the little porthole in the side made of stained glass, the mediterranean-bright canvas sunblinds across the front porch. The Evans family bungalow next door which gleamed in white stucco, a sundial in the front, an air of childlessness about it. The Johnstons on the other side, over-neat today, which once was merry with children playing with Rex, their spaniel dog. Across from my Grandma's house were Dig-for Victory pastures, and more further beyond. My Grandma had sort of scandalised all the neighbours by growing flowers in the first allotment but nobody ever argued with my Grandma. The trees across in Auchen Harvie. Forty years on the bungalows are still there but the post-war aspirations obviously aren't and the entire row of once vibrant near-prosperity has been replaced with an antiseptic cheerlessness, as though the houses were cleaned-up old age pensioners waiting for Alzheimers and the Great Beyond.

Outside my Grandma's house no rockery remains, none of that delight I once knew in the cascade of boulders and forget-me-nots, sweet williams, foxgloves, and nasturtiums. The eccentricity of the crazy-paving has been replaced by a roughcast concrete. The diamond panes out of which I once gazed when I was a little boy and thought myself the Aristocrat of the Breakfast Table (the symbol on the Chivers Olde English marmalade jar name after Oliver Wendell Holmes' eponymous essayist), the windows are now characterless and double-glazed. All the bungalows are quiet and without decoration though the present owners have retained the name of my

206

Grandma's house, which was 'St Piran', after a little Cornish village of my Grandmother's girlhood. The present incumbents haven't the imagination to call this undistinguished little harled dwelling any name of their own. This small stretch of what must be quite costly bungalows is bleak enough for any housing scheme.

All around are similar little houses built since my childhood. But at the back remain the rolling fields of the farm I remember forty years ago when I used to play with the Skeogh children and run after the geese. The family sold the farm a little while back and it was a pleasant, nice-looking lady who greeted myself and Angie as I gazed around looking at forty years on. Evelyn Long was the lady. She and her husband bought the farm some five years ago and have obviously worked very hard for the place looks lovely. Spick and span but obviously still a working farm. Evelyn tells me her husband is from Northern Ireland and I ask him how both of them like living here, in Stevenston. A bit too quiet she tells me but also that there are plenty of places near enough where they can have an occasional night out. If it was me it would be Northern Ireland. But the fields are fecund enough and just in the distance is the sea like silver and Arran rising out of it. So why doesn't such a beautiful setting in rich pastures make the other inhabitants in the rows of ticky-tacky want to settle into such dreadful dullness?

You could find out in Stevenston itself, at the Cross I remember being bustling, with a wee bridge over a little river where the old men used to congregate to reminisce and greet about the old days, just opposite what used to be Morrison's Bakery. There used to be horse-drawn bread vans there. The shops all around were neat and bustling. It isn't lack of money which produced this desolation, I think to myself as I look around the shuttered shops. It's lack of spirit. Plenty of spirit, corrupted, in the children who flock out of the local high school as I am being snapped in front of another row of empty shops. I am wearing a fedora. Maybe a bit well-dressed for this town. The town for toerags though, this is. I'm used to pass-remarkable weans in Glasgow, well used to dancing children when they see something unusual like journalists in gangster hats being filmed or photographed. But I'm not used to this. I never encountered, ever, such a torrent of abuse as I did from these schoolchildren in Stevenston. From first years right through to the sixth-formers, boys and girls. They have seen what is to them an alien, something out the pictures. Like inbred yokels from Idaho to Irvine they react as they would to any alien. They throw stones, this time metaphorically, at something they haven't seen in the flesh before. As I tell Angie to finish up here I cannot help but reflect what Julian Clary would find in this terrible little town. That's not fair. The elderly and middle-aged people we meet, like elderly and